Praise for
Writing the Thriller

"Skillman has written a brilliant dissection of the thriller novel—not just the structure but the soul. Not just for beginners, but for everybody. I've been writing for twenty years and I learned a lot!"

—Barbara D'Amato, author of the *Cat Marsala* mystery series and the *Chicago Cop* suspense series

"Skillman offers all writers—published or unpublished—a fascinating, instructive, helpful and discerning exposition on how to write suspense. In *Writing the Thriller*, Skillman shares the magic of other best-selling authors in addition to her insights. Superb from start to finish."

—Carolyn Hart, author of *Death on Demand* and *Henrie O* mysteries

"Even if you never plan to write a thriller, you'll enjoy reading Skillman's book. You'll be a smarter reader after looking over the shoulders of some of your favorite authors."

—Willetta L. Heising, Purple Moon Press, publisher of the award-winning mystery series reader's guides *Detecting Women* and *Detecting Men*

"Wow! I wish I had this book before I started writing thrillers. Skillman begins by creating a clear picture of the genre, then deftly defines the different suspense subgenres and their various elements. I found myself thinking her quite clever, indeed. In my opinion, *Writing the Thriller* is a must for any aspiring suspense author."

—Erica Spindler, best-selling author of *Cause for Alarm*

writing the THRILLER

T. Macdonald Skillman

WRITER'S DIGEST BOOKS
CINCINNATI, OHIO
www.writersdigest.com

Other fine Writer's Digest Books are available from your local bookstore or direct from the publisher.

Visit our Web site at www.writersdigest.com for information on more resources for writers.

To receive a free weekly E-mail newsletter delivering tips and updates about writing and about Writer's Digest products, send an E-mail with the message "Subscribe Newsletter" to news letter-request@writersdigest.com or register directly at our Web site at www.writersdigest.com.

04 03 02 01 00   5 4 3 2 1

Library of Congress Cataloging-in-Publication Data

Skillman, Trish Macdonald.
   Writing the thriller / by T. Macdonald Skillman.—1st ed.
     p.   cm.
   Includes interviews with experts.
   Includes bibliographical references and index.
   ISBN 0-89879-928-7 (pbk. : alk. paper)
   1. Fiction—Technique. 2. Suspense fiction—Authorship. 3. Creative writing. I. Title.

PN3355.S557   2000
808.3'872—dc21   99-053594
                                                           CIP

Editor: Michelle Howry
Designer: Sandy Conopeotis Kent
Cover designer: Matthew Gaynor
Cover photography: Ian Lawrence, © 1999/Nonstock (airplane) and Beverly Brown/Photonica (man on street)
Production coordinator: Rachel Vater

For Frances B. Macdonald, the librarian who gave me life,
then allowed me to dream.

And in memory of Miss Georgia Moore who made sure my mother and I,
and thousands of other Shelbyville High School students,
understood and appreciated the English language she so deeply loved.

ACKNOWLEDGMENTS

The author is greatly indebted to the following people: Evan Marshall, agent and cheerleader, for believing I could do it; Jack Heffron for giving me the chance; Dave Borcherding for steering me in the right direction; and Michelle Howry for her enthusiastic, on-the-mark editorial comments. Additional thanks go to Kathy Littekin for her transcription skills; and Margaret Anne Huffman, author and friend, for patiently answering dozens of questions about this business of nonfiction writing.

Special thanks go to the eleven authors who graciously agreed to be interviewed for part two of this book; to all the wonderful suspense writers whose work nourished my dreams and continues to challenge my talents; and, as always, to Jerry, who puts up with and loves me through all the weirdness that goes along with marriage to a writer.

Trish Macdonald Skillman
Wichita Falls, TX
May 1999

ABOUT THE AUTHOR

T. Macdonald Skillman has published two suspense novels, *Someone to Watch Over* (1994) and *Buried Secrets* (1995), both from Dell. She speaks often at writers conferences, usually on writing the mystery or the suspense novel. A member of Sisters in Crime and the Mystery Writers of America, Skillman lives in Wichita Falls, Texas.

TABLE *of* CONTENTS

INTRODUCTION . . . 1

> ## PART I
>
> ## *The Elements of Technique*
>
> 3

CHAPTER 1

Defining Suspense . . . 4

A discussion of suspense; the suspense novel and its subgenres; reading as a writer vs. reading for pleasure.

CHAPTER 2

Exploring the Categories of Suspense . . . 11

What distinguishes the various classifications of suspense; how some overlap; which categories require specialized knowledge to write; suggested reading to help you decide the category that's right for you.

CHAPTER 3

Characterization . . . 24

The need for reader identification and how to achieve it; bringing characters to life; the dreaded looking glass—how to describe viewpoint characters without using mirrors; avoiding stereotypes; why even villains need soft spots.

CHAPTER 4

The Basics of Plot . . . 41

The importance of conflict and tension; determining where your story begins; foreshadowing—the subtle art of teasing the reader; the rhythm of suspense—climax and resolution; suggestions for organizing scenes.

CHAPTER 5

Case Studies in Plotting . . . 50

Step-by-step development of a basic plot for each category of suspense.

CHAPTER 6

Setting and Atmosphere . . . 65

Effective use of these elements to draw the reader into your story; why research and believability go hand in hand; employing exotic locations without subsidizing your travel agent's retirement.

CHAPTER 7

Point of View . . . 80

Who should be telling your story and why; the pros and cons of first-, second-, and third-person narrative; tense options.

CHAPTER 8

Back Story . . . 95

What the reader should know vs. what the writer *must* know; how much to tell and when to tell it; the importance of playing fair without revealing too much; why less is usually more; when to rely on flashbacks and why effective transitions are the key to their use.

CHAPTER 9

Goals and Motivation . . . 106

Establishing believable reasons for characters to jump into the fray and then struggle on when logic insists all hope is gone.

CHAPTER 10

Dialogue . . . 122

Using dialogue to establish character, reveal or disguise critical information, and temporarily lead readers astray; the proper use of dialect and regional accents.

CHAPTER 11

Pacing . . . 137

The heart of a suspense novel; how to entice the reader into your story, slam the door, bolt the locks, and have them clinging to the edge of their seat till the end of the ride; mountains and valleys—the need for breathing room along the way.

CHAPTER 12

Theme . . . 151

Climbing a soapbox can involve more than an episode of vertigo; the need for an even-handed approach to controversial issues—how to achieve it and still make your point.

CHAPTER 13

Endings ... 157

Determining which outcome is best for the type of suspense you've chosen; the balance between truth, justice and reader satisfaction.

CHAPTER 14

Style ... 166

How style influences the type of suspense novel you choose to write—and vice versa.

CHAPTER 15

Words on a Page ... 173

How the choice of language and the placement of words, sentences and even paragraphs can strengthen or weaken a suspense novel; what to watch for in final revisions.

CHAPTER 16

The Mechanics of Submission ... 185

Researching the market; determining which publisher is right for *your* book; knowing when you're ready for an agent and how to find the right one; a professional approach to submission.

PART II

Interviews With the Experts

196

Author's Note ... 197

MICHAEL CONNELLY

Writing Crime-Based Psychological Suspense ... 198

CLIVE CUSSLER

Writing Action Adventure ... 205

JOY FIELDING

Writing Women-in-Jeopardy/Psychological Suspense ... 211

TESS GERRITSEN
Writing the Medical Thriller...218

JOHN GILSTRAP
Writing Issue-Driven Psychological Suspense...224

JUDITH KELMAN
Writing Issued-Driven Women-in-Jeopardy Suspense...230

SHIRLEY KENNETT
Cutting-Edge Technology and the Techno-Thriller...233

JOHN LUTZ
Using Urban Settings in Psychological Suspense...240

RICHARD NORTH PATTERSON
Writing the Legal/Political Thriller...245

MARY WILLIS WALKER
Writing a Series Character in Psychological Suspense...250

MARILYN WALLACE
Writing Romantic Relationship Suspense...255

BIBLIOGRAPHY...262

INDEX...265

INTRODUCTION

One of the first questions I was asked when I proposed this book was, "Do you know all these people on your interview list?"

The answer was no. I'd shared mystery convention panel rostrums with two of the writers and heard three others speak. But my main criterion for inclusion on my query list was an author's presence on my personal library shelves.

Still, the question gave me pause. Who was I to think such top names as Joy Fielding and Michael Connelly would agree to talk to me about their work? The only formal interview I'd ever conducted had been with a lawyer I'd known since high school. I'd also spoken with police and assistant prosecuting attorneys while researching novels, but we were talking the big time now.

"Do you think you could get at least six confirmations by this time next month?" my potential acquiring editor asked.

"No problem," I assured him. Then I mailed sixteen queries.

Eight days later, an agent for one name on the list called to request more information. "Doesn't sound like the sort of thing my client would be interested in," she muttered before hanging up. A second rejection came in the same day's mail. The clock was ticking and I was getting nervous. My husband the optimist issued daily pep talks. The next three queries came back marked "yes."

Confidence can be bolstered in strange ways. The morning of day twelve found me standing barefoot in my kitchen, making potato salad for that evening's meal. I answered the phone to hear, "Trish, this is Clive Cussler. When do you want to do this interview you wrote me about?" That evening I left the potato salad in the fridge and took my husband out to dinner.

Eighteen days after the queries had gone out, I forwarded a revised proposal that included ten confirmations. Joy Fielding had also responded via phone— from Toronto. Once my misdirected query tracked Michael Connelly to his new address, he became number eleven. Out of sixteen authors, only three failed to reply.

Those who agreed to be interviewed turned out to be gracious professionals who appreciated the time I spent tailoring my questions to their individual works. I had expected no less.

The responses proved insightful and in some cases poetic.

I thank them and I recommend their books to those who want to see for themselves exactly how thrillers should be written.

Part I

The Elements of Technique

Defining Suspense

L *ast night I dreamt I went to Manderley again.*

No, you haven't picked up the wrong book.

What better way to introduce a text on writing suspense novels than to begin with the opening line of *Rebecca*, Daphne du Maurier's classic 1938 narrative of gothic suspense?

I could have as easily begun with a passage from "The Pit and the Pendulum," Edgar Allan Poe's much shorter 1842 treatise on the Spanish Inquisition.

Most of you have read Poe's work. You're probably also familiar with *Rebecca*, if not the book, then Hollywood's interpretation. Though vastly different in terms of subject matter and style, both works have classic elements of suspense.

But how do you identify what is or isn't a suspense novel?

First things first. Despite Poe's unquestioning mastery of suspense, I won't be dealing here with short stories. Nor will I be dwelling on classic gothics like *Rebecca*, although I will cover categories that might be described as modern gothics.

Neither will I be investigating the horror/supernatural genre, such as the works of Stephen King and Dean Koontz. Other texts that provide insight into that specialized category exist, among them *Writing Horror*, edited by Mort Castle, also from Writer's Digest Books.

Now that we have that straight, what *does* qualify as a suspense novel for this book?

How about romance? Best-selling romance authors draw their readers into their stories by keeping them in suspense about whether, or at least when, the hero and heroine will rise above society's social restrictions, come to their senses or solve a myriad of other challenges so they can finally be together. A rich tapestry of characters, varied settings and often frightening complications that keep the protagonists from reaching their goal—doesn't that meet the requirements for suspense?

No, it doesn't.

In a romantic novel the author's focus must always remain on the two lead characters. Introducing them in such a way that the reader knows these two people are meant for each other. Creating the obstacle course that keeps them apart.

Romantic suspense novels on the other hand . . . but I'll get to those in a moment.

What about mysteries? They're certainly suspenseful. Taut prose following police detectives, private investigators or amateur detectives as they try to solve murders or other crimes. Surely those encompass all the elements of suspense.

Not exactly. But we're getting closer.

There are many differences between mystery and suspense. (See the sixteen-point comparison of the two by author Carolyn Wheat on page 10.) But one of the main distinctions between the two genres is this: The focus of a true mystery is on the puzzle. A crime has been committed. Whodunit? Howdunit? Whydunit?

Yes, there's usually a strong element of suspense. The hero or heroine is in various sorts of danger throughout much of the book. Other characters the protagonist cares about may also be at risk, may even become victims. But the majority of today's mysteries are series books. Since series characters rarely die, readers' concern about the fate of the book's most important character, the protagonist, is greatly reduced.

No one expects the climax of Robert B. Parker's next novel to end with the funerals of Spenser and Hawk and Susan.

Nor do they really believe Sue Grafton will bump off Kinsey Millhone before her intrepid heroine gets to *Z*.

Agatha Christie *did* do away with Hercule Poirot, but her publisher refused to release the book until Christie herself was near the end of her very prolific career. Popular demand eventually forced Sir Arthur Conan Doyle to resurrect Sherlock Holmes after killing him off.

Then what *is* suspense? Before things get any more confusing, I'm going to ask you to go through a short experiment with me.

Into the Woods

Imagine that you are walking along a forest trail. It's spring and you're alone. You can look up and see a shady canopy of leaves overhead and shafts of late afternoon sunlight filtering through the trees.

If you look closely, you'll probably see small animals, such as lizards or chameleons. The birds will be singing. Perhaps a gentle breeze will rustle the leaves.

At this point you're simply taking a peaceful stroll.

Suppose as you look around, you notice an area of trampled undergrowth that leads deep into the bushes, away from the trail? Your curiosity might be aroused, but nothing you've observed so far should trigger a sense of alarm.

But what if the birds suddenly stopped chirping, the forest creatures ceased scurrying and the woods fell unnaturally silent?

Without knowing exactly why, you'd begin to feel uneasy.

How would you feel if the next thing you saw was a large smear of fresh blood on that crushed undergrowth, and the next thing you heard was the sound of someone crashing through those bushes in your direction?

Your adrenaline would be pumping, your body would be tensed and you would be shifting your weight as if poised for flight.

The above exercise is a bit melodramatic, but I wrote it that way to make a point.

Suspense is *emotional.* It's surprise and confusion and fear and anticipation. And suspense is *danger.* Immediate danger. It's worrying about what's *going* to happen, not about the action taking place at that moment.

As the atmosphere changed and an element of the unknown entered the simple little scene, those peaceful surroundings and innocent observations took on new meaning.

Do you remember sitting around a fire at camp, telling ghost stories? Or huddling beneath the covers in your room, listening to the lightning crack and the thunder crash?

If the counselor or the camp director popped out of the darkness to yell, "Boo!" you probably jumped and laughed along with everyone else.

If Mom or Dad turned on the light, sat by your bed till the storm blew itself out or invited you to cuddle with them in the big bed, things looked a lot brighter.

So, do we know what suspense is now?

Truthfully, all we understand are the things that make up an *incident* of suspense. Which brings us back to the question—what is a suspense novel?

One explanation is this: A true suspense novel is a book about characters who find themselves trapped in a series of increasingly frightening incidents that force them to take extraordinary steps to survive.

A suspense novel can also be a book in which a strong lead character is charged with saving someone (a serial killer's next victim, for instance— Thomas Harris's *The Silence of the Lambs*) or something (the U.S.A.—Tom Clancy's *The Hunt for Red October*) from death or destruction.

Multiple variations on these two themes exist. Which brings us to a discussion of the various categories of suspense novels.

Making a Choice

Before beginning a suspense novel you have to know what type of suspense you plan to write. While there are dozens of ways to classify suspense fiction, for this book I've broken the genre down into eight key categories.

  Action-adventure
  Legal thrillers
  Medical thrillers
  Political thrillers
  Psychological suspense

Romantic relationship suspense
Women-in-jeopardy suspense
Techno-thrillers

Many suspense novels fall into more than one classification. Knowing the defining elements of each will help you understand how to construct a book that will keep both editors and readers on the edges of their seats.

We'll discuss the individual characteristics of each division in chapter two. You'll also find a list of authors whose work falls under the various categories at the end of that chapter.

To help you decide which type of suspense you want to write, read a few novels from each category. Once you find the category you like best, read— no, make that *devour*—as many books in that particular area as your credit card or library will allow.

The first rule of writing is to READ, READ, READ—especially within the genre you're contemplating. To be a good suspense writer, you have to first be an avid reader of suspense. The catch is that you must learn to *read as a writer.*

Consider for a moment the last good novel you read. When you put it down, your first thought was probably something like, *This woman's characters really come to life*, or, *I wish I could plot as well as he does.*

If your initial response involved sugarplum visions about the size of the author's advance, you're approaching the business of writing from the wrong end. As with the physician's creed of "First do no harm," the words scrawled above a serious writer's desk read "First write a good book."

Now think about the last *bad* novel you read. The one that made you wonder how things like that get published. Or perhaps the book wasn't really that awful; maybe it merely left you oddly dissatisfied.

As a reader you probably tossed that one aside or consigned it to the donation pile for the next library sale. The other book, the one that made you envy the author's talents, earned a place in your personal library and a shot at being read again and again.

Just as you didn't waste precious time critiquing what was wrong with the bad book, you probably didn't examine the good one too closely, either. But that's exactly what you need to do, and you need to do it *as you read*.

I'm not talking English Lit 101 analysis here. Guessing what was in the author's psyche as he put pen to paper won't help you write a good book. Learning how a particular passage or scene was constructed, why it did its job of pulling you into the story or what made a character effective could well be a first step toward that goal.

While it may feel a bit awkward at first, this isn't as hard as it may sound. The only downside is that once you master the technique, you become a more discriminating reader. Choosing a book may take a little longer, but I guarantee you'll enjoy what you do read even more than before.

If you can't bring yourself to dissect a suspense novel the first time you read it, put it aside for a few days, then read it again. Do this with a dozen books, primarily the well-written ones, but include a few bad eggs as well. (You also need to discover what *doesn't* work and why.) After a while you'll find yourself automatically looking for the underlying structure and defining characterization in any book you read.

I wish I could tell you exactly how to do this, but we each have our own learning curve. A good example of this are three of my friends who are also writers. Once that initial "So *that's* how she does it" raises the hair on the back of Paula's neck, the skills she's uncovered become part of her normal thought process as she tackles her own writing. A few notes on what he's reading are all Allen needs to get started. Carla, on the other hand, sometimes has to sketch an outline of a book before the light dawns.

The following chapters will teach you what you need to look for to master the technique of reading as a writer, as well as discuss what you must know before writing your own suspense novel.

If you'd like to learn more about reading as a writer, Lawrence Block addresses the subject in greater depth in chapter three of his *Writing the Novel: From Plot to Print.*

Sixteen Differences Between Mystery and Suspense
BY CAROLYN WHEAT (USED BY PERMISSION)

A mystery concerns itself with a puzzle.	Suspense presents the reader with a nightmare.
A mystery is a power fantasy; we identify with the detective.	Suspense is a victim fantasy; we identify with someone at the mercy of others.
A mystery can be likened to a myth.	Suspense is more like a fairy tale.
In a mystery the hero or heroine already has the skills he or she needs to solve the puzzle.	In suspense, he or she must learn new skills to survive.
In a mystery, thinking is paramount.	In suspense, feeling is paramount.
The most important action in a mystery takes place offstage.	In suspense, the important action happens onstage.
A mystery usually takes place within a small circle of friends.	The hero or heroine of a suspense novel often finds him- or herself thrust into a larger world.
Readers of mysteries are looking for clues.	Readers of suspense are expecting surprises.
In a mystery, information is withheld.	In suspense novels, information is provided.
The ideal reader of mysteries remains one step behind the hero or heroine.	Those who read suspense should be one step ahead of the hero or heroine.
Mystery readers expect a series.	Those who read suspense know a book can be a one-shot.
A mystery asks: Who done it?	In suspense the question is: What's going to happen?
The hero or heroine in a mystery is looking for suspects.	The hero or heroine in suspense looks for betrayers.
A mystery hero or heroine must confront a series of red herrings.	The suspense novel hero or heroine faces a cycle of distrust.
Mystery endings must be intellectually satisfying.	Suspense endings must provide emotional satisfaction.
Mysteries are usually three hundred manuscript pages.	Suspense novels can be longer.

CHAPTER 2

Exploring the Categories of Suspense

In this chapter we'll take an overview of the eight categories of suspense, discuss the basic features of each and note similarities between some of the classifications. We'll also explore what qualifications, if any, you as a writer must have to create a believable story.

Action-Adventure

Moviegoers get their kicks from Hollywood's latest version of menacing meteors (*Armageddon, Deep Impact*), psychopaths bent on blowing up city buses (*Speed*) and nature run amok (*Dante's Peak, Twister*). Readers look for similar stimuli between the covers of action-adventure novels.

Action-adventure does not involve metamorphosing aliens or giant insects. Those belong strictly to the realm of science fiction.

What you *will* find in action-adventure suspense novels are renegade cops or military men, cults holding America hostage and heroic citizens charged with rebuilding civilization following nuclear or natural disaster. Books involving Indiana Jones-type characters, whether operating in the recent past or modern times, also fall into this category, as do novels about secret government agencies established to handle political crises.

Romantic entanglements, if any, are brief and infrequent. In our politically correct world, the hero is usually less cavalier than he might have been in previous decades.

Sometimes action-adventure heroes are recurring series characters, such as Ian Fleming's James Bond and Clive Cussler's Dirk Pitt. Both authors created larger-than-life protagonists who repeatedly encounter wily villains with diabolical schemes for destruction. Readers know Bond and Pitt will survive; it's their exploits and the danger to other characters that have kept fans intrigued through multiple books.

Some may contend that action-adventure falls outside the guidelines for suspense fiction. I've included it for two reasons: (1) It fits the second definition of suspense—a book in which a strong lead character is charged with saving some*one* or some*thing* from death or destruction—and (2) action plots have seen a resurgence of popularity in recent years both in books and on the screen.

If you sense a potential overlap with the political thriller classification (see page 14), you're right. The difference here is that the action *and the adventure itself,* rather than fear for the hero's or heroine's or humankind's well-being, drives the suspense.

I included the feminine term in the previous paragraph to make a point. Given the popularity of Xena and other female action characters on TV and in the movies, the time might be right for an action-adventure novel featuring a woman. Of course, the first hurdle if you decide to tackle such a book would be proving to an editor that such a market exists.

While action-adventure often employs imaginative gadgetry or existing technology to save the protagonist or reach his ultimate goal, such use is always secondary to the action itself. For this reason, such books are not a crossover of techno-thrillers.

Legal Thrillers

At first glance the focus of legal thrillers seems obvious. But even here there are differences within the category.

Consider John Grisham's *The Firm.* Not a courtroom scene in the book. Though the story takes place against a legal backdrop, the emphasis is on the ambitious young lawyer and the predicament that ambition places him in. Characterization and the mafia-type adversaries are the keys to this story.

Now look at Grisham's first book, *A Time to Kill.* Set in the Deep South, it deals with the brutal rape of a young black girl by redneck young racists and the death of one of those men at the hands of the child's father. Again, characterization is paramount, as are atmosphere and setting. But this time the courtroom also plays a role. It's visible offstage as the hero, the beleaguered attorney for the unremorseful father, prepares for the trial. Everything that takes place in the book is leading up to that crucial moment.

Grisham doesn't disappoint his reader. The trial and the courtroom dominate the climax of the novel.

Other scenarios that can qualify as legal thrillers: jury tampering; lawyers, judges, jury members or witnesses threatened by defendants or their families; and investigations into legal ethics. Military court settings would also apply.

Must you be an attorney or have a background in some related area of law to write a credible legal thriller? It depends. Often the answer would be yes.

Legal thrillers have the potential to overlap into the psychological suspense category. If the story is told from the viewpoint of a jury member being stalked by a relative of a man sentenced to death row and the closest scene to the courtroom takes place on the steps of the judicial building, it could be done. Just be sure to research references to legal matters or procedures in depth.

Medical Thrillers

Medical thrillers are the stories that nightmares are made from. Doomsday viruses, chemical weapons, research scientists run amok, terrorists in possession of anthrax and God knows what other twentieth- and twenty-first-century plagues.

Other plots that fit this category might involve managed care providers who decide senior citizens should die early as a cost-cutting measure, or otherwise manipulate the system for the sake of the bottom line. Unethical medical personnel, power-hungry surgeons, nurses with vendettas, aides prematurely sending terminal patients to their final rewards. The list is almost endless.

As long as the book's primary focus is a medical crisis.

Say a medical-tech heroine believes that the newest staff member has been conducting unauthorized experiments on low-income patients. If much of the book revolves around the heroine's lab search for proof and her subsequent struggle to make someone listen, it's a medical thriller.

On the other hand, if the story focuses on a young doctor out to prove his patient's claims are being denied because a Medicaid supervisor in Washington has been altering paperwork, it's probably a political thriller. Or a combination—a medical/political thriller.

Is a medical background a requirement for writing a medical thriller?

"I think it would be very difficult for a layperson to write a 'true' medical thriller," says Tess Gerritsen, physician-author of the suspense novels *Harvest* and *Life Support*. "I define [a medical thriller] as a book in which the inherent conflict or crisis arises out of medical issues. In other words, these are not just simple murder mysteries set in hospitals—these are stories in which the solution to the mystery is intimately tied into the art or the science of medicine."

Political Thrillers

Mention the word *traitor* and students of American history would probably toss out the name Benedict Arnold. Religious scholars would immediately think of Judas Iscariot. Stories of treason have been around for centuries, but novels that deal with the subject really came into their own during the Cold War.

Spies, murder plots against presidents and prime ministers, coups to overthrow despots and dictators. All of these have formed the basis for political thrillers in recent decades.

Rather than die along with the demise of the Berlin Wall, this form of suspense simply mutated a bit. While a taut, well-crafted novel set during World War II can still find an audience, today's political villains come from a variety of places.

Tom Clancy found fertile ground with a South American drug cartel, power-hungry Washington advisors, rogue CIA agents and patriotic military mavericks in *Clear and Present Danger*. Along with some critical kudos came his usual over-the-top sales and another Hollywood blockbuster.

For those who protest that Clancy's work falls more under the techno-thriller umbrella (see page 19), you'll find no argument here. This is another place where categories overlap. As always, the dividing factor—if indeed there is one—hinges on where a book's emphasis lies. The term political/techno-thriller falls as easily from a reviewer's or marketing representative's lips as either description alone.

So what other plots qualify here?

Terrorist activities certainly do. Read your morning paper or turn on the news. If an article scares *you*, there's a good chance a reader of suspense novels will find a plot that's ripped from the headlines just as frightening. The goal of writing suspense is to keep readers awake late at night. Preferably because they're turning the pages of *your* novel.

Another popular topic for political thrillers is the American political scene itself. From Watergate to the Iran-Contra and Lewinsky scandals, the intrigue and behind-the-scenes shenanigans of elected or appointed officials is always fertile ground for political thrillers. For insight into plots of this nature, see political suspense writer Richard North Patterson's remarks about his novel *No Safe Place* (page 247).

Regardless of the plot you choose, unless you're willing to do extensive research, you'll need comprehensive knowledge of political science, world economics and history to write a political thriller. Fans of this category are savvy readers, familiar with all facets of the political scene; they expect an author to be equally well-informed.

Psychological Suspense

If indeed an umbrella category exists, psychological suspense is it. Every book that wears a suspense label must contain a strong element of psychological angst for both characters and reader. Books in this classification pound you over the head with it.

Not only do they keep you on the edge of your seat, they make you stop breathing for a moment.

Success here hinges on characterization. The mental state and motivations of both protagonist and villain must have been laid bare for the reader before the book's spine-tingling conclusion. Their pasts, their strengths and weaknesses, their darkest secrets must come to light—bit by agonizing bit.

The hero or heroine may be forced to match wits with kidnappers, pedophiles, serial rapists or killers, or simply a vengeful ex-spouse or spurned lover. Tormented law enforcement officials will face off with the world's most cunning criminals.

Visualize FBI agent Clarice Starling being taunted by the vile Hannibal Lecter in Thomas Harris's *The Silence of the Lambs* and you have psychological suspense at its best.

But this category doesn't demand an ultraevil villain. Credible plots have been constructed using an average Joe (or Jane) who finds himself pushed over the edge by circumstances beyond all endurance.

Consider a young, recently downsized father with a critically ill child. His health insurance benefits have run out. The hospital's social worker has done all she can, but none of the charitable or governmental agencies will pay for the experimental procedures his child needs to survive.

So far we have a heart-tugging little story.

But suppose the distraught parent decides on the spur of the moment to rob the bank that just turned him down for a second mortgage. What if something goes terribly wrong and the gun he thought was empty goes off? A bank guard is seriously wounded.

Panic ensues. The once sympathetic antagonist is now in real trouble. So are his hostages. If the bulk of the novel deals with what's going on in the minds of the reluctant villain, his captives and perhaps a hostage negotiator outside the bank, we have psychological suspense.

It's easy to see why this classification of suspense can encompass so many others. Medical, legal and political scenarios may in reality turn out to be psychological suspense in disguise. Once again, the emotional emphasis will be the defining element.

Psychological suspense also overlaps the next two divisions.

Romantic Relationship Suspense

In romantic relationship suspense, you'll find the modern version of the gothic suspense novels like *Rebecca*, which I talked about at the beginning of chapter one. *The American Heritage Dictionary* defines gothic suspense as "a style of fiction that emphasizes the grotesque, mysterious, and desolate." Fertile ground indeed for suspense.

Women drawn to mysterious men during weekend visits to old family friends. Wives who begin to believe that those attentive husbands the women's female co-workers envy may have hidden agendas. Professional women who find themselves in the middle of passionate affairs with men they've known only a short while.

In Marilyn Wallace's *A Single Stone*, a troubled wife begins to think her husband might be responsible for the death of one child and the disappearance of another. What makes this situation even more terrifying is that their own daughter died under identical circumstances a few years before—and our heroine had been charged with her own child's murder.

Overtones of a woman doubting her own innocence and, at times, her sanity infuse Wallace's plot with echoes of the classic gothic novel.

Is the husband guilty? I won't spoil the book's ending, but I *will* say this: In romantic or relationship suspense, the plot can go either way. Sometimes a second strong male character will be on hand to confuse things. As often as not, the protagonist will be on her own, forced to find her way through a maze of conflicting information and emotions.

A Single Stone also qualifies as an example of successful series suspense. Using multiple viewpoints, Wallace interweaves the heroine's emotionally wrought scenes with more routine ones involving her team of detectives.

The thing to remember here is that, unlike genre romance, the relationship that exists—no matter how passionate—will not be the focus of the book. And while the protagonists of such stories *could* be men (Hollywood's *Fatal Attraction* comes to mind), the overwhelmingly majority are female.

Women-in-Jeopardy (aka Fem-Jep or Child-Jep) Suspense

The characteristics of the women-in-jeopardy division and the one we just explored probably blur more than any of the others. Both require strong women characters who face increasingly frightening series of dilemmas, decisions and crises.

As usual, the difference is in the details.

Women in jeopardy always discover or suspect themselves to be in personal danger. Often their children are also at risk. The villains may range from family members to obsessive strangers. The heroines start out surrounded by family, friends and neighbors. As their problems escalate, they find themselves increasingly cut off from their usual support systems.

Others can't or won't believe their claims of danger. Authorities dismiss what the frightened protagonists see as patterns in a series of seemingly innocent or unrelated incidents. Evidence disappears before others see it, thus casting doubt over the heroines' grip on reality.

Right below that "First write a good book" adage that should be taped above every writer's desk should also be these words: "goals and motivation."

Those who don't care for women-in-jeopardy thrillers often complain that no intelligent woman would put herself into the situations most fem-jep heroines experience during the course of these books. Although establishing goals and motivation is critical in *all* good writing, it is the best response authors of women-in-jeopardy novels can make to allegations of unbelievability. Every fem-jep protagonist must have a compelling reason for her actions. So important are goals and motivation to all categories of suspense, we'll examine them in depth in chapter nine.

A closely related subgenre of fem-jep is child-jep, in which the main protagonist's child is in danger, either in tandem with the parent or alone. This danger may come from a stranger or an individual using the child as a pawn, such as an unstable noncustodial parent.

Child-jep plots often come under fire as exploiting children. Some critics have also suggested that writing about such situations puts ideas in the heads of dangerous individuals.

Sources such as the FBI profiles I consulted during the creation of my own fem- and child-jep books, indicate that the idea of harming children already exists in the minds of pedophiles and others who prey on those weaker than themselves.

Reading—or writing—about the dangers that move the plots in this category is not for everyone. Writers who tackle fem- or child-jep walk a fine line between empowerment and victimization. They're aware that graphic detail or description can signal a step in the wrong direction.

For another response to the critics, see Judith Kelman's comments starting on page 230.

Techno-Thrillers

The specialized classification of techno-thrillers has a reputation as being for men only. As a fan of Tom Clancy's early novels, I have to protest. According to statistics, more women than men read and buy books. Based on Clancy's sales, I can't be the only female to explore his world of techno-thrillers.

While I may not have completely understood the workings of the caterpillar drive that made a submarine's silent running a possibility in *The Hunt for Red October*, Clancy's taut psychological naval drama kept me thoroughly engrossed from beginning to end.

Since physics wasn't part of my educational curriculum, I'll admit to scanning a few of the more technologically focused passages. This only proves that all the other elements of good suspense must have been present.

So exactly what makes a book a techno-thriller?

Technology drives the plot.

Most of these books rely on, or at least involve, military or CIA-connected settings. Without access to the latest inventions, the hero would be reduced to an average man battling evil with a slingshot or a World War II-era rifle. Villains could not appear to have the advantage unless their scientific advances seemed to supersede his.

Knowledge and research are critical here. While there may be other readers out there like me, the true audience for a techno-thriller knows its stuff.

Using theoretically possible technology is allowed. But no quirky gimmicks or Star Trek-like transporter beams—unless they'll likely become reality in the very near future. Span too many years of technology and you wind up writing science fiction.

Is this another category where you need specialized skills or intimate familiarity with subject matter?

Not necessarily. Tom Clancy simply wanted to write a good suspense novel. He envisioned a plot, did extensive research on Soviet-American naval strategies and submarine technology, and the rest is history.

Learn From the Pros

The following list of suspense titles in each subgenre is by no means inclusive. Space limitations prevent me from providing a larger sample of the wonderful authors who qualify for each category.

Many of those listed have earned places on my own bookshelves. A few appear courtesy of a friend's recommendation. Others caught my attention during an afternoon at my local bookstore. Authors whose essays appear in part two of this book got a star (*).

For authors who write in more than one genre, I've tried to include one of their suspense titles.

While many published authors have books they wish they'd given more editorial revision, you probably won't find one of those really "bad" books here. For that you'll have to do your own research.

I have two final bits of advice before you head for your bookstore or library.

• This isn't Scriptwriting 101. *Read the book.* Don't watch the movie. Hollywood rarely follows the original version and Cliffs Notes won't teach what you need to learn.

• Some classifications of suspense are darker than others. Study the jacket synopsis and scan a few pages at random if graphic descriptions aren't your cup of tea.

Action-Adventure

Peter Benchley—*Jaws* and other titles (man against nature)

Mark Berent—*Eagle Station* and others (Vietnam War settings)

Clive Cussler*—Dirk Pitt series (lost ships and international villains on land and under the sea)

Ian Fleming—James Bond series (tongue-in-cheek espionage)

W.E.B. Griffin—Brotherhood of War series (combat situations)

Legal Thrillers

William Bernhardt—Ben Kincaid series of *Justice* titles

J.F. Freedman—*Against the Wind* (alcoholic lawyer defends outlaw bikers who may be innocent of murder charges)

John Grisham—*The Firm* (young lawyer vs. mob) and other titles

Perri O'Shaughnessy (pen name for sisters Pamela and Mary O'Shaughnessy)—Nina Reilly series, various titles

Richard North Patterson*—*The Final Judgment* and other titles (great characterization, psychological drama)

Scott Turow—*Presumed Innocent* and others (good courtroom drama)

Medical Thrillers

Robin Cook—*Coma, Toxin* and other titles

Michael Crichton—*The Andromeda Strain* (deadly virus on the loose)

Eileen Dreyer—*Brain Dead* (nurse heroine)

Tess Gerritsen*—*Bloodstream* and other titles (physician-writer)

John J. Nance—*Pandora's Clock* (passengers trapped aboard plane denied permission to land because it may carry deadly virus)

Political Thrillers

Eric Ambler—*A Coffin for Dimitrios* (classic—international intrigue in Turkey and Paris, set in 1938)

Tom Clancy—*Clear and Present Danger* and other titles

Ken Follett—*The Key to Rebecca* (classic—World War II intrigue, Nazi spy vs. British agent)

Frederick Forsyth—*The Day of the Jackal* (classic—Charles de Gaulle targeted by international assassin)

John le Carré—*The Russia House* (international espionage)

Helen MacInnes—*Above Suspicion* (classic—innocent-looking British couple sent into 1939 Germany to locate missing agent who was helping refugees flee)

Psychological Suspense

Michael Connelly*—*The Poet* (cunning murderer taunts FBI agents and journalist brother of victim) and other titles

Jeff Deaver—*A Maiden's Grave* (three killers, two teachers, eight deaf students, FBI negotiator) and other titles

John Lutz*—*SWF Seeks Same* (tense modern gothic in which woman's psychotic roommate plots to steal the other's identity)

John Sandford—Lucas Davenport *Prey* series (deputy police chief)

Mary Willis Walker*—*Under the Beetle's Cellar* (apocalyptic cult leader holds schoolchildren and their bus driver underground to await Armageddon) and others in the Molly Cates series

Romantic Relationship Suspense

Daphne du Maurier—*Rebecca* (classic gothic—young woman weds a stranger whose first wife died mysteriously)

Joy Fielding*—*See Jane Run* (woman goes to buy milk and eggs and forgets who she is) and other titles

Mary Roberts Rinehart—*The Circular Staircase* (classic gothic about a strange house and murder)

Karen Robards—*Heartbreaker* (wilderness trip becomes a nightmare for a mother and daughter) and other titles

Women-in-Jeopardy (aka Fem-Jep or Child-Jep) Suspense

Mary Higgins Clark—*Where Are the Children?* (woman accused of drowning her children starts over only to have her new kids turn up missing) and other titles

John Gilstrap*—*Nathan's Run* (twelve-year-old flees detention center after killing the guard sent to kill *him*)

Carolyn Hougan—*Blood Relative* (a man comes from Argentina to kill a teenage American girl for revenge)

Jessie Hunter—*One, Two, Buckle My Shoe* (nine-year-old tomboy matches wits with a killer of only young boys who took her by mistake)

Judith Kelman*—*Someone's Watching* (a mother fights to find the reason for her injured son's erratic recovery while someone plots to finish the boy off)

Marilyn Wallace*—*Lost Angel* (young mother flees danger only to have a friend killed and her child taken)

Techno-Thrillers

Dale Brown—*The Tin Man* (international terrorists, neo-Nazi bikers, top secret bulletproof fabric) and other titles

Tom Clancy—*The Hunt for Red October* (Cold War cat-and-mouse between Soviet and U.S. submarines) and other titles

Stephen Coonts—*Flight of the Intruder* (high-tech battles in the skies over Vietnam) and other titles

Patricia Cornwell—Kay Scarpetta series (forensic pathology)

Shirley Kennett*—P.J. Gray series (psychologist uses cyberspace and virtual reality to solve crimes)

CHAPTER 3

Characterization

A discussion of which comes first—character or plot—can be like debating the chicken and the egg.

I'm not referring here to what sparks the *inspiration* for a story. That can come from dozens of things. The key to writing a successful book from whatever first teases your imagination lies in how you *develop* that original idea. Many authors, myself included, believe that creating your characters should come before anything else.

My second book, *Buried Secrets*, was inspired by a setting. But as vivid as that locale was in my mind, the backdrop didn't really come to life nor did my nebulous plot truly coalesce until I envisioned the people.

I'm not going to attempt a general treatise here on how to create believable characters. If you've done your homework as a writer, you should have already studied that subject in depth. You should know the importance of reader identification—that bonding between the people who pick up your book and the people who live inside its pages. You understand that protagonists must grow and change during the course of a story.

If either of these concepts sounds like a foreign language, I suggest reading *Characters & Viewpoint* by Orson Scott Card, part of The Elements of Fiction Writing series from Writer's Digest Books. For those who simply want a quick refresher on character development, I recommend Michael

Seidman's "Creating Characters Who Create Your Story" in the December 1996 issue of *Writer's Digest*.

What I *am* going to do in this chapter is discuss the specific kinds of characters who populate our eight types of suspense fiction and what you need to do to make these characters work.

All heroes are not the same. Neither are all villains. The category of suspense dictates how much the reader will expect, or even *want*, to know about the characters you create for your book.

Let's begin by examining typical heroes from action-adventure and techno-thrillers, categories that on the surface seem somewhat similar.

Good Guys to the Rescue
ACTION-ADVENTURE AND TECHNO-THRILLERS

Heroes in both action-adventure and techno-thrillers often bend the rules to achieve their ultimate goals. Both types of suspense have been known to use touches of humor. In both, the good guys triumph over the bad. Both involve action.

So how is the hero of one different from that of the other?

What do we really know about Ian Fleming's action hero James Bond? He's suave. An impeccable dresser. Accurate with any weapon known to man, and a few that have yet to be invented. He's able to pilot anything from a ten-speed bicycle to the Concorde and beyond. He likes his martinis shaken—not stirred; his action fast and furious; and his women beautiful and challenging.

Other than his duty to queen and country, Bond's internal thoughts and personal data are nowhere to be found.

Does he have a mother? If so, does he think of her with affection or wish she'd quit nagging him to settle down and make her a grandma? What kinds of videos make him laugh? Does he even own a VCR? Did he need Q to program it? Was he a good student, or did he drive the headmaster to despair?

Now consider Tom Clancy's techno-thriller hero Jack Ryan.

From his first appearance in *The Hunt for Red October*, we know Ryan is a family man. He's concerned about finding the right Barbie for his little girl's

Christmas. Ryan hates flying, even on the Concorde, no matter who's in the cockpit. He thinks of himself as a paper pusher, yet feels excited, and more than a bit awed, to suddenly find himself briefing the National Security Council on what could become a major crisis.

There's not much in common between Jack Ryan and James Bond—except that both instinctively come through in a crisis, handle themselves with honor in the face of overwhelming odds and live to fight another day.

None of this means you can't have an action-adventure hero who has emotions or a techno-thriller protagonist whom the reader never really comes to know. What it *does* mean is that your characterization choices must make sense, based on the type of suspense novel you're writing and the decisions you make about plot.

Here's an example.

Let's take an action-adventure character I'll call Burke. His younger brother's wife, Jenny, and her daughter Amy are being held hostage by terrorists who intend to blow up a nuclear reactor if their demands aren't met. Common sense tells the reader this hero's reaction would be intensified by his sense of family duty.

The reader might infer, even if it's never actually spelled out, that keeping an eye on little brother has been part of what's toughened Burke and made him a leader. Little Amy's probably been the apple of her uncle's eye since the first day she grabbed hold of his finger. Perhaps Jenny dated Burke before she met his more domesticated brother.

Action-adventure by its very nature demands a relatively detached hero. So how do we show Burke's reaction to the kidnapping of Amy and her mother? How do we give him emotions?

Simply writing that Burke is mad as hell and stating the reasons is one option. But slowly revealing his boiling emotions through the things he does or says would be much more effective. That old rule of "Show, don't tell."

Here are a few subtle solutions—none of which should get in the way of the action. When a minor character questions the value of two lives compared to that of thousands, Burke could:

- Ball his fists and turn away, then whirl back around and slug the speaker.
- Grab the character by the shirt, then calmly let go without comment, revealing his icy control.
- The same point could be made with sound, like the crack when the pen in Burke's hand snaps in two.
- Facial expressions can also be effective, as when a concerned buddy attempts to bring Burke's family into a conversation. If Burke tightens his jaw, develops a tic on his eyelid or flashes a cold stare to warn that the subject's off-limits, readers will read between the lines.

Wound as tight as an addict in withdrawal, yet still stoic and controlled. This hero's emotions are there but remain beneath the surface. *And that's just where fans of action-adventure want the feelings to stay.*

Techno-thrillers permit a bit more leeway.

Clancy doesn't bother finessing the intro to Jack Ryan. We're introduced to the hero of *The Hunt for Red October* in a brief scene on page 23 of the novel. Using internal dialogue, Clancy *tells* us that Ryan is a Ph.D. who's writing a history of Fleet Admiral William Halsey. A quick exchange with Ryan's young daughter *shows* us that the child is concerned that Santa Claus might not find her at their new home.

A second passage *tells* us Ryan and his family live in England and that he will be visiting Washington, DC, during the coming week. When he abandons his writing to go play with his child, we're *shown* his devotion to his family. At this point we know nothing about Ryan's naval background or his connection to the CIA.

Ryan's next scene (at CIA headquarters) comes on page 45. Here the author takes an entire page to *tell* us Ryan's physical appearance, that he's an intelligent but low-keyed individual who takes pride in his work and how he feels about being employed by the CIA. Clancy also touches again on his hero's love for his family.

Clancy's reasons for this approach are simple. With all that's happening in a half-dozen separate locations, he doesn't have time for subtlety; so he goes for the throat and gets it over with. The reader learns about Ryan's emotions because it is necessary to know how much this rather ordinary-seeming man has at stake when things really get rough.

Other techno-thriller heroes may not require that the reader know much about their emotional workings. Knowing that the hard-as-Kryptonite pilot of an Apache chopper loaded with secret, advanced weaponry loves little kittens and phones his mother every Sunday is probably irrelevant to the story.

Lead characters in action-adventure novels change the least during the course of the story, at best becoming more hardened.

As with the glimpses of emotion and personal background, techno-thriller protagonists are more apt to evolve. Jack Ryan, for instance, learns that he's more macho than he thought. Still, subtlety reigns. You won't find this category's heroes gathered about a piano singing "Feelings" at the end of the book.

Discovering Exactly What Makes Protagonists Tick
PSYCHOLOGICAL, ROMANTIC RELATIONSHIP
AND WOMEN-IN-JEOPARDY

Speaking of feelings, the next three categories allow much wider latitude. Indeed, several of them *require* that the author crawl inside the protagonist's head. But to make the characters memorable, you must first make them real. With the possible exception of action-adventure, even heroes and heroines are not without character flaws.

Readers of romantic relationship, fem- or child-jep, and psychological suspense expect to experience uncertainty and terror right along with the protagonist. This can be achieved through *internal dialogue, physical reactions* (which should be much more obvious than those described in the previous example) and the *observations of other characters*. We'll talk more about these methods of characterization later in this chapter.

Another method of characterization involves the dialogue between the protagonist and the antagonist. We know how Hannibal Lecter's taunts affect the young female FBI agent in *The Silence of the Lambs* because Thomas Harris deftly draws us into that part of Clarice Starling's mind where her own demons dwell. Harris uses direct dialogue between Lecter and Starling to reveal much of what he wants us to know.

In *Under the Beetle's Cellar*, Mary Willis Walker takes a slightly different approach by using another character to let readers experience how eleven frightened schoolchildren react to being buried in a bus by an apocalyptic cult leader. Bus driver Walter Demming's internal dialogue provides the eyes through which readers watch the children survive day after day of captivity.

Both books are intense psychological studies. Harris and Walker also make sure their protagonists stretch and change and grow in various degrees during the course of their books. Clarice Starling identifies her fears, a first step toward conquering them. Walter Demming must overcome his own nightmares, related to his time in Vietnam, before he can complete his part in the story.

Growth and change are critical elements for both fem- or child-jep and romantic relationship suspense. These categories involve characters who've lost, if only momentarily, a level of control over their lives. Readers not only expect the protagonists to survive their ordeals, they want them to triumph. And if those characters exact a little revenge while they're at it, so much the better.

The important thing to remember here is that good fem-jep heroines may have weaknesses but they're never wimps. Growth comes as they conquer their deficiencies and fears.

Getting inside a fem-jep protagonist's thoughts also allows an author to justify the character's sometimes seemingly irrational behavior. "Because I say so" doesn't work here. Readers have to know *why* she's staying in that creepy old house—and then believe that her reason makes obvious sense in that particular situation.

The show-don't-tell rule applies here as well. "Character shows itself in behavior," says author Joy Fielding. "Don't tell me she's neurotic; *show* me what she's doing so I can figure it out for myself."

LEGAL THRILLERS

Character development in a legal thriller can vary.

An embattled juror should exert an emotional, this-could-happen-to-me pull on the reader. To create an attorney fighting the bottle, an ex-wife, disbarment and the case of a lifetime, an author would have to delve even deeper into the emotional pool. Pitting a sleazy but successful ambulance chaser against a novice female pro bono attorney might result in both deep emotional involvement and courtroom fireworks.

If a plot involved a staid old firm and a hotshot junior partner plotting to expose the company's unethical practices, an emphasis on intrigue and behind-the-scenes backstabbing could preclude deep personal or emotional revelations about the protagonist.

MEDICAL AND POLITICAL THRILLERS

Medical thrillers also run the gamut, but normally demand that an author focus on what's happening in the protagonist's head as well as in the lab. Political thrillers can go either way. Let's examine a suspense novel that overlaps the two classifications.

John J. Nance's *Pandora's Clock* pits a flight crew and passengers against a doomsday virus and an on-ground panic that prevents their plane from landing. Frightened officials shut down radar beacons, douse landing lights and block runways. Fighter jets warn them away from every nation's airspace. Politicians and generals discuss the strategy and ramifications of shooting down the jetliner.

Nance would have been cheating his readers if he hadn't provided some personal background for a few souls on the plane, as well as critical insight into the minds of the players on both sides of his deadly equation.

+>-<+

As you can see, the amount of characterization your thriller will need depends on which type of suspense you're writing. If you prefer to write plots that place less emphasis on the emotional side of your characters, action-adventure or techno-thrillers are your best bet. For the other six categories, you should be prepared to spend a varying amount of time inside the heads of the people you've created.

In subsequent chapters I'll discuss additional ways of revealing the emotions, background and even the warts of suspense protagonists.

Villains Who Love to Be Nasty

Think about the best suspense novels you've read. Which characters remain most vivid in your mind? If you answered, "The villains," authors of hundreds of thrillers will applaud.

So what makes a good villain? I'm going to let a couple of fellow writers tackle this one.

In her May 1995 *Writer's Digest* fiction column, Nancy Kress defined a villain as "a character who—from motives of selfish gain—knowingly seeks to injure, kill or loot another person."

Reviewer Lana Sweeten-Shults had this to say: "What makes thrillers so scary depends, for the most part, on the fear factor of the villain."

Villains are selfish people who want to frighten us.

Does this mean they have no redeeming qualities? No. Just like good protagonists, most villains' personalities contain shades of gray. Again the category of suspense dictates character development.

While stereotypes are best avoided, action-adventure often pushes this edict.

Clive Cussler's hero Dirk Pitt has been described as a cross between Indiana Jones and James Bond. Like Jones, Pitt makes mistakes and occasionally bleeds. Unlike Bond, he has an established cadre of cohorts he calls on when the need arises. The result is Pitt comes across as more of a flesh-and-blood human being.

Pitt's opponents, however, have included the following characters:
- Japanese extremists out to blackmail the United States
- smugglers in the Amazon jungle
- U.S. industrialists with a secret base on the moon
- an elusive billionaire with a God complex
- politicians trying to prevent discovery of a nineteenth-century document that could force the United States and Canada to merge

Obviously some of these people push the stereotype envelope. Just as important, they make great villains for a class of suspense in which readers are more concerned with what's going to happen next than with what's taking place inside the heads of the characters orchestrating the mayhem.

Readers learn about the villains who plague Pitt and company through their evil deeds and plans rather than by emotional descriptions. Note, too, that no gray areas exist here—action heroes are typically "good" and the antagonists they fight are "bad," pure and simple.

On the other hand, Marko Ramius, Clancy's Russian sub captain and antagonist in *The Hunt for Red October* is a complex study. In actuality he's an anti-villain—a good man in a bad situation, a villain of circumstance. He's the antagonist but not necessarily a bad guy.

Marko Ramius has valid reasons for touching off an international incident that risks nuclear war. Years of watching the dismal results of his country's programs have fed a youthful disillusion with Communism. The incompetency of pampered party medical personnel has caused the death of his beloved wife. Corruption, inferior equipment and his superiors' disregard for the lives of the seamen he trains have added to his discontent. Now, Ramius has devised a plan that will allow him and many of his officers to defect.

By using plot and characterization to justify Ramius's actions, Clancy succeeded in giving readers a sympathetic villain. Again, we learn much of what we need to know about Ramius through passages of telling, as well as from Jack Ryan's profile of the man and Ryan's conviction that all is not as it seems on the surface of the impending disaster.

Other techno-thriller villains may be more clear-cut and require less mental probing by the author.

• The setting for the Jake Grafton series by Stephen Coonts is the Vietnam War. Here the enemy is more one-dimensional. The emphasis remains on technology and heroes, as it should.

• Patrick McLanahan, Dale Brown's series protagonist, uses technology to fight international terrorists and neo-Nazis. If these guys have a gray-haired grandma somewhere, readers don't want to know it.

• Patricia Cornwell's look at forensic science in her Kay Scarpetta series sometimes investigates the personal aspects of a villain, but not always.

You may see a familiar pattern developing: In the action-adventure and techno-thriller categories, both heroes and villains are usually more clear-cut.

The books that normally take readers into the lives and minds of their villains tend to fall within the other six classifications.

Villains of the Stuff Nightmares Are Made of

Serial rapists, pedophiles and killers. Villains who make readers want to get up and check to be sure the dead bolt is on.

While they may represent the quintessential idea of evil, most suspense authors take great pains to fully develop such characters. Not to justify what they do, but to attempt to understand the *why* of their crimes.

At what point does a man's fantasy of settling the score with the women who've scorned or rejected him cross the line into the brutalization of other surrogate women? What makes one abused and traumatized child grow to become a caring teacher and another a vicious murderer? Are pedophiles products of their environment or strictly genetic quirks of nature?

Readers of psychological suspense (and to some extent, those of fem- and child-jeopardy novels) want to know about these things. So how do you make such creatures come to life?

INSIDE THE MIND OF A VILLAIN

Movie villains have to rely on exaggerated facial expressions or threatening behavior to convey how dangerous they are. Restrained descriptions of those things also work in novels. But on paper it's knowing what goes on inside their minds that really makes these villains so frightening.

The deeper a writer probes an antagonist's mind, the more likely a vulnerability within the character will be revealed. While this should not justify evil actions, it will prevent the character from becoming a one-dimensional figure.

The villain in Jessie Hunter's *One, Two, Buckle My Shoe* is a serial killer of young boys. When he snatches a nine-year-old tomboy by mistake, the reader learns that, initially, not only can't this monster imagine murdering the girl, he can't even touch her. "I won't hurt you," he tells his victim, "I can't."

Hunter gives readers a perpetrator as terrified as his captive, a villain, no matter how despicable, with a normal, panicked reaction to finding himself in an unexpected situation.

THE VILLAIN AS OBSERVED BY OTHERS

Samuel Mordecai, Mary Willis Walker's apocalyptic cult leader from *Under the Beetle's Cellar,* may be one of the more frightening antagonists in recent history. The author found even the process of creating this character unsettling: "Of all the research I've done, the most uncomfortable for me was reading the writings and subscribing to the newsletters of the extremist Christian groups I studied in preparation for *Under the Beetle's Cellar.* That scared me."

Instead of taking us inside Mordecai's mind for clues to his behavior and motivation, Walker takes another tact. Molly Cates, Walker's main viewpoint character is a journalist. Her interviews with Mordecai and others, such as the woman who raised him, allow us to see what has brought him to this point in time. Mordecai's own words, revealed in sermons to his hostages and to the frustrated negotiators outside his compound, emphasize his mental deterioration and foreshadow the impending disaster. Gradually, from a combination of all these different sources, a picture of the man emerges.

VILLAINS BY GENRE

Who are the most likely villains in each genre? Take a look at some of the most common.

Fem- or child-jeopardy villains may be stalkers or abusive partners who attempt to coerce the other party by taking or threatening her children.

Romantic relationship suspense novels often involve obsessive villains or those with profit motives. John Lutz's *The Ex* tells the story of an unbalanced woman who sets out to "take over" her ex-husband's new family. Of course his new wife is in the way. Again, multiple viewpoints provide a window into the mental processes on both sides of this struggle.

Legal villains (or more accurately, illegal ones) will either be uncaring corporate types, cunning shysters, criminal elements or, occasionally, desperate amateurs. The depth of development will vary here as it does with the category's protagonists.

Medical thrillers also employ a wide variety of antagonists. In Nance's *Pandora's Clock,* the real villain is the virus itself. Everyone else is reacting out of panic. This gives Nance an opportunity to shed light on the emotions we all have buried within us. Who knows how *we* would respond in similar circumstances?

In *Harvest,* Tess Gerritsen explores the grisly subject of selling human organs. The twist to this novel is that the greedy Mafia-type villains are recruiting and importing heart donors from the ranks of unsuspecting Russian street urchins. Rest assured these particular antagonists have no redeeming qualities.

Who are the villains in **political** thrillers? Pick a World War II-era espionage novel and the villains are Nazis or Japanese. Antagonists in books set during the Cold War are usually Russian. Choose John le Carré's *The Spy Who Came In From the Cold* and you enter a world of moles and double and even triple agents where the good guys may turn out to be the bad guys.

Writers of current political thrillers can make almost anyone a villain and decide how deeply they want to delve into their antagonists' psyches. Any of the methods for character development we discussed in the sections on psychological suspense can apply.

UNDISCLOSED VILLAINS

A villain who's part of a main character's daily life—or one who may be so innocuous as to be invisible—adds to the terror factor of a story. Masking the villain's identity until the end of the story without cheating the reader is the trick.

Such villains cannot make a single appearance early in the book. Nor can they suddenly show up three pages before "The End." To avoid this dilemma, try one of the following:

- Include several secondary characters as red herrings to misdirect a reader's suspicions.
- Never use scenes told from those characters' viewpoints.
- Write from the antagonist's viewpoint—without identifying that character by name.

This last option is the one Jessie Hunter chose in *One, Two, Buckle My Shoe.* Even in his internal dialogue, Hunter's serial killer refers to himself as "The Chocolate Man," the nickname the newspapers have given him.

I created a villain in much the same way in *Buried Secrets*, by using only the pronoun "he" when I was in my antagonist's viewpoint. One advantage—or disadvantage, depending on how you look at it—was that I had to provide my red herrings with backgrounds, surroundings and actions that seemed to correspond with that of the real antagonist.

Which leads us to the next section.

Supporting Players

Suppose we are writing a suspense story about Mary, a young mother and our main character. Though Mary is our protagonist, she does not exist in a vacuum. Other important characters:

- Wes, heroine Mary's old uncle, who never shuts up
- Mary's son, Davy
- His younger playmate Johnny
- Kevin, Mary's new husband and Davy's stepdad
- A woman with dyed red hair who lives in the apartment on the corner
- Mrs. Mardis, the elderly neighbor who takes a six-thirty stroll every morning, retrieves any newspapers the delivery boy tossed in the bushes, then puts them neatly on everyone's stoop
- Eric, the newsboy
- Mary's best friend, Carol Jean, who lives across the street

These are the types of minor characters who populate a book. Some are more important than others, but for various reasons they're needed in a particular story. Must the writer get inside each of their minds during the course of a suspense novel?

No. In fact, in many cases, it's best if she doesn't. Most will simply make walk-on appearances. A bit part with perhaps a line or two of dialogue while the real action's going on elsewhere.

These people rarely grow or change but still play key roles in making a story work. Their function is to lend support, get in the way, cause things to happen or distract the protagonist. They make someone miss a critical piece of information, delay a rescue, prevent discovery of clues that can save whoever is in danger. Often they become red herrings to mislead the reader.

Or they can do exactly the opposite of all of the above.

While a writer shouldn't waste *too* much time developing such individuals, each one should get his fifteen seconds (or fifteen lines) of fame. A plot may require some of these secondary characters to show up again and again. Making each memorable in a special way is the trick.

The first chapter of John Lutz's *The Ex* opens in the midst of a tornado. As his villain Deirdre walks away from a demolished mental hospital, a hand reaches from the rubble to grab the hem of her inmate's uniform. Lutz introduces Sam, the facility's injured attendant.

> *He looked up at her with pleading in his dark eyes.*

Twice Sam begs Deirdre not to leave "this place," to "stay where you belong." Her response is to stare down at him, with a brick held poised above his head. Again, Lutz gives the reader a glimpse of Sam's internal turmoil.

> *He understood her decision and his fate and merely stared at her with frightened but resigned eyes. He closed his eyes then, and his face was calm as she hurled the brick. . . .*

Two snips of dialogue, less than fifty words, and Sam is gone—yet he serves his chilling purpose well. The reader now knows exactly what Deirdre is capable of doing. The reader's fear for Deirdre's ex-husband and his new family will be enhanced when she reappears several weeks and a thousand miles later—because of a brief encounter with a character (Sam) *who was never actually described.*

Remember those people listed at the beginning of this section? Maybe talkative old Uncle Wes is following Mary around, driving her crazy while everyone is out searching for Davy, who's missing. A brief sketch of a balding man with baggy clothes and liver-spotted hands might be all the description a reader needs. Uncle Wes's constant chatter is his real identity.

Uncle Wes is the kind of person readers tend to overlook, but this dotty old man has an important role to play. He's an essential part of a good suspense novel. The bonus is that with careful scripting by a good writer, readers can visualize such characters without an itemized catalog of features.

Kevin, however, is a different story. As the protagonist's husband in the scenario just mentioned, he should be giving Mary comfort. But what if he's not? Small things, noted absently by Mary in her internal dialogue, would be most effective here.

Perhaps Kevin's a man with a standing appointment at the manicurist, yet he's gnawing a fingernail. It's been established that the only caffeine he'll touch is a mocha latté—now he's downing endless cups of instant coffee as black as his usually sculptured hair, which he's forgotten to comb. And not once since he walked in has he put his arms around Mary.

In other words he's acting guilty. Is *he* behind his stepson's disappearance? Hold that thought. I'll be using the characters I've described above in chapter five to illustrate how to build believable plots in each of our eight categories.

Mirror, Mirror on the Wall

Describing viewpoint characters can pose a problem. Some writers provide a laundry list description of the character through the use of an omniscient point of view.

> *Tim Winslow had piercing blue eyes, carefully coifed blond hair, a movie-star cleft in his chin, a glittering Rolex watch on his wrist, and an Armani suit on his back.*

While this detached approach can work, the author risks distancing the reader. There are better ways to convey information about your character.

Other writers offer a self-portrait of the people they want their readers to see by placing the characters in front of mirrors.

> *While she waited for Tim to make his appearance, Jeannie studied her reflection in the restaurant's mirrored doors. Her nose was a little too long, but her full eyelashes and pouty lips made up for the flaw, she*

decided. Her breasts were still firm. No serious wrinkles anywhere yet, thank God. Long hours in the gym kept her tush tight and the cellulite at bay.

This approach also has its drawbacks. Except when applying makeup, shaving, brushing teeth, combing hair or doctoring a blemish, real people rarely pause to study their features in a mirror. They take a quick glance occasionally to be sure they don't have literal egg on their faces, but normally they avoid their own reflections.

This is why such scenes often feel contrived or unbelievable. Whether implausible or just amateurish, there are better ways to get the same information across to readers.

One character can comment on another's features. This can be handled either in direct address or, in the case of multiple-viewpoint characters, through internal dialogue.

Kate, the protagonist in *Someone to Watch Over*, is a waitress. Her husband is long overdue from an out-of-town trip. A jealous co-worker who likes to push Kate's buttons tosses off an insensitive remark.

> *"Maybe Michael got tired of sleepin' with a dish-water blond and took a hike."*

In a second scene four pages later, the antagonist describes Kate as he observes her from a distance.

> *Rail thin and sad-eyed, at unguarded moments she looked more like an abandoned waif than a grown woman. Cal could easily imagine her on a poster, wearing faded jeans and a dirty T-shirt, advertising an 800 number for runaways.*

The picture these passages form of Kate will vary a bit from reader to reader. Still, the image will be much more vivid than if I'd said she was barely five feet tall, weighed ninety pounds and needed to visit a beauty salon.

Another way to describe a viewpoint character is through the book's narrative passages. A little of this goes a long way. Dropping in a visual detail here and there is less distracting for a reader than long paragraphs of physical description.

> *Arthur absently ran his hand over his head. Several strands of gray hair fell across the report he was trying to complete. Brushing them away with a scowl, he sighed in resignation. The Boy Wonder would have his ass if he didn't start concentrating.*

Readers can now surmise that Arthur is an aging businessman, rapidly balding and resentful that his boss is younger than he. By providing similar details about a character, any author can master this bit of writing sleight of hand—and he won't need mirrors to do it.

Many writers cite characterization as one of their favorite aspects of writing. This critical process lets them play God—at least on paper. Getting inside fictional characters' minds, uncovering flaws, imagining relationships with others, exploring secret desires, establishing just the right histories, then rearranging all or part of what they've created as needed provides a powerful sense of control.

As you go through that same process, you'll probably find that your initial story idea has expanded and gotten clearer. The choices you made in creating your characters are pointing you toward your ultimate plot. Which is exactly where we're going next.

CHAPTER 4

The Basics of Plot

H e was born. He lived a full life. Eventually he died. And somewhere in between birth and death he experienced something so terrifying he feared he might not survive.

As a reader of suspense, which part of this man's life would you want to be told about first?

Is the scuffle he got into the day he started first grade really that interesting? Would a story about a teenage escapade when he climbed a water tower to spray-paint his class year on the side of the tank really keep you on the edge of your seat?

Details like these are part of a character's back story.

Working such material into a book may be important—*when the information has a direct bearing on the story.*

If it turns out the book's villain was the kid who bloodied the hero's nose the moment he stepped onto the playground, that story might be relevant. Especially if the conflict has continued over the years. But such background rarely belongs in an opening scene. Or even in a first chapter.

Beginnings

So when does the story *really* begin? The basic thing to remember when choosing where to begin a suspense novel is simply this: Begin with a scene that evokes the specter of suspense.

While the first scene a reader sees *could* focus on a violent act, such as a kidnapping or murder, it doesn't have to.

If a writer can't begin in the midst of the action or danger, she *must* give readers a hint of what is to come. A tightly written scene that reveals an implied threat or centers on an argument between two people may be enough.

At the very least, a character's uneasiness about something in his life should be evident to the reader.

A protagonist should believe she, or someone she cares about, is or soon will be in danger. If she's receiving phone threats, chapter one should open with a ringing telephone.

Once again, we're looking for an incident that will engage the readers' emotions as well as their curiosity.

Multiple-viewpoint suspense often begins with action as seen through the villain's eyes. Clancy starts with Captain Ramius taking the *Red October* out to sea. Jessie Hunter opens with The Chocolate Man surveying his collection of little boys' shoes.

Opening with a scene from the victim's point of view is another way to grab the reader's attention.

Mary Willis Walker begins well into the action of *Under the Beetle's Cellar*, showing us the situation inside the buried bus on day forty-six of the confinement. Her opening line sets the tone for the book.

> *Walter Demming hadn't cried since September 2, 1968, but he sure felt like crying now.*

Walker has set her hook. Few readers of psychological suspense could resist being reeled into her explosive climax.

Conflict and Tension

Before there were fear and terror, there was conflict. With conflict comes tension. These two are the building blocks of any good story. In the case of suspense, they're also the foundation, the ceiling, the paint on the walls and the latch that opens the door.

Conflict and tension do their job by making readers care about what happens to the characters.

Consider the final scene of Peter Benchley's *Jaws* (the book ending, not Hollywood's version). In the novel, by the time Chief Brody finally finds himself eyeball to eyeball with the "fish," readers are ready to rip the harpoon from his hands and cram it into the shark's belly themselves.

Why?

Because every scene leading up to that moment contained conflict and tension, which grew from character and plot.

Plot-grown conflict and tension: Brody's battle with town leaders over closing the beach. Character-grown conflict and tension: Brody's terror of the water. The fear we all have of being eaten alive.

Conflict in a novel exists when the enemy is stronger, or at least perceived that way by protagonist and reader; for example, the town council had the power to take away Brody's livelihood.

Tension is created by conflict within a character or through interaction between characters; for example, if Brody had allowed his fear to rule his actions, he would have been unable to do what was necessary to make the beach safe for tourists *and* for his kids.

Scenes are the vehicles that drive conflict and tension. In writing a suspense novel, your job is to make every scene generate both conflict and tension at some level.

How does a writer create conflict and tension?

CREATE CONFLICT AND TENSION THROUGH DIALOGUE

Dialogue is one way to reveal conflict and tension. In a scene of a teen arguing with his stepfather, both aspects would clearly be present. Subsequent scenes, each building on the previous one, should then show the results of the encounter on either the teen or the stepdad, thus increasing the tension.

CREATE CONFLICT AND TENSION THROUGH PLOT TWISTS

Another way to create conflict and tension is to make sure characters are confronted by new obstacles at every turn. Every time the characters solve one dilemma, a new one occurs. These roadblocks should become increasingly more difficult to overcome as the book progresses. The continued failures Brody experiences in his quest to kill the shark are good examples of this.

CREATE CONFLICT AND TENSION THROUGH DEADLINES

Ask any student facing an end-of-term report, travelers racing between planes or a news reporter scrambling for a late-breaking story. Nothing increases tension more than a deadline.

Rather than pose problems, time-sensitive pressures work magic for suspense plots. Ticking clocks, dwindling food supplies or an antagonist's unreasonable demands create the ultimate obstacle for a protagonist.

• Mary Willis Walker lets readers know in the first chapter that Samuel Mordecai's plan for his buried captives is scheduled to be completed at the end of five days.

• In lieu of chapter numbers, Tom Clancy uses a day/date/location format in *The Hunt for Red October*. Because the book deals with military operations, the entries note the calendar dates in that form; for example, THE FIRST DAY. FRIDAY, 3 DECEMBER. THE RED OCTOBER. This subtle tactic keeps readers in the same mind-set as Clancy's characters.

As the story builds to its climax, scenes become shorter and shorter, matching the furious pace of the action. Here the captions serve two functions: They allow readers to keep track of where they are and which characters are involved at that location. And, since each scene switch represents the response to the previous action, tension all but explodes off the page.

Other authors have experimented with using the length of chapters to heighten dramatic tension. "The short chapters in my books are the result of both style and a conscious effort to generate suspense," says John Lutz. "Shorter chapters mean a faster pace [and] more opportunity for cliff-hanger endings."

CREATE CONFLICT AND TENSION THROUGH CLIFF-HANGERS

Just as the beginning of each scene must remind the reader of the conflict and tension within a character's life, the end of that scene should pose a question.

Beyond the expected, "What's next?" suspense writers strive for cliff-hanger endings. This is especially important if the scene falls at the end of a chapter.

Nancy Kress said it best in her November 1995 *Writer's Digest* fiction column: "The last line of any scene is the power position."

Imagine that argument between the teenager and his stepfather. We might begin to build a suspense plot with the following scenes.

CHAPTER ONE

SCENE 1: Argument; teen slams out of house; conflict remains unresolved.

SCENE 2: Boy's mother confronts husband about quarrel; stepfather refuses to discuss what led up to fight; mother asks why son always has to be the one in the wrong.

SCENE 3: Teen driving recklessly toward girlfriend's house; internal dialogue about conflict; wonders why stepfather seemed more volatile than usual; car suddenly careens out of control.

END OF CHAPTER ONE

CHAPTER TWO

SCENE 1: Stepfather's internal dialogue hints that boy knows something that could prove dangerous to both of them; inner conflict over how much damage control is needed; physical reaction to arrival of police; initial relief at discovery that visit is about teen's accident, not something else.

SCENE 2: Boy lies near death in ICU; stepfather tries to comfort wife who pulls away and blames him for situation; internal dialogue in which a conflicted stepfather realizes the danger to himself will dissolve if the boy should die.

END OF CHAPTER TWO

As this particular plot continued, subsequent scenes would reveal the reason for the stepfather's panic. The mother would begin to suspect her husband of sabotaging her son's recovery. Suddenly, she faces another roadblock: her son's sudden relapse just as the boy is about to tell her what the argument was about.

Each scene should bring her closer to the truth that her husband is hiding something and has become a danger to her son. Once she reaches that realization, a new set of problems should present themselves. Perhaps the boy disappears from his hospital room. Or the husband turns up missing only minutes before the police inform her that the wreck was not an accident.

Conflict and tension are the key elements of a suspense plot. Obstacles continuously thrown in the protagonist's path, ticking clocks and cliff-hanger scene endings keep readers turning the page. And that's what you want *your* plot to do.

"Where's Waldo?": Foreshadowing and Suspense

Foreshadowing is information that's there but unseen. Done well, it lays the groundwork for a reader to close the cover after "The End" and murmur, "I should have seen that coming," instead of, "Where the heck did *that* solution come from?"

So is foreshadowing the same as a clue? Not exactly.

Although similar, clues and foreshadowing are actually different things. Think of clues as tangible and foreshadowing as abstract.

Jessie Hunter introduces The Chocolate Man in a three-page prologue. In the next chapter we meet nine-year-old Emily. Engrossed in a favorite book, she's ignoring her mother's pleas to get ready for a trip to the park. Nothing too obvious here. Most girls Em's age would rather read than listen to their moms.

Also revealed in this chapter is that The Chocolate Man often abducts his young male victims from one of New York's city parks. Emily's divorced mother has her fears, but she's promised her only child this outing. She convinces herself that if she's vigilant, everything will be OK.

Except that the readers know (even if they haven't read the jacket copy) that things will *not* be OK.

The danger involved in visiting the park is fairly obvious. So where's the foreshadowing?

Emily's book is a Nancy Drew mystery. Drew and her pals are often described as courageous, resilient and resourceful. Without realizing it, these are the qualities Emily admires in her favorite heroine. As her own life unfolds, she will need them herself to survive.

Even the urban environment and the fact that she's an only child of a single mother lay subtle groundwork that readers may overlook. One-parent kids in the city must learn, often earlier than other children, to think problems through and reason situations out. So instead of panicking, Emily will cope by trying to mimic her heroine, Nancy Drew.

This was an example of foreshadowing a character trait. Events can also be foreshadowed.

The Chocolate Man has a fear of his own and a ritual to keep it at bay. Emily picks up on this in the midst of a scene that emphasizes other issues more apt to hold the reader's attention. Later, she's able to use that bit of knowledge to her advantage.

"You have to lay down the foundation before you can build the suspense," says John Gilstrap. "It's during that laying down of the foundation that foreshadowing often occurs. Foreshadowing is a promise that readers expect to be fulfilled."

Foreshadowing takes skill, but it's an integral part of creating suspense. Go back through the books you chose from the reading list and pinpoint places where the authors foreshadowed later events. You'll find many are simply throwaway references buried within conversations or narrative. Giving readers enough information that the solution makes sense—but not so much that the conclusion is obvious—is the key to writing great suspense.

The Rhythm of Suspense

Suspense has a flow. Imagine it as a river meandering here and there, rippling over small rocks, then rushing headlong over larger boulders to create dangerous rapids before dwindling back down to a benign stream.

Moments involving action or intense emotional conflict need to be balanced by calmer passages of short narrative reflection or tension-free conversation that allow readers room to breathe.

Think of the suspense itself as waiting beneath the surface during these lulls, momentarily snagged on a submerged branch or bobbing around near the shore in some little eddy. Just as readers catch their breath, the writer whirls them downstream once more toward the waterfall that awaits.

These moments of calm can be used to reveal character or introduce other key players. Personal history that provides needed information could be discussed here. Foreshadowing could be buried within a narrative passage that transitions the reader into the next period of sheer terror.

Whenever a segment of the plot reaches a climax, a writer needs to provide a scene of resolution.

Every time a protagonist overcomes one of those obstacles thrown before him, the plot fulfills part of a reader's expectations. A resolution scene can explore what that success means to the overall plot, the hero's own expectations or the potential outcome of the story.

Early on in *One, Two, Buckle My Shoe*, Emily manages to get away from The Chocolate Man for an instant. Her escape is short-lived, but her already distraught captor is slightly hurt in the melee. Emily's response to his injury takes place during the lull that follows.

The escape attempt is a climax—readers expected Emily to put up a fight. When she volunteers to tend The Chocolate Man's wound, we get a glimpse of how she will cope with whatever happens as the story progresses. This is the resolution. We'll be discussing a variation of climax and resolution in more—pacing—detail in chapter eleven.

Putting It All Together

How should you go about assembling the scenes you'll use in your book? Every writer has his own system.

Richard North Patterson sticks to a formal organizational system when writing his books. "I have folders for every scene," he says. "They're in consecutive order—about eighty-six folders. I'll change the order and something will surprise me as I go along, but I try and plot out my books as well as I can."

Mary Willis Walker doesn't outline, but she does keep track of her plots. "I take big chart-size paper and draw little diagrams of the various things going on. . . . It ends up being a very messy looking diagram of different running plots."

Still others have more relaxed methods of planning their novels. "I work from a synopsis written loosely enough that I don't close any mental doors," says John Lutz. "The key points of my books are developed during the plotting stage, added during revisions or sometimes simply inserted as they occur to me."

You may find one of the above methods works well for you.

I use a less formal outline consisting of short profiles of my main characters. Each contains biographical information as well as bits and pieces of scenes that eventually come together to make up the actual plot of the book.

Sometimes a particular book dictates its own special preparation. *Someone to Watch Over* is about a stranger whose anonymous efforts to protect a young widow and her children mutates from benign care to obsession. To make this work, I had to include a one-page sketch of the "accidents" my antagonist engineered for those he perceived as threats to my heroine Kate and her family.

I listed each incident in ascending order of menace—that is, a smashed greenhouse for a teacher who scolded Kate's daughter came before the more sinister fate that later befell the mortgage banker who'd refused to postpone foreclosure. This allowed me to plot Kate's growing terror as she realized how dangerous her "Good Samaritan" was becoming.

Books in which protagonists face deadlines or ticking clocks dictate their own organization.

Buried Secrets dealt with my heroine Nicki's repressed memory of a crime. The plot required that I create a schedule of events and activities that would trigger Nicki's slowly returning memory and eventually coincide with the anniversary of the traumatic episode.

Experiment until you discover what works best or feels most comfortable to you. Just be sure each scene is arranged so that life becomes increasingly harder for your protagonist and the reader keeps wondering what's going to happen next.

CHAPTER 5

Case Studies in Plotting

I n this chapter we're going to walk step-by-step through the development of basic plots for each of our categories. The first two involve the situation I sketched in chapter three (pages 26–27) for the character named Burke. Remember that Burke's sister-in-law Jenny and his niece Amy have been taken hostage by a group that has taken control of a nuclear power plant.

The Action-Adventure Plot

Our first chapter should deal with the takeover of the nuclear power plant by a villain we'll call Martin.

→─◄─

It's a weekend. Only a skeleton crew and a few guards are on duty. Jenny has come in to finish a report. Twelve-year-old Amy has tagged along.

Jenny hears gunfire. She warns Amy to hide but isn't able to do so herself.

(Right here we have a good opportunity for characterization. One of Martin's men has been injured and pleads for help. If Martin calmly raises his weapon and kills the man, readers will realize just how ruthless he is.)

Notified of Martin's demands, the police call in Burke. (To justify his involvement, we'll give him a background as a former commando turned security consultant.)

(Now we begin to throw up barriers.) Entrances to the plant have been mined. An open assault is quickly ruled out. Martin has vowed to kill a hostage every three minutes until any such attempt is aborted.

Meanwhile, Amy is crawling about the complex via the air-conditioning ducts. Using her mother's password, she's E-mailed her uncle about the situation. The tension moves up a notch. Until now, Burke didn't know she and Jenny were inside.

An old man from the original construction crew has been trying to get through to the police. He has a hard time getting anyone to listen to him but finally reaches the command center. This retiree remembers an old access tunnel that's not on the blueprints. When Burke finds the shaft, it's filled with rubble from a cave-in.

(Another obstacle, another delay. The rhythm of suspense—two steps forward, one step back.)

Amy continues to send updates. This contact remains one-way—an incoming message might be intercepted and endanger her position. Then, when she's unable to clear the screen before hiding, her presence becomes known. The hunt is on.

Martin's anger makes him foolish. He and Burke have a history. He taunts his old adversary that he's tracking Amy as he'd track a rabbit, a frightened, pathetic little bunny. Burke's internal conflict and determination rise another notch.

Burke will encounter a few more obstacles before he gains access to the power plant. By the book's climax, Martin will have found Amy. Jenny will have been roughed up. Frustration and his vendetta against Burke will have eaten away Martin's coolness, making him careless. And Burke will save the day.

The Techno-Thriller Plot

We laid the groundwork for this one in the discussion of the action-adventure plot. What's missing is the emphasis on technology. My suggestions are unsophisticated, but viable alternatives undoubtedly exist.

This time we'll focus on Martin's use of projected images to bypass security cameras and fool the guards so he can enter the plant. He's also found a way to override the thumbprint ID system, which we've already described in a short scene in which Jenny and Amy entered the building.

Mother and daughter were arguing about a trip to the mall. Amy wants to shop without Mom hanging around. (This lays the groundwork for internal conflict for both Amy and her mother. It also set the stage for their reconciliation at the end.)

We'll add other technology as we go, like a powerful, top secret drill that can quickly bore through the tunnel collapse with minimal noise. Burke is the only one with the credentials to obtain this item. He also has exclusive access to electronic equipment that will create holographic images to convince Martin the assault is being mounted from the opposite direction.

(Remember that time is a factor.) Martin will kill a hostage every three minutes after he discovers a rescue attempt is in progress.

To bring the tension to a peak near the end of the book, the actual rescue will hinge on the success of an untried prototype weapon. If it works, Burke will be able to quickly blast through the specially constructed doors of the reactor room where Amy and her mother are being held.

After a minor glitch here and there, Burke's plan works, leading to his final, face-to-face confrontation with Martin.

→>-<+-

Here's a reminder about our key players for the next six categories.
- Mary, our female protagonist
- Davy, her son
- Kevin, Mary's spouse and Davy's stepfather
- Mary's Uncle Wes, who rambles a lot
- Mrs. Mardis, early morning walker and newspaper retriever
- Eric, a teenage paperboy
- Johnny, Davy's younger playmate

- Carol Jean, Mary's best friend, who lives across the street
- A redhead who lives in the apartment on the corner

Because legal, medical and political thrillers require either specialized knowledge or extensive research, my examples for those categories will involve rather simple plots. Those of you with the appropriate backgrounds will no doubt be able to envision more complicated situations.

The Legal Thriller Plot

Attorney Kevin is certain the case he's just been given will be his ticket to a junior partnership in his new firm. The lawsuit pits his firm's clients, a small group of homeowners, against a waste disposal company. But what seems to be a golden opportunity rapidly becomes a nightmare.

After being granted numerous continuances, the attorney originally assigned to the case left the firm abruptly and the judge has refused a further postponement. Kevin's request for the full-time use of one of his firm's paralegals has also been denied. Others have managed similar cases with part-time help, he is told. It's a straightforward case; winning shouldn't be a problem. Unless, of course, he's not up to the task.

Kevin confides his fear about his ability to prepare a winning case to his wife, Mary, who's a law student. Although she'd hoped to spend her semester break with five-year-old Davy, she volunteers to help Kevin prepare.

Kevin's calls to the original attorney on the case are not returned. When he confronts her outside her current office, she nervously agrees to talk to him but only on her own terms. Mystified, but growing desperate, he and Mary agree to meet the woman at a remote location. There she tells them a wild tale of disappearing case documents and being followed, and says she quit after an attempt was made on her life.

Kevin suggests the opposition was to blame. She disagrees, hinting that someone in her own firm was responsible. Asked to explain, she murmurs something about the wrong person finding out she'd begun to put things together. When a car drives by their meeting place, she says she's never been a team player and that "these cases" aren't meant to be won anyway.

Deciding the woman is paranoid, Kevin begins rebuilding the case from scratch. Mary, a meticulous researcher, discovers that the defendant in Kevin's case (the waste disposal company) has been sued five times. The first case, handled by an out-of-town firm, resulted in a multimillion dollar judgment against the waste company. The last four plaintiffs, which Kevin's firm represented, all lost their lawsuits.

Studying transcripts of the losing cases, Kevin realizes each attorney (like him, newly hired by the firm) clearly went to trial unprepared. Yet all were offered junior partnerships within months of their losses. When he tries to talk to one of the other attorneys, he's told to "quit looking a gift horse in the mouth" and to not do anything to screw things up for everyone else.

The next morning the woman who'd walked away from Kevin's case is found dead in her apartment. That evening, although he's not allowed to have toy guns, Mary finds Davy playing with a realistic-looking plastic revolver. He insists he found the toy in the yard. Among the day's mail is an unstamped envelope. Inside is a catalog photo of a weapon identical to the toy and a note that warns, "Next time it could be a real one."

Frightened, Kevin sends Davy and Mary to her parent's home in a nearby city. As he continues to prepare his case, he receives a compliment on his dedication from the senior partner who sponsored the losing lawyers for their new positions.

Mary, using information supplied by Kevin, contacts the losing clients to determine how they chose his firm. She learns that in all four cases the same man brought the parties together. Digging deeper, she finds the evidence needed to prove that the firm has been deliberately losing cases in a secret deal with the defendants.

On the day opening statements in Kevin's case are set to begin, federal marshals escort Kevin and Mary into the courtroom and arrest the defendants in the case for obstruction of justice. One of the firm's senior partners and the go-between are also arrested. Although the firm's founder offers Kevin a junior partnership as appreciation for exposing the corruption, Kevin accepts a position with the firm that originally won its case against the corrupt waste management company.

The Medical Thriller Plot

Mary and Carol Jean are nurses. Mary's husband, Kevin, the hospital adminis-
trator, has become suspicious about the unusually high mortality rate on Mary
and Carol Jean's ward. Aware of the women's friendship, he's kept his fears
to himself. But Mary is concerned about the same issue, and Kevin's sudden
remoteness and frequent appearances on the ward have made her uneasy.

Then a relative of the latest patient to die accuses Mary of murder. An autopsy
confirms the man was smothered. Although off duty, Mary was seen outside his
room moments before the Code Blue alarm sounded. Since her excuse for being
there is shaky, the hospital suspends her pending an investigation.

Mary is reluctant to suspect her best friend and conflicted about Kevin's
possible involvement. The absence of any new deaths since Mary's suspension
seems to strengthen the case against her. Although Kevin argues in his wife's
defense, the police continue to concentrate on building a case against her.

Unable to verify or eliminate her own suspicions about Carol Jean or Kevin
because of the suspension, Mary tries to find out why her friend left her last
position. A former co-worker Carol Jean once mentioned is evasive, admitting
something happened but refusing to identify a now-retired supervisor who
might know the truth. To get the name, Mary must break into Carol Jean's
personnel records.

Someone sees Mary leaving the hospital in the middle of the night. Moments later an elderly patient who was expected to recover is found dead. Mary
is promptly arrested. Bail is set and Kevin takes her home. Finally she confides
what she was trying to do. Desperate to prove Mary's innocence, Kevin takes
over her investigation into the reason Carol Jean left her last job. But before
he's successful, his request for information gets back to Carol Jean.

Carol Jean truly believes that by ending her patients' suffering, she is helping
the Lord. Although she's never sent a healthy person to God, she knows
exposure will jeopardize her mission. She convinces herself that if Mary com-
mits suicide, the police will assume she took her life because she felt remorse
for her actions. Then Carol Jean can move on to another hospital to continue
her work.

Using the house key her friend had given her months before, Carol Jean finds an exhausted Mary asleep at home. As the lethal syringe Carol Jean is administrating enters Mary's thigh, Mary awakens and manages to knock the needle away before the plunger is fully depressed.

Fighting to remain conscious, Mary struggles with Carol Jean. Kevin and the police arrive just before she passes out. Carol Jean is captured as she flees out the back door. An empty vial in Carol Jean's purse identifies the drug injected into Mary's system and allows medical personnel to save her life. Later, a police search of Carol Jean's home uncovers a journal that supports Mary's claim of innocence.

The Political Thriller Plot

Kevin has taken a break from his graduate studies in economics to work for a charismatic state senator making a bid for governor. Edgar Nugent has made no secret of his ultimate goal: the White House in eight years. Despite her TV reporter friend Carol Jean's insistence that Nugent is not what he seems, Kevin's wife, Mary, signs on as a volunteer. While Mary answers phones, Kevin prepares briefs on economic issues for the candidate and Uncle Wes watches their eight-year-old son, Davy, after school.

Despite his dedicated staff, Nugent is behind in the polls. Tension in the office has been compounded by Nugent's recent uncharacteristic public displays of temper. One-on-one strategy sessions with his campaign manager, Dylan, do little to change the numbers and seem to aggravate rather than calm Nugent's tantrums.

Then Dylan chews Mary out in front of the entire staff for losing a transfer call from a big contributor. Uncle Wes, who has brought Davy by to see where his parents work, launches an angry defense of his niece. As Nugent rushes from his office to smooth things over, Davy takes advantage of the confusion to explore the senator's office.

When he hears Mary call him, Davy, without thinking, shoves the electronic game he's just picked up from a partially open desk drawer into his jacket pocket. Later he realizes it isn't a game after all. The next morning he slips the device into his mother's purse, hoping she won't notice it until she's at work and won't connect it with his visit the previous day.

But Mary has decided the campaign office can run without her. She's tired of Nugent's outbursts, and Dylan gives her the creeps. Not until she reaches for her checkbook in the grocery does she notice the mini tape recorder in her purse. Unsure whose it is or how it got there, she rewinds and plays the tape.

Kevin doesn't know what's going on in Nugent's office, but the senator is hotter than he's ever seen him, slamming drawers and pounding his fist on his desk. Dylan's normally soothing voice has also risen. Storming from his office, Nugent scans the room, his fiery gaze pausing a moment on each worker. When he reaches Mary's empty desk, his expression changes abruptly. Without glancing at Kevin, he returns to his office and quietly closes the door. The discussion within resumes at a lower level. When Dylan comes out, he leaves without speaking to anyone.

An obviously distraught Mary calls Kevin on his cell phone a moment later. Without explanation she says there's a family emergency and he's needed at home. Once there, Kevin listens in stunned silence to the tape of Nugent and his campaign manager discussing their planned "accident" for the opposing candidate.

From Nugent's behavior that morning, Kevin is sure Mary and Davy are in danger. The mention of a local cop's name on the tape convinces the couple the safest thing to do is to take the tape directly to the FBI office in the capital city. Uncle Wes always walks Davy home from school and they should be home any minute. Once they arrive, the entire family will leave together.

But time passes and Wes and Davy don't appear. Mary's frantic call to her uncle reveals that, because she'd taken the day off, Wes thought Mary would be picking Davy up. Kevin checks the school grounds as Wes traces the route home and Mary begins calling the homes of Davy's classmates.

Call Waiting alerts Mary to an incoming call. Rather than Davy on the line as she'd hoped, it's Dylan offering what he calls a simple solution. Meet him with the tape and any copies she may have made and she can have Davy. Kevin and Uncle Wes return as she's on her way out. After a quick conference, Wes suggests a variation on Dylan's plan. Mary and Kevin leave to meet Nugent's campaign manager at a seedy motel forty miles away.

After they hand over the tape, Dylan shoves Davy toward them. It's clear from the silencer on the gun he holds that he has no intention of letting any of them leave. Shielding Mary and Davy with his body, Kevin suggests that before Dylan does anything that could result in the death penalty, he might want to turn on the TV and check out the newscast on channel five.

With a long-range, real-time shot of the motel in the background, news anchor Carol Jean shouts questions at Nugent as he's led in handcuffs from his office. As the state police car pulls away, Carol Jean plays the incriminating conversation that Mary relayed over Kevin's cell phone as they drove to meet Dylan.

Dylan raises his weapon. Kevin shoves his family to the floor and lunges at the campaign manager. But Dylan's shot was aimed at his own head. State troopers break in and escort Mary and Davy and Kevin outside.

The Psychological Suspense Plot

Because this category overlaps so many of the others, I'm going to spend a bit more time detailing the plot.

→►◄←

Davy should have been home from his friend Johnny's house a half hour ago. Uncle Wes isn't home, either. The two are probably together.

Uncle Wes can be a pain, but other than his incessant rambling and his delusions about one day "making a million" from one of his electronic inventions, the old man is harmless. With Kevin on the road so much and Mary's home-based business just getting started, it's nice to have a built-in sitter.

Uncle Wes had lived with his younger sister Meg until her recent, sudden death. The family always thought Wes would go first. Aunt Meg had looked in such good health the last time Mary was here, although she *had* seemed a bit upset to learn that Mary was marrying a local boy like Kevin and moving back to town.

Of course, Aunt Meg had never wanted Mary to bring Davy along on her visits. Maybe that was it. Or it might have been Kevin's obsession with that day's TV reports on the discovery of the body of some boy who'd gone missing years ago.

Mary likes her new neighbors, except for the woman on the corner who hates kids. Last week she screamed obscenities at Davy and his friend Johnny just because they dripped ice cream on the sidewalk in front of her apartment building. Uncle Wes told Mary the woman was hard to get along with because Eric the paperboy and his buddies had been harassing her.

(As you can see, psychological suspense plots require a writer to deal much more deeply with the internal thought processes of a protagonist. The reader thus becomes the heroine or hero, going through the same deliberations and reaching the same, often erroneous, conclusions. By now readers should be wondering if Uncle Wes was involved in the old death that so fascinated Kevin or if he hastened his sister's demise.)

It's getting late. Johnny tells Mary he saw Davy meet Uncle Wes at the corner. But Johnny is only seven. He's not really sure whether the meeting happened today or yesterday. Johnny also remembers that Davy talked about telling the lady on the corner that they were sorry for messing up her sidewalk.

Mary goes to the woman's apartment but gets no response. Visits to places in the neighborhood where Uncle Wes and Davy like to go result in dead ends.

She considers phoning Kevin at his hotel but isn't sure how he'd react. They've only been married a short time, after an even briefer courtship. Sometimes Kevin seems a little put out by Davy's constant demands on her time.

Davy had no objection to her remarriage. Uncle Wes, buried in the blueprints for his latest electronic gizmo, had surfaced just long enough to wish them well. Only Aunt Meg had a negative reaction to the news.

(Our plot must provide readers with valid reasons why the various characters we've introduced might want to hurt Davy: Uncle Wes because he may have killed Aunt Meg or harmed a child previously; the woman on the corner because she believed Davy was harassing her; Kevin because he might have murdered that child.)

When Mary talks to her neighbors, they offer gossip or share snatches of overheard conversations. But how much of what they say are half-truths, one-sided views, or otherwise distorted in some way? It's time to report Davy and Uncle Wes as missing.

Before Mary can call them, the police come to her. To her dismay, they're not there about Davy. They're looking for Kevin. It seems the remains they found belonged to the kid brother of Kevin's high school sweetheart.

Suddenly a neighbor's observation that Kevin seemed upset when Davy interrupted Kevin's evening stroll with Mary the previous week takes on added meaning. Mary wonders if Kevin's occasional annoyance with Davy's demands on her attention mask a more deep-seated jealousy.

Mary doesn't know whom to trust anymore. To make matters worse, Kevin is not at the hotel where he told her he'd be. His company hasn't heard from him, either.

In the midst of all this, Uncle Wes comes home. He says he spent the afternoon playing dominoes with some men he just met down near the docks. When asked, he can provide only first names for his newfound friends.

The police notice a stain on Uncle Wes's pants and take him to the station for more intense questioning. After Mary insists, they also check the apartment on the corner. Still no response.

Davy is missing. Kevin can't be found. Uncle Wes is being questioned. Mary is slowly becoming isolated from those she might lean on for support.

Uncle Wes is released the next morning. His claim that the stain on his pants was paint sealer from a mishap at the docks has checked out.

The police widen their search. Their expressions tell Mary they don't expect to return with good news. The FBI and the Center for Missing and Exploited Children have been notified.

Uncle and niece drink coffee in awkward silence. A short time later Mrs. Mardis, the neighbor who takes early morning walks, drops by to tell Mary she's praying for Davy's safe return.

Before she leaves, Mrs. Mardis tells Mary that the woman on the corner left to visit her sister the day before Davy went missing. She also mentions that she talked to Davy last week in front of Johnny's house. Davy was showing the younger boy some electronic game he'd just gotten.

Mrs. Mardis doesn't remember what Davy said the game was called, but she saw Eric the paperboy with one just like it last night outside the supermarket.

Davy's game is a prototype that Uncle Wes gave him to try out. There is no duplicate. When Mary checks Davy's room, the game is not there. A call to Johnny confirms Davy had it with him yesterday when he left to go home. He also remembers that it wasn't Uncle Wes who met Davy on the corner; it was Eric.

(We foreshadowed the possibility of a game by noting Uncle Wes's preoccupation with electronics in an earlier scene. We also foreshadowed the possibility of Eric becoming a suspect by detailing his history of harassment toward the woman on the corner.)

The police want to question Eric, but he's not home. Uncle Wes has his own idea of where the paperboy might be. He and Mary head for a place near the docks where Eric hangs out.

(Somewhere about here we should reveal the reason for Aunt Meg's reactions to Davy's visits and Mary's remarriage. A conversation between Mary and her uncle on the way to the docks offers a logical opportunity. Perhaps she didn't really like kids and thought Davy would be underfoot when Mary moved back.)

Eric's not at the docks. But some other boys are. One admits seeing Eric near a boarded-up building the day before.

The nearby building is scheduled for demolition in less than ten minutes. Davy is inside, badly beaten but alive. A final check by the explosives crew minutes ago failed to uncover the unconscious boy covered by debris.

Uncle Wes slips by the security detail into the building; the demolition is put on hold; and Davy is whisked to the hospital. Kevin returns early from his business trip, having driven all night because he missed his family.

As they wait to learn whether Davy will survive, Kevin reveals that his uneasiness with Davy stems from an episode with the old girlfriend's brother. It seems the boy disappeared right after Kevin caught him spying on the pair making out.

Davy comes out of his coma and all is well.

(Note that we have tied up the loose ends of all the plot points we introduced during the course of the story.)

The Romantic Relationship Suspense Plot

Mary has been married to wealthy Kevin for only two months. During that time she's been secretly meeting Jim, her former boyfriend. Kevin's angst at learning Mary is still seeing Jim is compounded by his suspicion that one of them could be behind what appears to be a recent attempt on his life.

The more he questions Mary, the more evasive she becomes, denying, despite being confronted with evidence, that she's been unfaithful. Finally she admits to being with Jim but still denies any wrongdoing. Her excuse is that she's trying to diffuse Jim's obsession. She promises not to see him again.

Wanting to believe her, Kevin considers other suspects for the tampered brakes on his car.

Both a disgruntled ex-employee and a former client whose unethical business practices Kevin exposed seem good candidates. The first man, whom Kevin prosecuted for stealing, made threats at the time. He's recently been released from prison.

Further attempts on Kevin's life and another meeting between Mary and Jim complicate the situation. Kevin considers divorce. Mary, realizing she's losing Kevin, tells him the truth.

She and Jim have a son. Her aunt has been raising him out of state. Jim cares nothing for the boy but is certain he can make Mary return to him if he has their child. So far, he's identified the town but not the aunt's name or address.

Mary wanted to tell Kevin about her son. Something he said before their marriage kept stopping her. His comment that Mary was his ideal woman convinced her he wouldn't want a wife who'd had a child out of wedlock. She kept hoping to find the right time to break the news.

Then Jim showed up again and she knew she'd waited too long. Mary says she knows Jim's obsessive but can't believe he'd go so far as to try to kill Kevin.

In a taunting phone call that interrupts Mary's confession, Jim tells her he's decided their son would be better off without a lying, two-timing mother. He screams her aunt's name into the phone and hangs up. Caller ID tells them the call came from a local number. Jim does not have the boy yet. There may be time.

The aunt doesn't answer her phone. Mary and Kevin race from the house. Something alerts Kevin and he discovers dynamite wired to his car's starter. Jim has gone over the edge.

After overcoming several more hurdles, Mary and Kevin rescue her son. Jim is arrested. Kevin explains his remark about his ideal woman and forgives Mary for her deception. Davy comes to live with his mother and stepfather.

The Fem- or Child-Jep Suspense Plot

Davy did not show up in his classroom after Kevin dropped him at school this morning. Davy's friend Johnny says that local bully Eric the paperboy and his friends taunted Davy by saying he was "too little to hang with the big guys down at the bridge."

The only bridges nearby are the highway overpasses.

Eric's family left to go camping last night. His neighbors don't know where the family was going. The police decide to check every overpass within five miles. Davy is only nine and small for his age. His bike is still in the garage. How far could he have walked in a few hours?

Later Mary realizes Uncle Wes is rambling about how Davy always likes to hear about the time Wes found an arrowhead in the shallows beneath the old abandoned *railroad* bridge. That area is now a haven for transients and the homeless. Many are men with mental problems, hard drinkers who often carry knives to fend off the imaginary demons they believe are after them. Some are rumored to be child molesters. But the railroad bridge is over twelve miles away. The school is another six miles in the opposite direction. Could Davy really walk over eighteen miles?

Suddenly Mary realizes both Kevin and Carol Jean are conspicuously absent. She finds them in the kitchen. Kevin's head is buried in his arms and he's sobbing that he lied about taking Davy to school. He spent the morning somewhere else.

Carol Jean, the playmate Mary traded Barbie dolls with in second grade and has trusted with the emergency key to her house, is comforting Kevin. Her arms are wrapped around him and she's kissing him in a decidedly non-mothering way.

(As often happens in fem-jep, the plot overlaps somewhat with romantic relationship suspense. But our focus will remain on Mary and Davy.) Kevin's a cad. Carol Jean's no longer a friend. Mary is left with no emotional support.

When the police raid the shantytown under the bridge, Cranky, one of the more disturbed inhabitants, has already hustled Davy away. Expecting trouble, many others have fled. Those who remain deny knowing anything.

A homeless woman named Peggy tried unsuccessfully to rescue Davy. She knows where Cranky is but also knows that telling the police will only make matters worse. Cranky believes the police and the FBI and the CIA and the KGB are spying on him. Most of the time he's harmless, but he *can* get violent, usually whenever the police come around. Peggy knows Cranky has a soft spot for mothers; he remembers his own mamma fondly. But Peggy has a phobia about venturing away from the paths that connect her usual haunts. Now she must overcome this to find her way to Mary.

Mary is torn. Should she believe this filthy creature who appears at her back door in the middle of the night? Or should she alert the policeman sitting in the patrol car in front of the house? Our climax comes when Mary slips out to follow Peggy into the worst part of the city. Swallowed by the darkness and spied on by souls as unsettled by her presence as she is by theirs, she conquers her terror and talks Cranky into letting her son come home where he belongs.

--><--

As you can see, no matter which category of suspense you choose to write, certain common threads weave through each. All of the plots use foreshadowing and repeated scenes of climax and resolution to build their suspense. I'll be addressing these issues and many others in later chapters. But right now it's time to create the world in which your characters live and against which your plot will unfold.

CHAPTER 6

Setting and Atmosphere

While the setting of your book may not seem critical to you, readers like to know where they are. They need a sense of place and time to help them get into a story.

Setting is more than landscape and calendars and clocks. It can even have psychological meaning. In an October 1994 article in *Writer's Digest*, Michael Orlofsky points out that "Dawn suggests something is beginning, while evening suggests something is ending; the same can be said for the four seasons."

Long passages of description or "laundry lists" of what a character sees don't work well in suspense. The first slows down the rhythm. Beyond an occasional sentence that lists three or four items, so does the second. Neither really draws the reader into the story.

Another problem is that the rhythm of suspense demands a greater emphasis on atmosphere than on setting. Yet to build the ambience that's needed, the writer must first establish exactly where the action is taking place. This means doing more than simply sketching in a few physical details of a location.

Getting Our Bearings
SENSORY CUES MAKE A SETTING DISTINCT
Even a relatively generic setting—a farmhouse or old mansion, a cruise ship at sea, the inside of a hospital, or an abandoned warehouse—has its own personality.

Every farmhouse contains traces of its previous owners. A mansion on a windswept peninsula in Maine will have a very different feel than that of an old plantation in Georgia or the Hollywood Hills home that once belonged to a silent film star.

Waters that cruise ships sail may be as tepid as the Caribbean or as brisk as the inside passage to Alaska. The smells that linger in a warehouse that once served the canning industry will be distinctly different from those in one that stored leather jackets or crates of machine parts.

A medical thriller might be set in an inner-city hospital that serves welfare patients, drug addicts and gunshot victims. Or in an upscale suburban doctor's office that provides only limited services because the facility's clientele is affluent.

Readers would recognize the second location by its waiting room's calming color scheme, up-to-the-minute issues of trendy magazines and relatively tranquil environment. The same area in a Medicaid-driven ER might have dingy walls, wailing children, dull-eyed or angry patients snaking a line to an overworked receptionist, and a strong medicinal odor that mingles with that of unwashed bodies and building decay.

A brief scene in which an angry patient revolts and must be subdued by a security guard creates tension and establishes a vivid sense of place. Other than to set the stage, the episode itself may not serve a major purpose. However, if the same characters reappear in a later scene, so much the better.

SETTING ACTS AS A PLOT DEVICE

Setting can build that false sense of security characters should experience just before their raft plunges over the falls.

Here's an example.

In *At All Costs*, John Gilstrap's political thriller, hero Jake Brighton has just arrived at his job as a body shop manager. The opening scene touches on a traffic jam on the way to work, a brief exchange with the office manager and an even briefer passage of Jake's internal dialogue about the recent daylight robbery of a nearby service station that sets the stage for his next reaction. All this would lead the reader—and Jake—to believe this is just another average workday. Then the ordinary is replaced by chaos.

> *Jake reached for his blinking extension, but movement outside drew his attention to the front windows. People seemed to be gathering, even as they tried to stay out of sight. One of them had a gun.*
>
> *Shit!*
>
> *The lobby doors exploded open, releasing a flood of heavily armed men into the reception area. Jake instinctively jumped to his feet and yanked open the top right-hand drawer of his desk, snatching out his snub-nose .44.*
>
> *"Federal officers, don't move!"*
>
> *The words boomed like a cannon. Jake jumped as his stomach fell. He moved to drop the revolver back into the drawer but hesitated. Then it was too late.*
>
> *"Gun!"*
>
> *He watched in horror as a dozen submachine guns swung around to bear down on him.*

Unknown to Jake, his body shop workers have been running a drug ring. Because he pulled a gun, he's now assumed to be involved. No problem, the reader is thinking. Jake will explain; things will get sorted out; everything will be OK. And they might be, except for the fact that Jake and his family are living under assumed names, hiding from a false accusation in their past. Being fingerprinted by federal authorities is the last thing he needs.

What had seemed a tranquil setting has suddenly turned very dangerous. Jake and his family are soon on the run once more, racing to uncover the truth about the terrible events in his past before an obsessed FBI agent shoots first and asks questions later.

A sense of place can also create suspense itself. Most readers will associate danger with a broken light in the corridor that leads to a protagonist's apartment or with the observation that a subway platform seems deserted.

DETAILS MAKE THE SETTING VIVID

Little touches play major roles in establishing place.

Do characters walk or drive or ride city buses to get from place to place? Walking provides them the chance to closely observe their surroundings. A bus is a semirestricted environment that allows a character time to study fellow passengers, enjoy the elevated view or mull over problems through internal dialogue.

On the other hand, driving requires concentration. Vehicles and pedestrians become distractions that preclude extended daydreaming. Traffic jams or less traveled routes offer time for thought or force a driver's attention toward finding her way. Taxis or limousines isolate characters from the world around them.

Each distinction provides unique opportunities for plot development as well as establishing place.

SETTING CAN REVEAL CHARACTER

What does a protagonist think about as the bus rattles on? Does his internal dialogue in respect to other passengers give readers clues to his personality? How will he react when he realizes the kid who just slammed out the emergency exit left his switchblade in the old man across the aisle?

Habits, physical traits, social status and history all become a part of place. A woman displays a battered object from her childhood in the midst of a meticulously clean designer home. Is she making a statement to a demanding or controlling spouse? Will that willful defiance cost her dearly?

In the reverse, a character lovingly rubs his high school sports trophy for good luck every morning on his way out the door. If he's forced to retrieve that cherished keepsake from a drawer when he returns home every evening, the setting has conflict and tension and perhaps a foreshadowed murder weapon.

An organized work area hints that a heroine is in control of her life, or at least likes to think that she is. A silly party hat perched atop a bookcase filled with well-worn volumes on corporate law might indicate an urge to break free from a staid environment. Or simply an ability to keep life in perspective.

Character-revealing descriptions of setting can also be used to hint at plot developments to come. An art collector's display of prints featuring African blowguns and South American bolas could foreshadow knowledge that proves useful at the climax of the book.

It's All in the Details

Where you set your story isn't as important as *how* you depict that setting. Short, quick images stick in a reader's mind better than tedious narration. Pick a few salient points that establish where and when the action takes place, and then scatter them over the canvas your story provides.

Several U.S. cities have subways. Referring to specific stops such as Forty-second Street and Grand Central Station or Federal Triangle and Dupont Circle can clue readers in to whether they're in New York or Washington, DC, for example.

Passengers in each city will have distinctions of their own as well. Actors on their way to rehearsal in New York's theater district vary considerably from Washington lobbyists with their abbreviated, acronym-peppered speeches.

Try to find precise images and unique features that evoke empathy in the reader.

The escalators into and out of the Dupont Circle Metro station are especially steep, extremely long and partly exposed to the elements. On a sunny day, riding down toward that much dimmer underground area can feel like a descent into the maw of some giant prehistoric monster. An image like this creates a sense of foreboding—a heightening of suspense.

Reversing the trip from darkness to light brings a joy of release equal to the last day of school. Rainy days add an entirely different feel to the experience. These are the sort of details that perch a reader on a character's shoulders.

Special events can also provide useful settings.

The Fourth of July afternoon in DC brings two to three hundred thousand people to the Mall to await an evening concert and spectacular fireworks display. Individuals, families, straight and gay couples, foreign tourists and embassy workers come together to create a uniquely cosmopolitan audience.

Frisbee matches, dueling cheers between rival college students, random bursts of patriotic song, impromptu waves à la sporting events, even catered picnics complete with china plates and crystal champagne flutes. A cunning villain, perhaps an assassin, might find such a setting the ideal place to blend in.

The sweat and noise and crowded bodies, some with wet T-shirts draped over their heads for relief from the heat, could just as easily swallow up and shelter a frightened protagonist.

Mardi Gras on Bourbon Street. Spring break on almost any U.S. beach. Infield shenanigans at the Indy 500. A hog-calling contest at a county fair. These and dozens of other settings can be twisted to fit the needs of suspense.

Dropping bits and pieces of such specialized images throughout a book adds continuity as well as the power of place to a story.

Take care not to cross the line into a geography lesson. As Nancy Kress warns in her July 1993 *Writer's Digest* column, "Put in enough description to make your setting vivid and real, but not so much that the setting upstages the people in it."

But *do* get things right.

One Reason to Sweat Those Same Details

When it comes to setting, accuracy *does* matter. Sloppy writing is not only unprofessional, it can do long-term damage to your credibility as an author. I once heard a well-established editor of western novels discuss this at a writers conference.

This editor pulled a manuscript from the slush pile to take home one evening. Although it wasn't Louis L'Amour, he thought the writer's style showed some promise.

Over the Kansas prairie rode the hero, pursued by the villains. Then, just as the hunted man decided to seek cover behind a rocky outcropping at the foot of the mountains . . . the editor said he hurled the manuscript across the room.

It seems the writer hadn't done his homework.

Three minutes with a AAA TourBook just told me that the topography of Kansas "transitions from eastern prairie to high plains." My source goes on to discuss areas of low hills "marked by sandstone and limestone outcroppings" in the far northern part of the state. So far, so good.

Unfortunately, at the beginning of his book, the writer had established that his story was taking place in a particular part of Kansas. *A part the editor knew consisted of nothing but gently rolling plains.*

Experience also told him that so obvious an error warned of others yet to come. And here's the sad part. He told the assembled group of aspiring authors that the name of that lazy writer was now burned into his memory.

Thus slammed a door on future submissions at that house—or any others the editor might move on to.

Unfair? Not really. Publishing, like any other industry today, is looking for the best. Hundreds of less careless writers are always out there, waiting to be discovered.

And even if an error does make it past the eyes of an editor, you can bet your readers will notice, says author Marilyn Wallace. "In *A Case of Loyalties*, I had a character ride a bicycle across the Oakland Bay Bridge. I got several annoyed letters pointing out that, while you can ride across the Golden Gate Bridge, you can't do that on the other bridge across San Francisco Bay."

A writer never knows what particular knowledge an editor or reader might have. More to the point, anytime *any* reader is jarred out of a story by a blatantly incorrect fact, the author destroys the rapport he's established. He also interrupts the rhythm of suspense. Facts do count.

Which Way Did They Go and How Do I Get There?

If you've decided to set your book in Kansas; New York City; the Cuban enclaves of Miami; Altamont, Illinois (pop. 2,300); Del Rio, Texas; or its corresponding border town of Acuna, Mexico; and you've never been to any of those places, you'll need to gather some research materials.

Maps, auto club tour books, documentary and even travel videos can help. Try interlibrary loan if your local branch doesn't have what you need.

Write the Travel Bureau or Chamber of Commerce for tourist packets. Better yet, ask friends and relatives if they know someone who lives in the area. Get an introduction and invest in a phone call.

Best of all, use the Internet. If you're not computer literate, ask a friend who is for some help. This is also a great way to include more exotic locales without applying for a passport or visa.

If you *are* good friends with your travel agent, explain what you need. She might just have that elusive bit of info that could make your setting come alive. My family doctor once gave me a guided tour of CCU (Critical Care Unit—a level below the more familiar ICU, or Intensive Care Unit) after her evening rounds. An assistant DA I'd met through a club affiliation arranged for me to view an empty grand jury room on a day that group wasn't in session.

When using maps, make note of one-way or dead-end streets and directional logistics. Just as jarring as mountain ranges in the middle of a prairie is a trip down a north/south highway with the morning sun directly in your eyes.

If your story takes place during a prior era, watch out for modern changes as well. You won't want to have a critical scene in your World War II thriller take place on a busy street that was actually a cornfield until 1955.

Making up a location or place name is another option—and a good idea if your politico villain bears any resemblance to an official in your own hometown. Check a comprehensive atlas at your library to be sure the name you've chosen for your fictional city doesn't actually exist elsewhere in the state.

Readers have little problem with fictional buildings and businesses popping up along existing streets. But what if you need to use a real area and a major feature is missing? I used a tongue-in-cheek approach to this by noting the following on the acknowledgment page of my first novel.

> *Brook County and the town of Brookton, Indiana, exist only in the imagination of the author, who also constructed the rest area above the Ohio River at no cost to Hoosier taxpayers.*

Once you've researched your setting, you're ready to begin creating the atmosphere that will convince readers their steps are following those of the viewpoint character.

In the Mood: Creating Atmosphere

It was a dark and stormy night when Greg's car wound up in the ditch.

Very little there to pull the reader into Greg's world.

When the storm finally hit, a curtain of rain kept the headlights from penetrating more than a few yards into the darkness ahead. As his car began to skid, Greg cursed his decision to hold off replacing the Camaro's balding tires.

Better, but something's still missing.

With an earsplitting crack of thunder, the road ahead disappeared in a torrent of rain. Greg's balding tires skidded erratically on the suddenly slick pavement. Barely missing an eighteen-wheeler that loomed out of the darkness, the Camaro slid toward the drainage ditch as if in slow motion.

As Peg's scream echoed in his ears, Greg could visualize the zigzag tread pattern of the all-weather tires he'd rejected in favor of new irons and a monogrammed leather golf bag.

That just might do it.

While the first, clichéd example may be short and to the point, it fails to perform the first duty of atmospheric description. Nothing in those fifteen words evokes *extreme* danger or the sense of place we discussed earlier. Few readers would feel as if they had a part in what's happening.

The second version tells the readers more but still lacks the precise visual images needed to put them inside that Camaro.

In the third variation readers know where they are—on a rain-slicked highway, fighting for control of a skidding car. They've met the protagonist and learned he's a guy who places more value on his golf equipment than on the safety of himself and his passenger. They might also surmise that what just happened will be only the beginning of Greg's troubles.

Atmosphere is not just weather, although the relentless presence of continued rain or a blizzard that traps characters inside *can* build conflict and tension. Think of atmosphere as mood—the emotional side of setting.

The surprise of being a country mouse unexpectedly waking up in the city. Getting lost in a dangerously unfamiliar area. Venturing into a peaceful neighborhood only to discover all is not what it seems. These are the kinds of things that set the tone and the mood of a story. The kinds of things that evoke an *atmosphere of suspense.*

Consider your own memories, good and bad, of the places you've seen and the situations you've been in. Which ones evoke strong emotions?

Jessie Hunter's Chocolate Man reacts to the same things as you and I—just not in the same way. Even James Bond's cool exterior masks a man who passionately loves his adventurous life.

To write successful suspense you must be able to put your characters, and draw your readers, into situations you yourself may prefer to avoid. When you find yourself shying away from writing about a particular topic, try this exercise.

Gather as much data from your research as you can, then immerse yourself in your setting. Study the material, then close your eyes and visualize where you are.

Walk those mean or tranquil streets and decide what might unsettle or frighten *you.* Pay special attention to the details that lend themselves to suspense. Recessed doorways as you walk home from the movies. Shadowy shrubbery between the sidewalk and your house.

What about sounds or smells or people that don't belong?

The lingering presence of pipe tobacco inside a smoke-free building might signal something amiss. An overpowering aroma of men's cologne in a women's locker room could mean something's off-kilter. An unfamiliar guard outside a high-security area can warn of trouble ahead. Situations in which something is out of place create an atmosphere of suspense.

Sometimes you have no way of projecting yourself into the situation you want to create. This is where experts come in.

Finding and Approaching Those in the Know

Aspiring authors often voice two problems when it comes to experts: The authors either don't know where to find the experts or fear their request for information will be dismissed because they've not yet published.

"Why," you might ask, "would someone in the medical profession, law enforcement or scientific community agree to talk to me?"

Why indeed?

Because as a professional writer, you want to get it right. Because you're going to go in with a short list of well-prepared questions and then *listen attentively to*, as well as tape, the responses. Because you're going to offer to take an expert to lunch if it seems appropriate. And because you always send a written thank-you for the interview.

Most people are flattered to be asked to help a writer, as long as you work around *their* schedules. "In general, people are happy to talk to authors," says Tess Gerritsen, "as long as we don't abuse the privilege. So I try to know ahead of time everything I need to find out, and I read up as much as I can about the topic before I go around asking dumb questions."

Mary Willis Walker, author of *The Red Scream* and *All the Dead Lie Down*, has visited reptile houses, ridden along with police officers on patrol and interviewed crime victims while researching her books. She, too, finds that most people are happy, even flattered, to be asked about their particular areas of expertise. "I find it very hard to ask people for help," says Walker. "Then I'm always delighted and surprised by how willing and eager people are to share what they know when you're a writer."

Even if a writer has researched term papers or a thesis, finding the one person with that obscure bit of technical data can prove daunting. What does a real precinct interrogation room look like? How do you find someone who can describe how it feels to experience an acute allergic reaction? When a local cop or the family doctor can't help, where do you go?

Professional organizations, hobbyists, retirees. Every town has history buffs and retired teachers who love to talk about their specialties.

If appropriate, ask for names of other people who might be helpful or who could provide more information. A defense attorney, intrigued by my plot premise, once stopped in the middle of our interview to call the local DA to discuss the tricky question I'd just posed.

What you should really be looking for is something beyond mere facts. Watch for anecdotes or experiences that can be transferred to your characters. The more research you do, the more your plot will unfold.

Many hobbyists have learned their crafts the hard way. Ask any weekend carpenter about hammered thumbs or expensive boards scrapped by mistaken measurements. Such failures may suggest a scene that could bring a hero's struggle to life. Retirees often have great stories to tell. A senior citizen's memory may not be pristine, but a parallel character who relates a similar tale to the heroine can add color to a story. And color means atmosphere.

Witnesses make good sources. Talk to people who've lived through a disaster or visited your story's setting. What impressed them about the area or event? What did they *feel*?

A writer doesn't have to be Barbara Walters. Libraries can provide articles and books on how to conduct an interview. Practicing with a friend also helps. Asking if an expert objects to being taped is the professional, and often legal, thing to do.

As for that dreaded question, "Have I read any of your books?" a beginning writer's answer should be this: "I've not yet published. But I feel very good about this project and I'm certain your expertise can help me make it to my goal."

The details you can gain by talking with an "expert" or eyewitness not only provide a realistic sense of place, they often offer suggestions for atmospheric details that can increase suspense. Sometimes you get much more than you expected.

Because of a family connection, I have a fascination with Mount Saint Helens. Needing more than PBS's *In Search Of* series on volcanoes provided, I wrote several Washington State members of a national group I belong to, asking for their memories of specific details about the then decade-old eruption. A nurse and a librarian wrote wonderful letters sharing their impressions.

Then a man I'd never met volunteered to loan me his eight-hour videotape of local news coverage during the event.

From the first hiccup through the aftermath of the blast, I suddenly had it all. Including posteruption footage in which a foolhardy cameraman recorded what he thought was his final report as he struggled to escape from the ash-laden atmosphere of the restricted area near the volcano.

Much later, an actual visit with a park ranger in the area added a rare pre-eruption map to my material. Unfortunately, my book premise was rejected. But I know that someday I'll find another plot an editor *will* like.

I also know my readers will feel that mountain tremble and breathe volcanic ash right along with my characters. All because I wrote a few letters in a quest for atmosphere.

Here are a few more tips on researching.

• **Know when to stop.** I have a research-loving writer friend who set out to verify a few details about the accelerants used by arsonists and amassed hundreds of articles on arson in general. Days went by before she realized what was happening—days she could have been writing.

• **Verify facts.** Information gleaned in an Internet chat room is fine if it deals with an individual's experience. Check with a second source if it involves something more concrete.

• **Don't compound the mistakes of others.** Another fiction writer may not have researched a subject as thoroughly as she should have. Even a single nonfiction source for technical information can sometimes be in error. Consider the importance of the detail you're seeking and follow through accordingly.

How the Professionals Create Atmosphere

Perhaps the best way to understand atmosphere is to take a look at how some successful writers have created suspense through setting.

In *Airport*, Arthur Hailey describes the tense atmosphere in air traffic control.

The radar room had no windows. Day and night . . . ten radar controllers and supervisors labored in perpetual semidarkness . . . beneath the calmness at all times was a constant nervous strain. Tonight, the strain had been added to by the storm and, . . . a flashing red light and alarm buzzer.

We, the readers, are cloaked in that darkened atmosphere, seeing that red light, hearing that persistent warning buzzer. As a result, we also feel the adrenaline rush and shiver of fear Hailey's character experiences.

Judith Kelman opens *More Than You Know* this way.

> *At the entrance to the set, Dana Saunders hesitated. The topic of today's show gave her a rotten feeling in the pit of her stomach, a racing pulse. Like the onset of a sickness she was powerless to prevent.*

We didn't need a description of lights and cameras and tiers of seats filled by an anxious audience to know we're in a TV studio. We've all seen enough Springer or Oprah that we can visualize what wasn't said. Kelman also revealed enough about Dana's state of mind that we know she hosts a controversial show that's probably going to be even more contentious than usual.

> *The waves turned vicious and worsened with every rush of wind. The calm weather of the morning transformed from Dr. Jekyll into a vehement Mr. Hyde by late evening. Whitecaps on the crests of towering waves were lashed into sheets of spray.*

So begins Clive Cussler's *Flood Tide.*

Although Cussler has yet to introduce us, we know the character through whose eyes we're seeing this display of nature's power is cold and wet. A slug line at the beginning of the chapter has noted the date and that we're in unknown waters. Caught at sea in the midst of a storm. Afraid and shivering. Atmosphere aplenty to keep us reading on.

One final example, this time from the acknowledged master of suspense. See how, in a single opening sentence of *The Cradle Will Fall*, Mary Higgins Clark identifies her heroine, creates tension and lays the foundation for suspense.

> *If her mind had not been on the case she had won, Katie might not have taken the curve so fast, but the intense satisfaction of the guilty verdict was still absorbing her.*

In thirty-three words, Clark's readers have learned that the protagonist is a successful prosecuting attorney and her latest case was especially important—so important that, even though she won, she can't keep her mind on her driving.

Many things are available to help create atmosphere. The plants and trees and animals native to your setting can be useful. Remember those birds that suddenly stopped chirping during our imaginary walk in chapter one?

The architecture of a city can play a role. Compare the steel and concrete buildings of downtown New York to the pastel houses in the Florida Keys. Or the ethnic makeup of the rural Midwest to an inner-city neighborhood in Los Angeles.

Words play a big part in setting the stage and building the atmosphere of suspense. In chapter fifteen, we'll discuss how to make your prose work to establish both.

CHAPTER 7

Point of View

Before you can write your thriller's first sentence, you must make an important decision: Through whose eyes will your readers be watching your plot unfold?

Your viewpoint choices are omniscient, first person, second person, limited (or singular) third person or multiple third person. Let's examine how each one affects suspense.

Omniscient Point of View

The omniscient viewpoint permits the writer to see into all characters' heads—to play God, jumping from one viewpoint to another at random within scenes and even sentences. It also allows for authorial asides.

At first glance, writing a book from an all-seeing, all-knowing point of view (POV) might sound like a good idea. In reality, it's tough to do. And, while there may be suspense novels out there written entirely in this POV, my research failed to find one. Perhaps this example of omniscient viewpoint will explain why.

> *Farley had dreamed in color for as long as he could remember. Then he married Doris. From his wedding forward his nightly visions played in his mind like a 1930s grade D movie, an endless parade of dull mono-*

*chrome images. No more glorious magenta. Good-bye cerulean blue. So
long luscious lemon yellow.*

   *Doris, of course, had no clue as to the disaster her softly murmured
"I do" had caused. In fact, she loved being married. Loved every minute
of every day she spent as Mrs. Farley P. Janus. Each morning she rose
with a spring in her step and a smile on her lips. It was that smile that
finally drove Farley to buy the assault rifle.*

These people are as remote as the images playing out on Farley's dream
meter. Omniscient viewpoint disrupts readers' identification by placing them
outside the book's action, making them spectators rather than participants.
Since they are not a part of what's happening, readers are less likely to empathize with what the characters are experiencing.

Remember that suspense is emotional. To feel that emotion, we must be
privy to a character's thoughts. Omniscient viewpoint prevents us from achieving that intimacy. By seeing into all characters' minds only briefly, we lose the
chance to really identify with any of them.

Occasionally, a writer will open a thriller with a brief narrative passage
written from an omniscient viewpoint. If the material revealed is especially
moving or startling enough, this can be effective.

Joy Fielding did this in her women-in-jeopardy novel *See Jane Run.*

   *One afternoon in late spring, Jane Whittaker went to the store for some
milk and some eggs and forgot who she was.*

Fielding's omniscient opening works because it's so shocking. And because
she immediately switches to Jane's viewpoint for the rest of the scene.

The thriller is first and foremost a commercial vehicle. Omniscient viewpoint is most often found in books with a literary slant. Because it doesn't
really allow readers to identify with the protagonist, this POV is not a good
choice for suspense.

Second-Person Point of View

I'm taking this viewpoint out of order because it is even less common than omniscient—in thrillers *or* other books. In second person the author speaks directly to the reader. In essence, *you*, the reader, become the unnamed protagonist.

Consider the following opening scene.

> *Your heart is pounding and you feel like you've forgotten how to breathe. Just a few more yards and you can rest. Unless he's still following; then you'll have to keep going.*

Right about now most readers of suspense will be thinking, *I'm not out of breath. Who is this person?* Rather than make the readers feel a part of what's happening, second person makes them aware of the writer's style. Achieving and sustaining suspense thus becomes much harder.

Second person is best reserved for quirky, offbeat stories that don't rely on suspense.

First-Person Point of View

> *Death is my beat. I make my living from it.*

So begins Michael Connelly's *The Poet*, a taut psychological suspense novel whose protagonist is crime reporter Jack McEvoy.

First person allows a writer to remain in one viewpoint character's head. It also *requires* a writer to remain in that same character's head.

Let's look at these requirements.

• First-person POV immediately signals a reader that this character has survived whatever is about to happen.

• Readers can know only what the character knows, see only what he sees, learn only what he learns.

• The language and tone of the book must remain consistent. If I'm telling the story, I can't suddenly slip into another character's speech pattern or wander into his thoughts. As I write this passage I know what *I'm* thinking. I have no way of knowing what's in *your* mind as you read it.

• Because readers view only what goes on inside the mind of one character, that character, her thoughts and what she sees must be interesting enough to hold their attention throughout the entire book.

• Other people can tell a first-person viewpoint character about things that have already happened, but action in real time can take place only when that viewpoint character is present. For example, if the suspected villain drives past the viewpoint character's house, she can become aware that he had done so only if she looks out her window as his car goes by. If other plot considerations call for her to be away, knowledge of the drive by must come to her after the fact, through conversation with another character who *did* see the villain's action.

• First person can make it hard for a reader to picture the viewpoint character's expressions, and thus his reactions. Some passages can sound stilted.

I grimaced and felt myself grow tense as I listened to William's version of what happened.

• A writer's personality can seep into a viewpoint character's persona, substituting the writer's own traits and opinions for those he originally intended and perhaps needs the character to display.

Now for the good news.

• Readers are privy to everything the viewpoint character thinks and does. This includes her motivation, her personal history and her thoughts and suspicions about others in the story.

• First-person POV is easy to control. A writer is less apt to stray into another character's head in the middle of a scene.

• Use of "I" can make readers believe the action is happening to them. Because of this, if the plot is intriguing enough, readers will stay with the hero or heroine through the end of the book.

• First person can make stories with limited settings feel even more intimate.

Ask yourself the following questions.

1. Does my plot allow my viewpoint character to be present during the critical action scenes?

2. Would the intimacy achieved by the use of "I" be enhanced by my story's setting?

3. Are my plot and my viewpoint character intriguing enough to sustain a suspenseful narrative and a single internal dialogue for an entire novel?

If you answer yes to these questions, first-person POV may be the right choice for you.

Limited (Singular) Third-Person Point of View

While not quite as intimate for a reader as first person, limited, or singular, third person comes very close.

After opening with the brief and extremely startling omniscient statement about Jane Whittaker forgetting who she was in *See Jane Run*, Joy Fielding moves quickly into Jane's POV using limited third person.

> *It came to her suddenly, without prior hint or warning, . . . that while she knew exactly where she was, she had absolutely no idea who she was.*

Fielding remains in this POV throughout the book, taking the reader inside Jane's mind as she is introduced to a husband and friends she can't remember and struggles to find the reason for her loss of memory. Readers go where Jane goes. They experience what she does. And, when Fielding wants them to, they feel Jane's emotion.

Some of the same restrictions of first person apply to limited third.

Readers can know, see and learn only what the POV character does. The writer cannot slip into another character's thoughts. Real-time action can take place only in the POV character's presence. It's almost as if the writer is the POV character's shadow—not inside her head but always at her heels.

But in limited third, readers cannot be absolutely certain the POV character will survive the unfolding ordeal unscathed.

The distance that comes with limited third allows a writer to show the viewpoint character's appearance, expression and physical reaction. Read this example.

> *His choice of cutoffs and Bud Light tank top for Davy's "casual little get-together" was a bit underdone, Nick decided. The out-of-date Miami Vice stubble was definitely a Class A goof. Everyone else was in cocktail attire and the only facial hair in sight was a severe Vandyke on a wizened old man who could have doubled for Freud. For a guy who was desperate to fit in, he'd really screwed up this time.*
>
> *What the hell, he thought, taking a deep breath. He'd just bluff his way through the evening the way he usually did. The decision sounded good, but his hand was shaking so badly, it took him three tries to light a cigarette.*

In the above passage we are clearly inside Nick's head, seeing him as he sees himself, viewing the others through his eyes and feeling his hand tremble.

While the writer's personality is less apt to invade the viewpoint character's persona in limited third person, the tendency to accidentally stray into another character's POV is greatly increased. As with first person, in limited third the viewpoint must remain consistent.

Limited third allows a writer to control when and how much she wants to emphasize action, movement or thought. It permits the author to pull back from the character when the action is more important than the internal dialogue.

Phrases like *he knew, she thought* or *Jay tried to remember* indicate shifts into a character's internal dialogue.

Action and regular dialogue in books that use limited third person are written as if the reader were seeing and hearing it through the viewpoint character's eyes and ears.

> *"Tully wants to talk to you," Carol Ann said, breaking into Kate's thoughts.*
> *"When?"*

"Ten minutes ago. He had steam comin' out his ears."

Tully Pitcher's stained undershirt and glistening bald pate reflected the heat buffeting the narrow kitchen. The truck's stop's chunky owner had demolished Tran's neatly arranged vegetable bins and dumped the spice rack. Grease dripped from the exhaust fans, splattering every surface. . . .

In Tully's mind, good food and orderly kitchens were incompatible. The only thing he and his Cambodian cook agreed on was the importance of sharp knives. He was underscoring that tenet now, with a cleaver and an odd assortment of vegetables. When Tully got angry, he got creative.

Kate cleared her throat.

"Need a double outta you. Rae's sick," Tully said, without looking up as he added eggplant and zucchini to the onions and peppers already ravaged by his blade.

Kate felt her headache blossom.

"What about Carol Ann?"

"Been bitchin' 'bout your hours. You takin' it, or not?"

In the above exchange, I wanted readers to see Kate's action as she entered Tully's kitchen. I did this by pulling back a little. We remain in Kate's viewpoint, yet distanced from her internal thoughts. Because of this viewpoint and distance, we can also see what Tully is doing. The next line momentarily pulls us close again so we can experience Kate's emotional reaction (her headache) before conversation continues. Limited third person allows this kind of flexibility.

By distancing readers from the viewpoint character a bit, an author can focus more on the movement and reactions of the other players within each scene. This in turn places more emphasis on the plot itself than on the main character.

While it can be used for all categories of suspense, limited third person works especially well when the plot involves a limited number of characters or locations.

Limited third-person POV is the choice for many thrillers whose authors like to create their tension through a balance of the action, movement and internal dialogue of one person.

Ask yourself the following questions.

1. Can my plot be revealed through the eyes of a single character?

2. Will my viewpoint character be present during the plot's critical scenes?

3. Do I want my readers to be aware of that character's expressions and physical reactions as well as his internal dialogue?

4. Would a greater emphasis on plot strengthen my story's suspense?

5. Can I consistently write "he said" or "she said" without drifting into another character's thoughts?

If your response to all five questions is yes, this POV may be a good choice.

Multiple Third-Person Point of View

The night may have a thousand eyes; a good suspense novel does not. However, this POV offers an author many advantages.

Multiple third person allows a writer to take his readers anywhere he wants them to go. Individual scenes or entire chapters can be written from the viewpoint of characters other than the protagonist. Readers can even see parts of the story unfold through the eyes of the villain. Dangers and events can be revealed before the protagonist learns of them, raising the reader's level of concern for the hero or heroine's well-being.

While every category of suspense can be written in first, limited third and multiple third person, novels with the biggest scope are most often told from multiple viewpoints.

Tom Clancy could not have done justice to submarine warfare and political maneuvering without taking his readers inside a variety of locations.

Clive Cussler always opens his novels with a fascinating look at the origin of whatever shipwreck Dirk Pitt and his salvage team are attempting to locate. This abridged example from *Raise the Titanic*, set in the historical past, would not be possible without using multiple POVs.

April 1912

The man on Deck A, Stateroom 33, tossed and turned in his narrow berth, the mind behind his sweating face lost in the depths of a nightmare. . . . The physical grind and mental torment of the last five months had exhausted him to the ragged edge of madness. . . .

He wasn't sure how long he'd dozed. Something had jolted him awake. Not a loud sound or a violent movement, it was more like a trembling motion from his mattress and a strange grinding noise somewhere far below his starboard stateroom. He rose stiffly to a sitting position and swung his feet to the floor. A few minutes passed and he sensed an unusual vibrationless quiet. Then his befogged mind grasped the reason. The engines had stopped. . . .

The scene goes on to detail the man's strange behavior in reaction to learning the ship is sinking. In addition to such opening sequences and Pitt's own viewpoint, other scenes are often viewed through the eyes of a member of Pitt's team or his current love interest.

The trick to writing in multiple viewpoints is to avoid alienating the reader by jumping around too much. Several things can be done to prevent this from happening.

• Restrict each viewpoint character to her own scene or chapter. Readers become frustrated if they can't tell or lose track of whose POV they are in.

• Identify the viewpoint character by name within the first sentence of a new scene, even if the previous one was also told from the same person's POV. After this initial identification, you can refer to the character as he or she. However, if a scene is especially long or several other characters are involved, you should repeat the name every few paragraphs to help keep readers oriented.

• If you decide to use a location ID at the start of chapters or scenes, be consistent or readers may become confused as to where they are. The rule for immediately identifying the POV character within such scenes also applies with location IDs.

• Try to maintain a balance between viewpoint scenes. While it's not necessary to alternate one for one, writing two-thirds of a book from only two or three viewpoints then switching almost entirely to a different character's POV for the remaining third isn't really fair play.

• Avoid writing scenes from the viewpoint of a dozen minor characters who each appear only once during the course of the book. Leaving the established viewpoints tends to diminish tension and dilute reader identification.

• If you believe you've encountered a situation in which writing a scene from a onetime character's POV is necessary, determine whether the same information can be conveyed through an established viewpoint character. If it can't, and the scene is critical to the plot, you're looking at the exception to the rule. (Novels with an especially broad scope sometimes make bending this last guideline necessary.)

Multiple third-person POV is especially effective in plots in which the writer wants to explore the mind of the villain. Jessie Hunter's *One, Two, Buckle My Shoe* is a good example. Any story with a strong psychological tone is a candidate as well.

Tess Gerritsen (see page 218 for her interview) also uses multiple POVs: "I've always used multiple viewpoints in my writing—I think it may have to do with my own short attention span. In a thriller, multiple viewpoints help to move the plot along. It gives readers the sense that there's a 'bigger picture' to the story, that this tale is going to involve a number of people and that their lives will weave together in intricate ways."

If you're considering multiple third-person POV, ask yourself these questions.

1. Does the scope or psychological aspect of my novel justify multiple POVs?

2. Is it important that action occur simultaneously in two or more places?

3. Does my plot dictate that my protagonist remain in the dark about certain events that I want my reader to know?

4. Are my antagonist's internal thoughts equally as important as those of my protagonist?

If you answer yes to any of these questions, your book calls for multiple POVs.

Mixed Points of View

A few books combine first- and limited third-person POVs. Michael Connelly's *The Poet* is an example. The book begins, and the majority is written, from the first-person viewpoint of Jack McEvoy. Certain chapters, however, are told from the POV of the serial killer McEvoy is determined to find.

While Connelly is certainly not the only writer who has mixed POVs within a novel, you should think carefully before following his example. *The Poet* works because Connelly, an experienced writer, was able to maintain the exact viewpoint balance the story required.

Another author who has experimented with mixed POVs is Marilyn Wallace: "Many writing teachers and most books about writing would advise beginning writers to stay consistent with regard to point of view, tense and voice, but I believe that a writer must keep herself interested in order to keep her readers interested. If playing with such variations is intriguing, then by all means go ahead and do it. But if literary pyrotechnics get in the way of telling a good story, it's time to examine your intentions as a writer."

Tense

The majority of thrillers, regardless of viewpoint, are written in past tense. There are, of course, as Marilyn Wallace mentions above, exceptions to this.

When an author chooses present tense for a suspense novel, he usually maintains that tense for the entire book. In these cases POV will be either first or limited third person.

Some readers find the present tense distracting. Obviously an author takes a chance of alienating such readers when he makes this choice. Still, done skillfully, present tense can create and sustain suspense equally as well as past tense.

Now and then an author will go a step further by mixing both tenses and POVs within a book.

In Marilyn Wallace's *The Seduction*, two sisters, Rosie and Lee, are waiting to confront the person who has been stalking them. Chapters that deal with this vigil are told in first-person present tense through the eyes of Lee and begin with a notation of the time of day rather than a chapter number. This serves to trigger the reader to the change as well as heighten the tension.

> *We face each other, two sisters, one dark and edgy, the other a pale, serious redhead, both slender and watchful. We know that even if we*

seem to be talking to each other or entertaining only tranquil thoughts,
we are really waiting. Waiting for him to make his move; waiting, too,
to make ours.

First-person present tense chapters open and close the novel. Only three or four other strategically placed chapters use this tense and viewpoint.

The remaining chapters, which deal with events leading up to that point, are numbered and told in past tense from Lee's limited third-person POV.

The subway station always felt the same when I stepped off the F train,
dank and gloomy, as though time and seasons didn't exist so far below
the ground. I fell in with the crowd snaking between the tile walls toward
the trickle of light beyond the exit sign, my purse tucked against my side
and my eyes on a nonexistent object in front of me.

In *The Seduction*, mixing viewpoint *and* tense works because it increases the tension for readers. Even as they're absorbing the back story revealed in Lee's limited third-person past tense POV, they're anticipating the tense/POV switch that will signal a renewed escalation of the immediate threat against the two sisters.

Few authors choose to attempt what Wallace has successfully done. For less experienced writers, choosing first person, limited third or multiple third person and writing in past tense is usually advisable.

The Final Decision

The question remains. *Who* should be your POV character(s)?

FIRST-PERSON POV

Because reader identification is so intense, choosing the **protagonist** as the POV character is usually best when using first person. But exactly who should the protagonist be?

Consider a plot about a second wife (Alicia) who's hired a hit man to arrange "accidents" for first her adult stepdaughter, Suzanne, and then her husband,

Walter, in order to inherit an estate. Either Walter or Suzanne could be the protagonist. Told in first person, each story would have a different slant and tone.

What about an **antagonist's** first-person account?

Dame Agatha Christie tried this with *The Murder of Roger Ackroyd* in 1926 when she waited until the last chapter to reveal that the book's narrator was the murderer. At the time, critics denounced the tactic as unfair. Reader reaction was mixed. Over the years the book has become a classic. But that novel was a puzzle mystery, not a thriller.

My research, which included a query to dealers of used mystery and suspense books, did not turn up a true suspense thriller written in first person from the villain's POV.

Such a book would certainly offer a challenge. Few suspense readers have the strong desire to be a stalker, a serial killer or even a onetime murderer. This presents a problem of reader identification: While readers appreciate an occasional glimpse into these people's minds, they might find living with one for an entire novel overpowering. (An exception might be a book written from the POV of a parent or other family member stalking the acquitted killer of her child. Films have dealt with this plot, but the POV in movies involves a different set of rules.)

While first person can be used in any category, it lends itself best to legal, psychological, romantic relationship and women-in-jeopardy suspense. The scopes of many action-adventure, medical, political and techno-thriller plots usually call for another choice. As always, reading examples of the category you've chosen is the best way to learn what's most effective.

LIMITED THIRD-PERSON POV

Singular third-person suspense is also most often written from the **protagonist's** viewpoint. But, because this POV provides readers with a bit of distance, a story seen through the villain's eyes might be possible. The trick would be making the reader believe the viewpoint character was in as much danger as the real victim until the climax of the book. Most writers would find this a daunting proposal.

When deciding which character should be the protagonist of a thriller written in limited third person, ask yourself the following questions.

• Which character will be present during critical action scenes?
• Toward which person will the villain direct his anger?
• Which character has the most to lose?

In a fully developed plot, the answers to these questions should point to your protagonist. Limited third person can work with any of the categories, although the requirement of revealing only action actually viewed by the POV character often makes it better suited to plots with limited characters and locations.

MULTIPLE THIRD-PERSON POV

Even when a novel has multiple narrators, there should be one primary protagonist with whom the reader most closely identifies. (The above questions should also be helpful in determining the primary protagonist of a thriller written in multiple POVs.) In multiple third person, however, you can also include the viewpoint of several secondary characters. The key is to choose these various people carefully.

I've already discussed the danger of jumping around too much when using multiple POVs. Your primary viewpoint character should appear in a majority of your scenes. This person should be the one who changes the most during the course of the story.

In addition to the protagonist, a majority of multiple POV novels include the antagonist as a viewpoint character as well. A glimpse inside the villain's head is one way to heighten suspense. This person's identity may be either revealed or disguised. The most common exception to including the villain's POV is action-adventure. Although Clive Cussler uses multiple POVs in his Dirk Pitt series, his antagonist is never one of them.

Once the primary POV has been established, the main consideration in choosing other POV characters should be (1) the category of suspense and (2) the scope of the plot.

Romantic suspense and women-in-jeopardy usually have limited multiple-viewpoint characters. This is because these books take place in a more confined setting. Often the protagonist, the villain, and one or two others are all that are needed.

In *Someone to Watch Over*, I chose as viewpoint characters my protagonist Kate; my revealed antagonist Cal; Park, a deputy sheriff who's an old friend of Kate's; and, in a limited number of scenes, Kate's two children.

I also broke the rule of no single-scene viewpoint characters by showing the results of one of my villain's arranged accidents from his victim's POV. My purpose was to underline how unstable Cal had become in a very short time. That makes six POV characters for a 388-page novel.

A techno-thriller's scope is much broader than most fem-jep plots. My quick count of Clancy's *The Hunt for Red October* found a dozen viewpoints in a book just eighty pages longer than mine.

Psychological suspense, on the other hand, can have as few as two POV characters—usually the protagonist and the villain—or as many as Clancy's techno-thriller. The remaining categories fall anywhere in between.

In the end, my best advice is to choose the POV that feels most comfortable when you begin your suspense novel. You'll know rather quickly if you've made a mistake. Starting a book over because of a viewpoint problem is no picnic. But, as any writer can tell you, each book is a learning experience.

CHAPTER 8

Back Story

Back story refers to an individual character's history. Every character—from the protagonist to the villain to the checkout clerk who appears on just one page—has a history. But it's up to the writer to determine how much of the back story the reader needs to know.

Much of the background that writers create for their characters is for the writer's own benefit. To make these people come alive on the page, an author has to know what makes them tick. He must understand why they *act* as they do before he can show how they *react* to the events in the plot.

Not all character development has relevance to the final plot, however. Long narrative passages that force-feed readers information on how or why an existing situation came to be are known as "dumps." The author is, in effect, "dumping" back story onto the reader all at one time rather than integrating the material elsewhere within the story—in essence, she is telling rather than showing.

So how do you decide what to share with readers? And when or where is the proper time or place to reveal it?

Revealing Character Background: A Case Study

I discussed in chapter four why you should never open a suspense novel with historical data. Let's use our Burke and Martin, multiple POV, action-adventure/

techno-thriller plotline to explore alternative ways to logically insert the information readers need to know. For a quick review of the plots we created for these categories in chapter five, reread pages 50–52.

CHAPTER ONE

Chapter one will consist of four tightly written scenes.

If we open with Martin and his men studying blueprints and photos of the power plant as they go over their plan of assault, we've met the requirements for a thriller's first scene. Action is taking place and a threat has been established.

Right now all the readers know is that Martin is the villain. They have no idea what he wants or why he's chosen this way to get it. The identity of our protagonist is also unknown.

Our second scene follows Jenny and Amy into the plant. Mother and daughter are negotiating the ground rules for their trip to the mall. Jenny introduces Amy to the security guard, points out where things are located and explains the various security procedures. Amy, anxious to get to the mall, resents the stop's intrusion on their Saturday plans. She complains about how dumb all the precautions are.

Jenny mutters under her breath that things wouldn't seem so stupid if Amy's precious uncle were leading the tour.

The readers now identify with Jenny and Amy as typical parent and child. They are also acutely aware that the pair is about to become involved in a dangerous situation. At this point either mother or daughter could be the book's protagonist. But the reference to Amy's unnamed uncle has not gone unnoticed.

Burke's name has not been mentioned. His position as a security consultant has been foreshadowed but not established. His prior relationship with Jenny remains undisclosed.

Only the writer knows this historical data.

Our third scene in chapter one describes Martin's assault on the power plant. It ends with the shoot-out between Martin's men and the guard Jenny and Amy met as they entered the building.

Scene four begins when Jenny hears gunfire and the sound of running feet in the corridor outside her office. She shoves Amy under the desk and whispers for her to not make a sound, no matter what happens. The chapter ends with Jenny's capture.

Action and danger have been well established. A question as to what role Amy's unnamed uncle might play in the plot has been raised. Martin's demands and the reasons behind them are still to be revealed.

CHAPTER TWO

Scene one of chapter two finds Burke taking the day off, fishing from the dock of his lakeside cabin when his cell phone rings. It's his brother Tim, who's out of town. Tim can't locate his family and wants to know if his big brother has kidnapped them for the day.

No need to confirm that Jenny and Amy are the family in question; readers will make the connection on their own.

After some brief brotherly bantering, the call is interrupted by the landing of a chopper in Burke's front yard. Burke mutters that duty seems to be calling and hangs up.

Readers now know Burke has a personal stake in the power plant takeover. When he's identified as a security consultant and told that only a skeleton crew was at work, readers realize Jenny's presence has not yet been discovered by those in charge.

Burke's history with Martin would best be disclosed in scene two of this chapter when the villain learns Jenny's last name. He says he and Burke go back a long way, then tells her his version of the playground story and hints at other more serious clashes over the years. Then he casually tosses out the information that he chose this particular target because Burke designed its security system.

Both Jenny and the reader now suspect that luring Burke into a trap is as much a part of Martin's plan as the money he's about to demand. Catching Jenny has upped the stakes. If Amy is discovered, things can only get worse.

In scene three we'll return to Burke's viewpoint. Martin's use of Jenny to phone his demands provides an opportunity to reveal her presence to our hero. If Jenny is only allowed to say what Martin has dictated, Burke will assume

Amy is also being held. Martin ends the call by shooting his own injured man, leaving Burke to worry about exactly who was shot.

Information about the adult clashes between Martin and Burke that really led to this moment remain unrevealed. We have three options available for making the reader privy to this data: (1) Burke's internal dialogue; (2) continued exchanges between Martin and Jenny; or (3), as discussed in chapter three on characterization, dialogue between Burke and a member of his rescue team.

Martin should also be the character who remembers Burke's past relationship with Jenny. His later hunt for Amy then offers an opportunity for him to goad Burke that Amy is the child Burke and Jenny should have had.

During the character development stage, the author would probably have considered possible reasons for the couple's breakup, but those reasons need not be revealed. *Unless that knowledge affects the plot in some way.*

Action. Danger. A frightening villain. Mental anxiety for a hero to whom failure means the loss of people he cares about. All the elements of suspense are on the table. And readers were never subjected to a history lesson.

The Hows and Whys of Plot Background

Most of the information detailed in the scenes I've outlined above deals with historical data that affects a character's motivations, actions and emotional involvement. But not *all* the reader's questions are answered.

Nothing in this example explains why the plot's premise is taking place or what brought the characters to that time and place. Martin's hatred of Burke may simply be a facet of his twisted personality that injects additional tension into the story. Or it might be the catalyst that set off the chain of events that led to the takeover.

Withholding how and why material serves several purposes. What the reader isn't told, she wonders about. Things only hinted at assume added importance. And a reader's need to know increases the element of suspense.

John Gilstrap is an author who understands the value of hand-feeding his readers this type of critical background.

Gilstrap's *Nathan's Run* begins when police lieutenant Warren Michaels is called away from a family outing to investigate a murder at his county's juvenile detention center. At this point readers might assume that Michaels is the primary protagonist.

This belief is reinforced when they learn the details of the murder. Twelve-year-old Nathan Bailey has stabbed a guard and then escaped. Given recent publicity surrounding preteen murderers, few readers would expect the real protagonist of Gilstrap's plot to be the boy in question.

To reveal Nathan's version of what happened, Gilstrap uses a series of phone conversations between the boy and a radio talk show host whose listeners have been debating his case. According to Nathan, he acted in self-defense.

The question in readers' minds then becomes: Why would a guard have been trying to kill a twelve-year-old boy?

Although Nathan doesn't have an answer, his manners and personality soon convince the host and her listeners that he may be telling the truth. His revelations about mistreatment while in the juvenile facility add yet another dimension to the story.

They also let readers understand why he keeps running. Listening to the broadcasts as he digs into Nathan's history, even Michaels begins to suspect things are not what they seem.

As Gilstrap slowly parcels out the how and why back story, he throws additional obstacles in the path of Nathan's run to safety. Among these are a district attorney using Nathan's case as a political stepping stone, multiple police departments determined to track down a cop killer they feel is mocking them in a public forum and a man sent to finish the job the detention center guard was unable to carry out.

Nathan's reactions to events surrounding each obstacle seem to argue he's guilty. Yet after each episode, readers learn a bit more of the how and why. Each specific background detail Gilstrap chooses to reveal is directly related to Nathan's valid motivation for running.

Jittery cops. A hired killer. One sympathetic policeman. Each using every available means to find a single confused and frightened boy. A child whose only hope lies in trusting one of the very people he's come to believe wants him dead.

Now well beyond their initial reaction that Nathan was the antagonist,

Gilstrap's readers find themselves pulling for secondary protagonist Michaels as he tries to get to Nathan before the boy is caught in the cross fire. An excellent example of how to reveal crucial information without dumping it on the reader.

Using Flashbacks

In addition to conversation between characters, back story can be revealed through flashbacks. But the transitions leading into and out of a flashback must be seamless, or a writer runs the risk of losing a reader's interest.

Poorly placed flashbacks can also interrupt the rhythm of suspense. Still, used infrequently, carefully constructed flashbacks can be effective.

This device can be handled in several ways.

Linda Orett, Marilyn Wallace's protagonist in *A Single Stone*, has been acquitted of murdering her own child due to a finding of reasonable doubt. Readers learn this information through a series of unusual flashbacks.

Haunted by her inability to remember what happened the day her daughter was killed, Linda often carries on brief mental conversations with herself. Each episode is a mini flashback in which Linda questions her reaction to current experiences in relationship to her past.

Since these thoughts are in response to the action going on around her, readers have no difficulty following the narrative. This approach works because Wallace uses italics for the internal exchanges and keeps each one brief.

The first few times Linda converses with herself the reader isn't quite sure exactly what event she's thinking about or reliving. Initial references consist of only a few words.

> *Baby shampoo; she* couldn't *be smelling it, not really.* Your imagination is working overtime, *Linda told herself as she dropped a rye bread into the wire cart and continued on her way.*

Then, seven pages into chapter one, Wallace injects an eight-line flashback of courtroom questioning.

Unbidden, an image of the three little girls in the market rose before her.

None of them was blond, *she told herself.* I'll be all right. *She fed the car more gas; suddenly, she was in a hurry to get home.*

—and didn't your mother-in-law become so alarmed that she came to stay with you when your daughter was two weeks old?

(I must hide my hands. I cannot put her down. The chair is hard. The room is spinning.)

—A month after the birth of your daughter, your husband took you to see Dr. Gorchik. What did the doctor find on that visit?

(Find. Nothing to find. Nothing lost yet.)

—Please tell the court. . . .

"The past is behind me. I can move forward," she muttered to herself.

This passage does not actually indicate who was on trial or for what, only that Linda was the one being questioned. What *is* obvious is that this same type of internal conversation was part of her thinking even during that past experience.

None of the details surrounding Linda's past are described. It is not until the final line of the first chapter that Wallace reveals the underlying query that torments her protagonist. She does this via Linda's jolting cliff-hanger thought.

How could anyone think I murdered my own child?

Linda's back story continues to be disclosed through her internal thoughts and through dialogue between the two detectives trying to solve the identical murder of a second child.

Because Linda's mental conversations are brief, they quickly become part of the novel's rhythm.

Normally, flashback passages are not as pronounced as those Wallace created. A simple transition—often using a tense change—signals the reader that the flashback has begun. When the action returns to the present, another tense switch reverses the transition.

The example that follows is from *Someone to Watch Over*. My protagonist and her young son Cody are waiting for her daughter to come home from school. A neighbor's cat wanders over and begins to purr.

> *"Motor-sickle."*
>
> *Kate laughed. The contented rumble did remind her of the motorcycle Buck Perry sometimes rode. Buck had given Michael a ride home [and] the children had begged for rides. Kate, remembering a schoolmate who'd lost a leg in a motorcycle accident, had been frightened by the massive machine. Michael had sensed her fear and told Buck they'd wait for another day. It was one of the few times they'd communicated without conflict in several months.*
>
> *She held the memory close, wondering if her recent fears were rooted in something similar.*

A tense transition from ***did*** remind her to ***had given*** Michael a ride signals the start of this brief flashback.

At the end the tense switches back from, *the few times **they'd communicated*** to *She **held** the memory close*, and ***wondering** if her recent fears **were rooted**.*

Isolating the Past Into Sections

Richard North Patterson is another author who skillfully builds suspense by taking readers into the past to dispense back story one piece at a time.

Attorney-client discussions and courtroom testimony reveal the back story in many of Patterson's character-driven legal thrillers. However, his *Silent Witness* is an example of yet another method that can be used for disclosing prior events.

The novel's premise revolves around events that took place during attorney Tony Lord's teenage years. After a ten-page prologue, Patterson divides his book into four separate parts. The prologue begins in the present and ends with a phone call that sends Lord's thoughts tumbling back in time.

Part one concentrates entirely on the events of Lord's senior year, when he was suspected but never charged for the rape and murder of his high school sweetheart.

The second part details Lord's investigation and preparation for the eerily similar murder trial that forces him to return to his old hometown. This time it's Tony's best friend who's under suspicion. His buddy, now a high school teacher, had been having an affair with the victim, one of his students.

Patterson moves ahead a few months for part three to take his readers into the courtroom as Tony Lord defends his old friend. The final section addresses the aftermath and consequences of the hung jury verdict.

The back story revealed in part one permeates the other three divisions. The explosive climax shocks the reader. It also changes Tony Lord, relieving him of an old nightmare only to replace it with a new one.

Many variations of divisions such as these have been used to reveal back story. Usually a plot's structure dictates when they will work and when they won't. Stories like Patterson's that revisit major events in a protagonist's life are often good candidates. Intense action plots that take place within a short period of time usually aren't. Before deciding whether divisions will work for your book, study the above thriller and others using the same construction.

What to Put In; What to Leave Out

Now that you know *how* to insert back story in a novel, the tough part is *what* should be included.

Back story can play many roles in suspense. It can reveal important character traits, establish critical plot points, foreshadow events and character reaction, cast suspicion or supply misdirection.

If something in a character's background affects her reaction to the plot, work it into the narrative. Preferably well in advance of the point where it applies.

I used the flashback from *Someone to Watch Over* (on the previous page) not to reveal historical information, but to illustrate the crumbling relationship between my protagonist and her husband prior to his death. This was important because Kate's initial reaction to being stalked is tied to her already shaky self-esteem.

In the case of our power plant story, Amy's knowledge of her mother's E-mail password would need to be established as soon as she and Jenny enter the office. Then, when she contacts her Uncle Burke, technologically astute readers will not question her access to the computer.

If the plot's climax hinges on a villain's weakness, include a subtle reference to this in the midst of an earlier, equally tense scene. The Chocolate Man's fears and rituals, exposed quite early in Jessie Hunter's plot, return to haunt him in later chapters.

When historical background common to two or more characters is used to throw suspicion on both, it should be introduced without interrupting the story's flow at whatever point seems most logical.

Early in the unnamed villain's internal dialogue in *Buried Secrets*, he made a reference to having been in Asia. Different supporting characters then mentioned in separate conversations that each of my potential suspects had spent time in Asian countries.

The references to each character's Asian connection were planted within casual conversations between my protagonist and the friendly neighbors she meets after being thrust into a new environment. This kept readers off balance while events and action built the suspense and moved the story forward.

Sometimes what you leave out at certain points in a plot is more important than what you put in. Stringing a protagonist along also teases the reader. But you must play fair with the reader as well.

You cannot introduce a new character or set of circumstances near the end of a book just because you failed or couldn't figure out how to include a key piece of information earlier. In the same vein, telling a reader too much too soon reduces the story's tension and spoils the suspense.

The key is to balance the when and how much against the book's action.

If a minor character hints that something that's just been said has deeper meaning but refuses to explain, tension deepens. Should that person then disappear or be killed, readers learn that whatever wasn't said would be dangerous for the protagonist to find out.

To recap, here are some guidelines for revealing (or concealing) back story in a suspense novel.

- Introduce past events only if they can be used to reveal character, create conflict or increase tension.
- Reveal the minimum amount of detail needed to peak readers' curiosity at specific points in the story.
- Bury important aspects of historical references within dialogue or action.
- Keep flashbacks brief and their transitions seamless.
- Divide a book into sections only if doing so will not weaken the suspense.

The best passages of back-story revelation add a new dimension to the suspense itself. An increase in tension. A conflict that was previously unknown. Additional reasons for a protagonist's fear or an explanation of his actions.

Applying the above criteria to inclusions of historical information will insure that your character's back story does all of these things.

CHAPTER 9

Goals and Motivation

N*obody is that stupid!*
How many times have you thought this about a hero or heroine
while watching one of Hollywood's blockbuster thrillers?

Suspense movies rely on visual action to pull an audience into the moment.
When Bruce Willis or Mel Gibson decides to do something no sane person would
even consider, what invariably happens? Viewers see a heart-stopping rooftop
chase or an exchange of gunfire that sends the hero's stand-in diving for cover.

The creators of celluloid thrillers don't have four hundred pages of script
in which to delve into a character's motivation. To compensate, they quickly
whisk viewers beyond a hero's unbelievable decisions and into the next physical
action.

At best, a sidekick or partner may offer a weak protest. Danny Glover
wouldn't have to see a script for *Lethal Weapon Umpteen* to know he'd have a
line that reads something like, "Riggs, that's crazy!"

Even movies with less frantic action often fail to justify protagonists' reasons
for acting as they do. Fem-jep films, especially those made for TV, are probably
the worst offenders.

In today's atmosphere no intelligent career woman invites a man she's just
met into her bed. Mothers don't give permission for little Joey or Susie to take
a weekend trip with the family who just moved in down the block.

Yet similar plots reappear again and again.

There are exceptions of course. The initial motivation for Michael Douglas's character in *Fatal Attraction* is clearly sexual gratification. Only after he's learned that antagonist Glenn Close's motivation is obsession are his actions governed by a more noble need to protect his family.

Screenwriters are not inept. The problem lies with the medium itself. Direct dialogue can only do so much without becoming a dump of forced information. Novelists have other tools available that make establishing goals and motivation easier.

Book authors often use a **flashback** to reveal character motivation. In film the visual transition into a flashback is more obvious and thus more distracting. Because the action in a movie thriller is so fast and furious, flashbacks interrupt the rhythm of the suspense.

Film lacks two other important things novelists use to construct and reveal character motivation: **time** and the access to **internal dialogue**. This is why, in movies, motivations often grow out of circumstance rather than characterization as they do in novels.

As watchers we expect instant gratification. When we read, we prefer to savor the moment. This gives novelists a window of time in which to establish motivation. Internal dialogue helps by revealing a character's thought process, thus making readers privy to *how* as well as *why* a decision is made.

Because print writers have these tools available, readers should never find themselves questioning the intelligence of a novel's hero or heroine.

When critiques of their work cite weak motivation, novice writers sometimes cite a published author, protesting that, "So-and-so's character reacted that way." Usually the author of the book in question is an established writer whose loyal readers are more forgiving.

Breaking into print has never been easy. Without built-in audiences, writers *must* pay attention to such details as character motivation if they want to be published.

Editors are first of all readers. The stronger each facet of a manuscript, the better its chances are of rising above the hundreds of others that cross an editor's desk.

Something to Strive For

While both movies and books offer opportunities to show a protagonist's or villain's goals, novels again have the upper hand. The goal of a movie thriller's hero or heroine has to be presented quickly and changes little over the length of the film.

Save the people trapped in a burning skyscraper. Rescue the kidnapped child. Win the case. Find the antidote. Prevent the assassination. Sink the sub. Track down the origin of those threatening E-mail messages.

Readers expect to be presented with a dangerous situation just as quickly, but as with motivation, novel writers are allowed more time to establish their characters' goals. A hero's goal can also change dramatically during the course of a book.

The more obstacles a writer puts in front of characters, the harder they'll fight for whatever they want. Along the way their original goals either strengthen or mutate in some way.

Consider a struggling young attorney who accepts a tough but high-profile case. Initially, creating enough publicity that a prestigious law firm will take note of her strategy skills might be more important to her than winning.

Her client thus becomes a means to an end. But as she researches the situation, she discovers things that stir her emotions. Someone makes anonymous threats. Now she's angry. Determination to see justice done replaces her original goal. Here, goal and motivation merge.

The bonus of such a plot is that a borderline heroine with selfish motives is changed into a more sympathetic character—someone the readers are rooting for.

Protagonists are not the only ones who need reasons for the things they do. Villains, too, have goals and motivations. Even minor players may have their own agendas. As usual, category determines what constitutes logical goals and believable motivations for the characters in a thriller.

Action-Adventure: Goals and Motivation
PROTAGONIST

Dirk Pitt is an old-fashioned hero whose goal is to right whatever wrong he's uncovered at the moment. James Bond strives to defend and protect queen and country. Other action-adventure protagonists' goals may have narrower focuses such as completing assigned missions.

Whether they're trying to save the world, an oppressed segment of society or a single individual, these heroes must be larger-than-life. Fans of this category expect bold actions and plots that push all the boundaries. Characters themselves may have rough edges, but their ultimate goals will be noble ones.

For such a hero, motivation can be as simple as the knowledge or belief that the proposed task is his job, or the right thing to do, or that he is the only one qualified. Personal reasons are acceptable as long as readers won't see the hero as selfish.

Motivation can also be more complex, as with our character Burke. Stopping Martin from blowing up the power plant may be in his job description, but the presence of family members and the identity of the villain also play a part.

These heroes are men who plan carefully and rarely charge in without a backup plan. Faced with the unexpected, motivation and bravado override any trepidation they may have.

Regardless of how lofty the goal or how far out an action-adventure plot, fans expect the protagonist's motivation to seem reasonable for the situation. Readers might never tackle the challenges Pitt or Bond or the others accept; they do want to believe that those characters would.

ANTAGONIST

Villains must have motivation, too—or at least goals they're hoping to attain.

The goal of an action-adventure villain can be as basic as the theft of an armored car payroll. His motivation: greed. A goal to wreak havoc on a city or kill a bureaucrat might be motivated by anger over what a former civil servant sees as an unjust layoff or firing.

Books that deal with terrorists or secret agencies spend little time exploring the antagonist's motive. These villains do evil things because they're the enemy or simply bad people. In-depth discussions of political motives are usually reserved for political thrillers. Other types of suspense, however, may require the villain to have just as much motivation as the protagonist.

Legal Thriller: Goals and Motivation
PROTAGONIST

The goals and motivations in a legal thriller are usually a bit more complex. If the plot involves a trial, the obvious goal is to win. But legal thrillers traditionally investigate more than lawsuits. A protagonist may discover something about herself—or her client—that changes her goal.

For instance: A defense attorney's initial goal is to win acquittal for her client. How does this attorney fulfill her role as defense counsel once she suspects her client might be planning a crime much worse than the one of which he's currently accused? Actual knowledge must be reported. Suspicion falls within a much grayer area.

If this suspicion grew from a remark made during privileged communication, a new goal has arisen: finding a way to prevent a crime that may or may not happen without—jeopardizing the legal rules of ethics.

Attorney protagonists are less apt to act out of character. They narrow their focuses, look for opponents' weaknesses and prepare carefully. Their knowledge of the law becomes the means of reaching their goals. Sometimes the legal process itself becomes their motivation.

John Grisham's Jake Brigance in *A Time to Kill* loves the law. He wants the things a successful practice can bring. So far he hasn't achieved them, but that could change with the right case. Perhaps with the client he's just accepted. A man who admits he's guilty. A man who all but told Jake he planned to commit murder.

Jake is about to defend a father for killing the men who brutally raped his ten-year-old daughter. A black father. White rapists as his victims. A Mississippi courtroom setting. Jake's goal is to make a name for himself by winning an acquittal.

But Jake has a young daughter of his own. Because of this, his motivation for wanting a not-guilty verdict is more complex.

Other legal thrillers involve threatened jurors, whose will to survive is their goal. Such protagonists are more apt to do things out of character. Their motivation for this uncharacteristic behavior must be that the situations they find themselves in leave no other options.

ANTAGONIST

In plots with a lawyer protagonist, such as *A Time to Kill*, the villain is often a prosecutor whose goal and motivation is political. In that book, Jake also faces off against members of the rapists' families, the Klan and various factions of the town's residents, all of whom have very personal motivations for wanting Jake to fail.

Plots that concentrate on legal ethics pit attorneys against themselves, large corporations or other law firms. Such conflicts require complex goals and motivations.

When the protagonist is a threatened jury member, motivations and goals for the villains will be more basic. A goal of wanting a guilty defendant to get off may be motivated by such things as loyalty or revenge (by a family member), greed (the accused knows where the money's buried) or fear (if convicted, the accused may name names).

Medical Thriller: Goals and Motivation
PROTAGONIST

The stakes in a medical thriller are high. The protagonist's ultimate goal is to prevent death. Other goals may also be present, especially when the story is told from multiple POVs.

In John J. Nance's *Pandora's Clock*, the pilot's goal is to find an airport willing to let his plane land. His motivation is his desire to save his passengers and crew. Other characters' goals are to verify that the virus is really on board, where it was contracted and how to contain it. Their motivations vary.

Goals may be clear, but often motivation needs further explanation. A researcher who injects himself with an untried antidote obviously does so to save others. But readers will expect a more detailed and reasonable explanation for his action.

- Does he think of himself as the next Pasteur?
- Did someone he love die of the disease?
- Was he responsible for creating or releasing the germ in the first place?

For the character and his actions to be believable, readers need to know these things.

Instinct may govern a person's motivation. A nurse might rush to the aid of a patient being smothered without thinking of the danger to himself. If the assailant escapes, however, a deeper motive must be established before readers will believe that the nurse's attempt to find the assailant on his own is justified. Perhaps he himself has become a suspect.

Righting a wrong can be the goal of an intern who sneaks access to restricted files in an effort to prove an HMO has been falsifying records. The motivation for wanting to do this must be more than mere curiosity. The logical thing to do would be to file formal complaints rather than risk her career. Readers will want to be convinced why she sees this as her only choice.

- Does she believe the person who would process her complaint is involved?
- Has she already been accused of "crying wolf" in a previous matter?
- Has an accusation of negligence on her part in the matter damaged her credibility?

ANTAGONIST

When the "villain" in a medical thriller is a virus, goal and motivation are moot. When corporate entities are cast as antagonists, greed is both the goal and the motivation. Individuals may be motivated by revenge or operating under diminished mental capacities.

Political Thriller: Goals and Motivation
PROTAGONIST

Prevent a coup. Uncover the mole. Rescue the double agent or political prisoner. Protect the leader. Save the local environment. Stop the plunder of public lands or funds. Expose corrupt officials.

All these are logical goals for the protagonist(s) of a political thriller. Motivation will depend upon who is cast as the heroine or hero.

In the case of government agents, motivation will be tied to the job itself. Readers of these books are less apt to question what initially seems like a dumb move from a protagonist. Why? Because they know that agents must often put themselves in harm's way to achieve their goals.

But the reason for the agent's questionable action must be made clear fairly quickly. Heroes cannot continue to react against type or readers will suspect they're incompetent.

In *Clear and Present Danger*, Jack Ryan flies to South America to salvage a covert operation gone bad. In this novel Ryan has risen to a position within the CIA of acting Deputy Director (Intelligence). At heart he's a scholar who prefers to operate from the confines of an office. So why doesn't he send someone else?

The answer lies in his motivation. The actions of power-hungry bureaucrats within Ryan's department caused the mission to go sour, but Jack himself gave the command that launched the operation. Using Ryan's internal dialogue and an exchange with the leader of the rescue team, Clancy underlined his hero's motivation.

> We sent them in there, *Jack told himself.* My agency sent them in there. And some of them are dead now, and we let somebody tell us not to do anything about it. And I'm supposed to be. . . .
> *"Might be dangerous going in tonight,"* [Ryan said.]
> *"Possible. Looks that way."*
> *"You have three minis [machine guns] aboard your chopper,"* Ryan said after a moment. *"You only have two gunners."*
> *"I couldn't whistle another one up this fast and—"*
> *"I'm a pretty fair shot,"* Jack told him.

Ryan's motivation seems logical to readers because it grew out of his characterization.

When a political thriller pits a common man or woman against a corrupt government agency or official, however, motivations can become tangled.

John Gilstrap's *At All Costs* introduces Jake and Carolyn Brighton, a couple who has spent fourteen years on the run from accusations that they slaughtered sixteen people and touched off an eco-disaster. Jake's false arrest on another charge puts in motion the process that will uncover their true identities. Once again, they're forced to flee.

The problem is that the couple now has a son, a boy who has no idea who his parents really are. Resentful of his family's nomadic lifestyle, Travis is a troubled teenager.

In this story Jake and Carolyn's primary goal is to protect their family *at all costs*. The desire to remain free, and together, fuels their motivation. But immediately several secondary goals come into play. There are steps they need to take.

- Get away before the check of Jake's fingerprints reveals who he really is.
- Find a safe place to stay.
- Establish another identity.
- Explain to their angry and rebellious son what's going on.

Their goal of survival is equaled by their need to make Travis understand that they are innocent of a horror he's been taught about in school. Backed into a corner, they see only one way out. They must return to the quarantined disaster scene to find the evidence that will prove someone else was to blame.

Once again, Jake and Carolyn's goals have changed, as has their motivation. Their desire for freedom has been joined by their long-buried desire for vindication and an end to their nightmare.

ANTAGONIST

Clear and Present Danger contains multiple villains. One is a member of the drug cartel playing different factions against one another in an effort to gain control. Ryan's corrupt co-workers are using the situation to their own advantage as well. Throw in a spineless U.S. president willing to accept whatever scapegoat is handy and Ryan clearly has his hands full.

Gilstrap's *At All Costs* provides a variety of antagonists who block the Brightons' path to their goals. The person really responsible for the eco-disaster and an ambitious FBI agent head up the list. Multiple jurisdictions want a piece of the action. The danger of exposure to the chemicals that contaminate the site create yet another goal—gaining access to the proper protective gear.

Creating obstacles for his protagonists was not a problem here. Gilstrap's concentration focused on establishing logical reasons for every desperate action and tortured decision Jake and Carolyn have to make.

Psychological Suspense: Goals and Motivation
PROTAGONIST

A psychological suspense plot involves mortal danger, directed either at the hero or heroine or at someone that character loves or is charged with protecting. In these intense dramas the line between goals and motivation can blur.

Someone in authority, such as a detective or FBI agent, may face off with a sociopath or other violent criminal. The protagonist's goal will be to stop future killings. If the pair has crossed paths before, the additional goal of professional pride or personal vengeance may be present.

Motivations are usually more complex than just doing a job. Because readers expect an in-depth investigation of both parties' psyches, back story plays a major role. Why the heroine became a cop or the hero an FBI profiler will be explored, revealing motivations that predate the immediate confrontation.

In other psychological thrillers, the protagonist is an average person and the conflict will be personal. The antagonist may be a family member, a friend or a perfect stranger who's chosen the protagonist at random. Whatever the threat derives from, the protagonist's goal is to survive emotionally intact. The will to live becomes the prime motivation.

Because they are not law enforcement professionals, these protagonists are often bewildered by or angry about what's happening to them. Cunning villains avoid leaving evidence that might give credence to their victims' claims of harassment or danger. Left on their own, the protagonists must learn to control their anger or to resort to the same tactics as their tormentors.

ANTAGONIST

Many times the purpose of the villain's existence is to destroy her opponent—physically or mentally, preferably both. But a psychological suspense antagonist's real goal is to prolong the process of inflicting mental anguish.

These villains enjoy their work. Picking their victims, planning their attacks, watching their prey twist and turn at their whim. The process itself is as much a turn-on as the envisioned moment of death. What they hope for most is a worthy opponent.

How this focus came to be is examined, again through the use of back story. If written in multiple POVs, passages of internal dialogue take the reader deep into motivations that have been shaped over long periods of time. Mistreatment as a child is a common denominator, but other explanations abound.

The girl who was continually belittled by classmates may harbor a desire to some day pay them back in kind. If she then experiences similar reactions in her work and love life, that earlier goal might become a dangerous obsession. A chance encounter could result in someone becoming a surrogate victim.

In psychological thrillers, giving the villain sufficient motivation is just as important—if not more so—as establishing a valid incentive for the protagonist. But no matter what events from her personal history triggered the villain's twisted attitude or view of the world, her ultimate motivation now is always the need to control. Not only her own environment, but also that of her prey. Her primary motivation thus becomes the goal of total domination over her victim's actions, reactions and, most of all, thoughts.

Once her victim's every waking moment is spent either in fear of the villain or trying to outwit her, the antagonist reaches her goal. Once that victory has been achieved, the euphoria of power begins to wane, leaving her wanting more. If the writer has laid the foundation for this through believable motivation, readers will see this outcome as logical.

Good psychological suspense is a battle of wits. *The Silence of the Lambs* is a classic example.

Hannibal Lecter taunts Clarice Starling, hinting he has the answers she desperately needs. By offering snips of knowledge in exchange for glimpses of her personal history, Lecter draws out her secrets. Like a squirrel gathering nuts for the winter ahead, he stores these visions away until he can use them against her at a time of his choosing.

Such mind games are the ultimate in psychological suspense.

Romantic Relationship Suspense: Goals and Motivation
PROTAGONIST

Someone who begins to question her romantic partner's intentions should previously have been blissfully secure in the relationship. Then some unrelated incident convinces her things may not be as they seem. She discovers her mate is harboring a secret or has done something out of character.

Suspicion begins to grow. Eventually she comes to believe the person she loves may be a threat.

Proving or eliminating doubts about a spouse or lover is the protagonist's primary goal. Her motivation is a need to calm her fear, return to the status quo or end the relationship.

ANTAGONIST

Con men or women, unhappy or about-to-be-ex-spouses, or sexual predators make good villains here. Money, freedom from a stifling relationship, a desire to inflict emotional or physical pain, and sexual conquest are all valid goals.

Motivations range from greed (the victim controls the money), revenge (child custody issues) or control (sexually or emotionally abusive partner) to selfishness or obsession (previous lover believes, "If I can't have him, no one can.")

Spouses or lovers may turn out to be the real villains. Or, they may not.

A partner's suspicious actions may simply be attempts to cover up an affair or some illegal activity not related to the protagonist's troubles. The spouse could be a loving mate who fears that sharing professional or personal problems will jeopardize the relationship.

Whether the current lover is guilty or not, other suspects must be introduced early in the book. These characters must share some of the suspicious behavioral patterns of the current romantic interest.

An affair speaks for itself. But what if the paramour is behind the protagonist's problem and the cheating mate doesn't know it? A partner's illegal activity might be connected to the danger the protagonist faces or simply a red herring for the reader.

Separate motivation must be established for a partner's unwillingness to share intimate details. Has the loss of a child affected a spouse more deeply than outward appearances indicate? Is he afraid his wife might leave if financial circumstances changed or a child from a previous affair came into their lives?

An old lover who reenters a protagonist's life may or may not be a threat. Perhaps he knows something about the current mate and is trying to protect his old love. Then again, if his professed knowledge proves to be false or a figment of his imagination, he may be the villain.

Whatever the particulars of the plot, each of these major characters must have clear goals and motivations. Only when all the pieces come together and the real truth is known will the protagonist—and the reader—learn who can be trusted.

Women-in-Jeopardy (Fem-Jep) Suspense: Goals and Motivation

PROTAGONIST

The way to convince readers that a woman in jeopardy's actions are logical is to build a believable character. Put her into a predicament her experience has not prepared her for. Back her into a corner with no means of support and little hope of escape. Then make sure the motivation for her reaction fits the circumstances you've created.

In *See Jane Run*, Joy Fielding has put her protagonist Jane Whittaker into a unique situation. When the book begins, Jane does not know who she is. Someone identifies her and still nothing seems familiar. Not the well-known surgeon whom everyone says is her husband. Not the beautiful daughter who smiles back at her in dozens of family photos.

Has she had a nervous breakdown as a psychologist suggests? Is the medicine the doctor in the emergency room prescribed causing her continued confusion? And why won't anyone let her talk to or see the child she doesn't remember?

Is her daughter really with her paternal grandparents? Or does the bloody dress she was wearing and then hid when she first realized she'd lost her identity have something to do with her child's absence?

Bit by bit Fielding isolates Jane from all avenues of escape until she's forced to confront the horror that caused her to forget who she was. By that point readers know the kind of woman Jane was before the incident. They also know how her experience has changed her, so her reaction to learning the truth seems natural and expected.

See Jane Run is a combination women-in-jeopardy, romantic relationship and psychological suspense novel. For insight into the book's creation, see Joy Fielding's comments in the interview on page 211.

ANTAGONIST

The primary goal of a woman-in-jeopardy villain is usually control—either of the heroine or a situation. Convince a judge that your ex-wife's tormentor is a paranoid figment of her imagination you win the custody of the children. Discredit a fast-rising co-worker and *you* step into her shoes. Harass your sexual rival into a mental breakdown and the object of your affection will choose you.

When the antagonist is an obsessed lover, or stanger, the motive lies within the character's psychological pathology and the goal they seek is total control of a heroine's thoughts and physical actions. If the villain can't have her, no one can. In this instance, the writer's goal is to explore the whys behind a villain's obsession and to make his actions as frightening and twisted as possible. Again, the movie *Fatal Attraction* is probably the most familiar illustration of this situation.

Techno-Thrillers: Goals and Motivation
PROTAGONIST

The technology in techno-thrillers is no longer limited to military or security-related issues. Medical and computer sciences have entered the picture. Forensic pathology is the technology Patricia Cornwell uses to catch killers. Shirley Kennett applies virtual reality toward the same end.

The goal of a techno-thriller protagonist is to prevent war; rescue MIAs, POWs, kidnap victims or other hostages; stop a threat to a city, a nation or the world; catch a killer; clear his own name; or regain his stolen identity.

Most often a techno-thriller protagonist is motivated by a sense of duty or an acknowledgment that the assignment is his job. Pride in his technological skills or track record also plays a part. In the case of an individual such as a computer hacker who's using technology to right a personal wrong, part of his motivation might be that extra thrill he gets from proving he can outwit whomever is on the receiving end of his quest.

ANTAGONIST

Because the antagonists in techno-thrillers must be as accomplished as their opponents, these villains will not make stupid mistakes. Parts of the plots will involve the art of one-upmanship. The standard motives of greed, ego and a need to be in control are most common in this category, but others are being discovered.

Shirley Kennett explored a new source of motivation in her third virtual reality-based techno-thriller: "When creating the villain in *Chameleon*, I wanted to explore a character who got himself lost in the violent world of computer and video games at an early age and never grew out of it, a boy who confused reality and VR. Unfortunately, the idea isn't all that far-fetched."

Things to Remember

• Minor characters should have their own goals and motivations and should not react simply because it is convenient to the plot.

• Goals should be unique to each character and situation.

• Motivations must be built over the course of the story. Just as goals change, motivations evolve based on the responses of others and the plot's turns and twists.

• The best motivations grow out of character.

—Protagonists react as they do because of things in their backgrounds and their previous experiences as well as their current circumstances.

—Villains may appear to be pure evil. But except for the true sociopath, antagonists behave the way they do because of flaws in their characters that have evolved over time.

• Strong villains have depth that's reflected in their motivations. Their goals may be basic—get money, eliminate rivals, terrorize or hurt or kill their victims. The reasons for their goals' existence should be more complex.

• A villain's goal and the motivation behind it can be based on benign intentions. *Someone to Watch Over* deals with an anonymous Good Samaritan who sets out to protect and care for a widow and her family. Only when he begins to take his job too seriously does he become a real threat.

How to Test Goals and Motivations

Consider whether, under similar circumstances, you would take whatever action your protagonist is considering. If not, why not? What might make you do it? If you had your character's background and situation, would it change your decision?

Now ask why your character *should* do this. Not only why should he do it, but why should he do it *in this situation*. If the responses aren't satisfactory, you need to reconsider your character's goals, establish deeper motivations and adjust the plot so that you leave him no alternative.

Do this and readers encountering your characters will never have reason to think, *Nobody is that stupid*!

CHAPTER 10

Dialogue

"I'll see a doctor," he said finally. "A shrink, if that's what it takes."

An insect kissed the screen and disappeared into the yard.

"Donna? Is that what you want?"

She lined and glossed her lips, waiting until she'd wiped a speck of color from a front tooth before turning to face him.

"I want it like it was a year, hell, even eight months ago. I want you to take me shoppin', and dancin'. Do crazy stuff like you used to."

"I can't. I'm not that person anymore."

"You sure as hell ain't! I know guys drawin' pensions got more in their jeans than you do."

"Dammit, Donna. I lost my wife, my kids, everything." He shook his head, covering his face with one hand. "Something like that eats at a man's guts."

"I didn't start the . . . fire. Why should I act like some weepy old woman? I'm twenty-three, dammit, not eighty. I deserve some fun. I deserve a man who can get it up, not some little boy cryin' on my shoulder every time we go to bed. You won't spend the insurance money. Your head's [messed] up. You're dead from the waist down. Hell, Cal, you might as well been sleepin' with Kelly that night."

"But I wasn't, was I? I was with you!" He hurled the beer can toward the bathroom. A thin stream trickled across the carpet as it rolled to a stop against the doorframe.

The above exchange is from *Someone to Watch Over*. This excerpt from the opening scene introduces the protagonist Cal Jefferies and his second wife. It sets the stage and the tone for the book and reveals enough back story that the reader wants to know more about the relationship and what's going to happen.

Used wisely, quotation marks are a writer's most powerful tool. Readers search for passages of dialogue. They consider dialogue to be the meat of a story.

Dialogue makes a story come alive. People who began as ink on a page suddenly become flesh and blood. The invisible barrier between reality and imagination crumbles when an articulate character opens her mouth. And—despite her crude language—Donna Jefferies is very articulate.

Dialogue plus conflict equals tension. And remember that conflict doesn't necessarily mean arguments or fighting. Two people talking around a subject neither wants to address can be just as riveting as a verbal brawl.

Dialogue is a window to characters' inner selves. What they say—and don't say—tells readers more about them than pages of narrative prose. Dialogue in thrillers does its job best when it conveys the underlying tone of suspense. Conversations might be gossipy or jarring. Secretive. Conspiratorial. Adversarial or threatening. Confrontational or angry.

Compare the following exchanges between an attorney and a potential witness. The first is a terse Q&A that tells readers little about the character's or their emotions.

> *"None of it's true, you know."*
> *"How do you know?"*
> *"I was there."*
> *"So what happened?"*
> *"It's not my place to tell. Ask one of the others."*
> *"I could* put you on the stand. *"*
> *"I don't think I'd make a very good witness."*

This first exchange is vague: Such a conversation might be important to the plot, but nothing in what was said gives that indication. Now an edgier version of the same conversation.

"You think you know all about it, don't you? Well, none of it's true."

"Sounds like empty bragging to me."

"Yeah, right. Well, I know what I'm talking about. I saw the whole thing."

"So tell me about it."

"Why should I? You'll just twist it around until it fits that legal mind-set of yours. Till she sounds guilty as hell when you know damn well she's not."

"I could get a subpoena."

"You'd have to find me to serve it. Why don't you pick on one of the others? They're used to your games. A shark like you should be looking for bigger fish, anyway."

Same basic information, but with this version you as the reader know much more about both speakers. The lawyer is obviously a prosecuting attorney. Probably a good one, if the other character's opinion is any indication. The potential witness is defensive, distrustful, protective of the "she" in question—and perhaps a little afraid.

The word choice alerts the reader to a conflict between the two speakers. Once the tone became adversarial, the true atmosphere of the scene emerged. The first speaker has information. Information the second speaker wants and, more importantly, needs to know. The revised exchange created goals for both characters as well—keeping the secret for one; discovering what really happened for the other.

Dialogue is also a tool for characterization. Such exchanges establish the characters' attitudes, social statuses, demeanors and places in the story.

- A stronger, more aggressive reaction from the attorney might have altered our perception of both speakers.
- A demanding response might indicate the bullying personality of someone who intends to win at any cost.
- An attempt to cajole cooperation would tell us the case is weak or the attorney is unsure of her capabilities.

Who Said That?

Each character must have his own voice. His manner of speaking, inflection and word choice must be unique to his background and personality.

Giving each character his own tone and speech pattern helps readers keep track of who's who. It also allows a writer to limit those annoying *he said* and *she asked* tags. By making each character's voice distinctive, such identifying tag lines become less necessary.

AGE

Age can be determined by the use of slang or throwaway references—to Glenn Miller, Elvis, the Beatles, Talking Heads, etc. Word choice and inflection can also betray attitudes most often identified with a person of a certain age.

What age would you associate with the speakers of the following unrelated sentences?

1. "I don't give a f—— what the old fart next door thinks. It's my room. I'll play my f——ing music as loud as I want."

2. "I'll be darned if I'm going to let something that looks like a glorified TV get the better of me. Hand me the user's manual for this goldurn thing."

3. "I know it sounds silly, but I used to pretend it was me out on that dance floor with John Travolta."

4. "Everyone's going to be there but me. You'd think I was still in diapers or something."

5. "Seeing their names on that black granite wall . . . I tell you, man, for a second I was right back there with 'em. The noise of the choppers; the smell of that stinkin' jungle. Jesus, I tasted the damn blood."

In order, these are the implied ages and reasoning.

1. A teenage boy, because of the strong language and the obvious reference to objectionable music.

2. A man in his late sixties or older, because of the antiquated word *goldurn*.

3. A woman in her thirties, because she would have been in her teens to early twenties when the movie *Saturday Night Fever* came out in 1977.

4. A preteen to early teenage girl, because of the diaper reference. An older teen's speech usually reflects current slang.

5. A man in his late forties to early fifties, because of the references to the Vietnam Veterans Memorial (The Wall). Most of the men drafted during the Vietnam War were eighteen to twenty years old.

DICTION

Diction denotes more than education. In the example at the beginning of this chapter, Donna Jefferies drops the last letter from every word ending in *ing*. A character who does this only once or twice or who stumbles over grammar choices might be trying to project an image that differs from his true background.

Dropped *g*s can indicate a person's regional heritage or educational level, but should only be used for characters who appear infrequently. Maintaining such inflection throughout an entire book can be exhausting. Trigger words or phrases are also more effective than quirky spellings.

PHRASING AND WORD CHOICE

Phrasing and word choice help readers get a visual "fix" on a speaker. Compare the following three versions of the same sentences.

> *"There may be more to this than first impressions indicate. I really think we ought to talk with William's parents before we phone the police. I'm sure they wouldn't want anyone to get the wrong impression."*

> *"Things probably look a lot worse than they are. We'd better check with Bill's mom and dad before we drag the cops into this. They're not the kind of people who'd appreciate their name being dragged through the papers."*

> *"This is sure some sorry mess. Seems to me we'd best ring Billy's kin, 'fore we drag the sheriff outta bed. Boy's ma and pa ain't gonna be happy if this hits the fan 'fore they get a handle on things."*

TONE

Tone is equally important. By this I mean not just the tone of a speaker's words, but that of the entire conversation.

Here, Terry McCaleb, a retired FBI profiler who's the protagonist of Michael Connelly's *Blood Work*, is talking to his doctor during a checkup. Notice how the tone of the conversation shifts from feigned innocence to accusation. (To illustrate my point I've edited out narrative sections important to the story but not to our topic.)

> *"Do you ever wonder if we should be doing this?" he asked.*
>
> *. . . "Whether we should be doing what?"*
>
> *". . . Taking out organs, putting in new ones. Sometimes I feel like the modern Frankenstein. . . ."*
>
> *. . . "What's really wrong?"*
>
> *. . . "I guess I want to know how come you didn't tell me that the woman whose heart I got had been murdered."*

A subtle change in tone can also be used to signal that a character is under stress. If the tone of the dialogue is contradicted by a character's actions—say an offhand remark that's accompanied by a nervous habit—what's been said becomes suspect.

When a character who's been portrayed as a frequent interrupter or chatterer appears silent or withdrawn in a subsequent scene, readers will assume she's either worried or hiding something.

CATCH PHRASES

One way to help identify a particular character whose appearances within a story are critical but infrequent is to give him a signature word or phrase. A football fan might refer to "the whole nine yards" now and then. Make that character a woman and she'll stick in readers' minds even more.

An eager-to-please character will often begin sentences with the word *right*, as if agreeing with whatever the previous speaker has said. Just be careful not to overdo such quirks. The aim is to make the character's voice memorable, not annoying.

What a character says should reveal something the reader needs to know. This can be information about the speaker or other characters, their motives or back stories, or some action that took place when a primary character wasn't present. Spoken words can also set the scene for what's yet to come or misdirect a protagonist in some way. Except for the lack of involvement by my protagonist, the illustration from *Someone to Watch Over* at the beginning of this chapter accomplishes all of these.

Dialogue should provide a glimpse of a character's emotional state or her opinion of a situation, herself or others (both those present and those offstage). Anger, confusion, worry, impatience, boredom, fear, cruelty. These are all valid emotions and traits that work well for suspense. They're also guaranteed to add tension and conflict.

After the book is finished, to assure consistency of tone, word usage and diction, do a separate "speech" edit for each character who appears more than once.

Secrets, Threats, and Moments of Panic and Terror

Broken-off sentences or changed subjects suggest secrets.

> *Jean lowered her voice. "Maybe we should tell Mary."*
>
> *"Tell me what?" Mary asked, pausing in the doorway.*
>
> *"Nothing important," Don said. He gestured toward the dining room. "Everything ready? No last minute, pre-party jitters?"*

As a reader, I know that whatever Don and Jean have been discussing is important to the story and Mary needs to know it.

> *"I know what you did and I'm going to tell."*

If such a warning doesn't bring a sudden flicker of fear or unease, you've led an unusually uneventful existence. From a childhood prank that backfired or the test answers we penciled on our fingernails in fifth grade to the stop sign we ran last week, all of us harbor something we'd rather not have revealed.

You don't have to be paranoid to feel a twinge of guilt at the sight of that blank computer disk you accidentally brought home from the office. Even the threat of *false* accusation can bring momentary pause.

"I have your son."

Four simple words that would strike panic in any parent's heart. Add "Don't call the police unless you want him back in little pieces" and you recognize true terror.

Arguments bring out characters' baser traits. The loss of control and how they handle the aftermath reveals facets of their personalities that are usually hidden. Scenes that follow the excerpt from *Someone to Watch Over* at the beginning of this chapter explore just that. And both Cal's and Donna's actions after their fight are key to what happens throughout the book.

The speech of characters already revealed as villains will usually be unsuspicious in public. It's their internal dialogue that reveals their much darker sides.

Readers trying to identify an *unrevealed* villain don't want things too easy. Such antagonists' dialogue should not draw undue attention or single them out. Better to have them say things that could be taken two ways. Or to reveal something later in the story that they obviously should have mentioned much earlier if they are who they pretend to be.

People don't always say what they mean. Manners hold us back. This is why words spoken in anger are so revealing.

Societal conventions are out of place in confrontational scenes. Blunt language reinforces the tension. Even a control freak will slip up in the right situation. Anger and fear make us say things we'd never utter in polite company. Given what all she'd put him through, Rhett would never have told Scarlett he didn't give a *darn*.

Just remember that a few carefully placed four-letter words make a stronger impact than those that litter every sentence a foul-mouthed character utters.

Doing What Comes Naturally

Avoid using dialogue for information better told through narrative. Short gossipy exchanges are fine for revealing snips of back story; anything much longer becomes a forced info dump. Let one character hint at an important bit of history, then have the person he was talking to dig for the rest. Better yet, have that person confront the character being talked about.

Anecdotes told to one character by another allow a writer to insert back story without resorting to the riskier flashback. Authors Hal Blythe and Charlie Sweet refer to this technique as "a story within a story."

In this excerpt from *Stillwatch*, Mary Higgins Clark's heroine, TV reporter Pat Traymore, is researching background on Abigail Jennings, a powerful U.S. senator who is about to become a vice-presidential candidate. The senator's bio says that her mother was the housekeeper for a wealthy family in Abigail's small hometown. Pat is about to discover otherwise. (Again, I've edited out the narrative passages.)

> *"The* cook," *Ethel repeated emphatically. "She and Abby had a little apartment off the kitchen. . . ."*
>
> *"Tell how Mrs. Saunders caught Abby coming in the front door and told her to know her place," [Ernie] suggested.*
>
> *"Oh, yeah. That was lousy, wasn't it? Mama said she felt sorry for Abby until she saw the look on her face. Enough to freeze your blood, Mama said."*

A short but revealing anecdote. And regardless of where Abby fits into the story, Pat Traymore *and* Clark's readers now know something about the senator's character and background they might have otherwise never learned.

When you use dialogue to reveal back story, the conversation must have another purpose as well. In the example above, Pat's visit to Senator Jennings's hometown is a natural step in the preparation of the documentary series she's doing. Questioning people who knew Abby is routine research.

Don't rely entirely on anecdotal exchanges between characters to reveal back story. Vary circumstances. Present one or two as memories relayed through internal dialogue. Use straight narrative for others.

What's said and when it's said must also fit the character, the time and the situation. Never include an exchange simply because you need the reader to know some piece of information. All dialogue needs a purpose.

In *Buried Secrets*, I wrote a party scene that let my heroine Nicki meet several new neighbors at one time. To justify the party's purpose, I made it clear that the hostess often put together impromptu gatherings. I also described her as the local matchmaker, something that added to Nicki's discomfort.

During the course of the evening, various characters revealed key information or referred to events that later had a bearing on the plot.

Group scenes are a good way to mask the meaning of such information. The social discussions between characters of varying generations seemed natural rather than forced. Nicki's curiosity about her new home and its history were also a logical story progression.

Make Dialogue Sound Real—But Not Too *Real*

Dialogue must sound natural to the reader. But "normal" conversation actually sounds dull on paper. Readers don't want to wade through extraneous material. Good dialogue is natural conversation tightly compressed. This is especially effective in suspense where what's spoken aloud often has double meaning.

"One of the first things I learned is that writing dialogue is not replicating speech," says author Marilyn Wallace. "Most people don't go directly to the heart of their point, don't use complete sentences, don't say something once when they can say it three or four different times. In fiction, that would become tedious, a chore rather than a pleasure to read, so writers try to indicate that without boring the reader."

Tape or listen to an actual conversation. Write it down verbatim if possible. Now highlight the essence of what was really being said. Rewrite the highlighted sections and consider how you would react to reading each version in a book. You'll find that hearing is not the same as seeing.

Note that people often speak in incomplete sentences. Use of the other speaker's name once identities have been established is also rare.

Unless you're trying to portray a cold or stuffy character, avoid precise diction. Most of us use contractions and verbal shorthand. The speech of an impoverished immigrant or recently naturalized citizen might be a mixture of precise words, misused slang and hesitations spent searching for the right word. An educated expatriate from the same country would have less trouble with the language.

Street people sometimes know proper English but use slang to fit in. Revealing their ability to speak properly shows readers another side of these often-stereotyped characters. Such intriguing contradictions heighten suspense.

But street talk can also be confusing for the reader. Pick two or three trigger words or phrases that denote background rather than attempt weird phonetic spellings.

You can also surprise readers by having a character casually use words or phrases usually associated with another ethnic or racial group. The words *girl* or *girlfriend* are often thought of as common forms of address between African-American women. In truth, many young southern white women use the term as easily.

Dialogue Can Also Reveal Emotion

Dialogue is a good way to reveal a character's emotional state. Too much body language becomes repetitious. How many times can someone raise her eyebrows or twist her hair before the word *boring* comes to mind?

Because tension means stress, speech patterns may change during especially tense scenes. Stammering and run-on or fragmented sentences are common. Carefully placed, these can fuel a book's overall tension and increase the suspense.

Listen to my protagonist's reaction to being told by a sheriff's deputy (and former love) that her husband was with another woman when he died in an auto accident.

> *"Did she tell you why they were together?"*
> *"She's dead, Kate. They're both dead."*
> *"Then, where's his truck?" she demanded. Comprehension swept*

away denial, eroding her self-control, allowing the fragmented thoughts swirling about her to tumble out.

"He drove the truck to Cleveland for an interview . . . he left on Monday . . . said he'd be back by yesterday morning . . . it's a really good job . . . we'll be able to pay the bills . . . and get a good mitt for Sarah and some Mickey Mouse sheets for Cody . . . and I might get a permanent . . . I used to have my hair done in a salon every week . . . I know I'm a mess right now, but I don't always look this way . . . when Michael gets back and we get on our feet, we'll have you over for dinner . . . you can bring a date."

Her hands slipped from her hair to her face. Sobs racked her body, threatening to jar her from the sofa to the floor.

A long passage to be sure, but one that paints a vivid portrait of a woman trying to avoid the reality that her world has just fallen apart.

When something is said can also be critical. An anecdote related early in a book might contain foreshadowing. Placed later in the novel, the same exchange might reveal secrets that were foreshadowed in some other way.

How a person responds to another's remark can show readers a lot about his mood or attitude or demeanor.

Dana frowned. "You're talking normal stresses, Doctor. The kind all of us face every day."

"Precisely. Which is why we can never be a hundred percent certain that an offender won't repeat his crime," Mosher said firmly.

"Nonsense!" Patterson Graham bellowed his objection. "With all due respect, Dr. Mosher. It's obvious that the offenders you sampled lacked the benefits of a proven treatment program such as the one we offer at Cambridge. My clients benefit from intensive work, expert counseling, and long term follow-up support."

"Then, why won't you allow outside investigators to confirm your result?" Dana asked.

The exchange above is from Judith Kelman's *More Than You Know*. The speaker Dana is a TV talk show host. The subject of the day's episode is whether convicted rapists can be "cured."

Even without the author's description of Patterson Graham's tone of voice, his words provide the reader with a clear picture of his demeanor. Contrary to his protest, it's clear he holds no respect for the skills or opinion of Dana's other guest.

The contrast of Dana's calm rebuttal is equally effective in conveying her position.

Matching Dialogue to Category

The dialogue in action-adventure and techno-thriller novels is usually spare—short and to the point, sometimes with an injection of humor. Snappy patter and restrained responses, especially during action scenes, fit both the characters involved and the genre itself.

Demands and their responses will be delivered in blunt exchanges. Technical and prototype or obscure military references usually require brief explanations.

When necessary, such dialogue should take place between a main character and someone outside the world he's operating in. Dirk Pitt doesn't have to tell his pals Al Giordino or Rudy Gunn how a piece of underwater equipment works. He might, however, be required to fill things in for love interests or other laypeople.

Dialogue in legal and medical thrillers may take place on several different levels. Lawyers or health professionals talking to one another sprinkle their speech with jargon. While it would be unrealistic to eliminate such references entirely, limiting these exchanges to a few choice words or phrases will avoid alienating the reader.

Explain terms that would normally be foreign to a layperson. Many of us have heard the Latin terms used within the legal profession, but few outside the court system know or understand their exact meaning. Thanks to *Chicago Hope* and *ER*, acronyms such as EEG, CT and EKG are equally familiar. A definition for each or explanation of why the particular procedure is appropriate in a given situation can be more elusive.

Attorneys and medical personnel may use insider terms when talking to clients or patients. This is where providing explanations fits smoothly into the dialogue. Nonprofessional characters, however, will use more common speech in response.

Dialogue between laypeople will vary depending upon their own backgrounds. A trucker, a waitress and a college student each has her own vocabulary. As with any other character, create a voice and tone to fit each one.

The dialogue in political thrillers often consists of innuendo and contradictory statements. Governmental jargon and references to international events are common. Just don't try to recreate such terminology exactly.

I once eavesdropped on a conversation between two men in business attire during a Metro (subway) ride between Washington's National Airport and a station near the Capitol. Several of the names and abbreviations they dropped struck a vague chord. The rest of their acronym-splattered exchange was all but incomprehensible. As with medical and legal thrillers, provide enough background information in the political thriller for the layperson to be able to follow the conversation.

The speech and demeanor of average citizens caught in a web of political intrigue will verge on panic and focus on their disbelief about what's happening.

Psychological suspense calls for emotional language. Nothing will really be quite as it seems. Conversations have double meaning. One character who tells another a story about a situation with similar circumstances that ended badly may be issuing either warning or threat.

Things that sound innocuous or trivial may wind up haunting the protagonist. Those that remain unsaid can cause the same reaction in both hero and reader.

In a romantic relationship plot, a protagonist will be hesitant, doubting her own interpretation of things. She's reluctant to admit her fears; if she tells a friend about her suspicions concerning her mate, she may talk around the subject. She'll find logical explanations for things, then complain that she's making excuses for obviously questionable behavior.

The friend's response will depend on her own view of the man in question. If she's having an affair with him, her dialogue will be comforting and dismissive.

"Of course he still cares about you. You're making yourself crazy over nothing."

Note the choice of the word *cares* rather than *loves*.

To a woman with an unfulfilled crush on another woman's lover, a ready defense of his actions might be more appropriate. Other characters' interaction would depend on their places in the story. Schemers and cheaters always try to sound sincere.

Women in jeopardy are usually shocked and bewildered at the beginning of their ordeals. Even the strongest woman feels off balance when faced with a threat that suddenly appears from nowhere. As the story progresses her response will turn first to anger and then to determination. Each of these emotional changes will be reflected in her dialogue.

Putting It All Together

Make every word your characters speak serve a valid purpose. Dialogue should never put the reader to sleep. Nor should it contain irrelevant information. Each character should assume his own voice, remain consistent throughout the book and offer readers an insight into what's taking place.

Dialogue has one more important role to play in your thriller: The balance you create between dialogue and narrative controls your book's pacing.

CHAPTER 11

Pacing

S ometimes you can have wonderful characters, an intriguing premise and plenty of conflict and ongoing tension and still wind up with a thriller that doesn't quite work. How? By failing to control the story's pacing.

Each genre of commercial fiction has its own rule of pacing.

• A **romance** usually involves multiple encounters in which the lead characters match wits in verbal exchanges. While action scenes are not excluded, the pace of such sections is rarely designed to frighten the reader. Emotional fireworks and an adventurous journey on the rocky path to true love are what keep fans of this genre coming back for more.

• Traditional **mysteries** follow the often frustrating routine of a detective (police, PI or amateur) in search of clues that may turn out to be dead ends. Action scenes are common; yet again, the emphasis is on the quest and the puzzle itself rather than the psychological or physical aspects.

• An **epic saga**, such as *Gone With the Wind*, allows for the occasional leisurely descriptive scene such as the Twelve Oaks barbeque that opens the book. Historical data about either the setting or the people is as important as the action that takes place during the story. When it does happen, action may be edge-of-the-seat engrossing. But it will not be the novel's focus.

Though each of these examples differs from the others, none of them are wrong. And some romances, mysteries and sagas are written using a pace that leaves their readers breathless. The point is that the authors of such books have greater leeway in choosing the appropriate pace for their particular plots.

The pacing demands of a suspense novel are less forgiving. Readers who pick up a thriller expect to be kidnapped by fear and action and dragged along on a wild ride. They're looking for a breakneck journey that rarely slows down long enough to explore dead ends or enjoy a plate of fried chicken served up with a side of flirtation.

A thriller's pacing is like climbing a long, steep series of stairways. Visualize the interior stairwell of the Statue of Liberty or a high-rise office building.

You start your climb with some trepidation but breathing easily. By the second or third landing, you're panting a little. Halfway up, despite occasional rests, you're gasping for breath. At the three-fourths point there's a stitch in your side and a weight on your chest.

As you cling to the railing at the bottom of the last set of stairs, your heart is pounding; your lungs are burning. You stare up at that last long expanse, knowing there's no way you can take another damn step.

Then a final surge of adrenaline kicks in and you find yourself standing at the top feeling like Leonardo DiCaprio on the bow of the *Titanic*.

The scenes and chapters and climax of a suspense novel explore how you reached that pinnacle and chronicle what you had to do along the way to keep your feet moving. If the pacing is right, the reader's breathlessness equals your own.

Defining the Parts

The components of pacing are often referred to as **scene** and **sequel** or **conflict/crisis** and **resolution**. In an earlier chapter I used the similar terms **climax** and **resolution**. Regardless of what you choose to call them, for a thriller to succeed, you must maintain a balance of these elements throughout the book.

A detailed discussion of scene and sequel can be found in Jack M. Bickham's *Scene & Structure*, part of Writer's Digest Books' The Elements of Fiction

Writing series. For the purpose of this discussion, I've chosen to use the terms conflict/crisis and resolution.

Nothing decrees that conflict or crisis must alternate one on one with resolution. Writers of multiple-viewpoint suspense often, before writing a scene of resolution, include several scenes of simultaneous crises or conflicts as seen through different characters' eyes. But rarely does one scene of resolution follow another. The reason: pacing.

A story's scenes must build upon one another until their cumulative effect creates the momentum that moves a plot forward. You control that momentum through a balance of conflict or crisis (dialogue and action) and resolution (narrative).

Conflict and crisis are the towering mountains. Resolutions are the narrow valleys in between. It takes time to climb a mountain. Crossing a valley is a much quicker trip. Thus a scene of conflict or crisis should be longer than the resolution that follows.

Every scene will have a different pace than the one that precedes it, depending on what the scene is supposed to accomplish. A chapter with multiple scenes will have an individual pace of its own. Each chapter will in turn feed the overall pace of the novel.

Scenes should make readers curious. Chapters should leave them wanting more. The well-paced novel should reward them with satisfaction and a heck of a trip along the way.

The obstacles you've created for your characters lead to action scenes of crisis or conflict. Unless you're writing the climax to the book, your protagonist must emerge from such scenes still short of his ultimate goal.

During scenes of resolution the temporarily defeated protagonist may consider giving up. Because you've created a strong character whom readers can identify with, this period of self-pity should be short-lived.

These lulls after defeat should be used to briefly contemplate what went wrong and to plan new strategy. By the end of a resolution scene your hero or heroine should rise like a phoenix from the ashes, with determination stronger than ever.

As you remember from chapter ten, spoken dialogue moves quickly; narrative ambles.

Resolution is composed of introspection and reflection. Both require a slower pace that provides a moment for readers to catch their breath. Both are best served by narrative, internal dialogue or brief spoken exchanges that contain little conflict.

Reserve the majority of spoken dialogue for action and conflict scenes that build tension or lead to a crisis.

Tick, Tick, Tick

A suspense novel consists of a series of escalating crises that build to a final, explosive climax.

Each of these crises must be more threatening and dangerous than the previous one. The result of each crisis should also eliminate an avenue of retreat, point toward another opportunity or direction, or reveal a previously unknown fact or facet of the main plot problem.

Old axioms apply. Just as it's always darkest before the dawn, the crisis immediately prior to the final climax must appear to close the door on all hope.

The use of a time frame or a deadline that the protagonist must meet to prevent disaster is one way to build toward a final climax. Author Marilyn Wallace often uses this technique. "Our hurried, harried society is so engaged with time that it feels natural to me to use the ways we measure it to organize my storytelling. One of the essential components of suspense is the urgency factor. If a character has all the time in the world to figure out what to do, then the suspense is much less compelling."

The already relentless pace of a thriller should increase even more as the climax nears. Shortening the length of chapters and the length of each scene within those chapters does much to accomplish this goal. Writing shorter sentences, even choosing shorter words, can also add to the feeling of impending doom.

When it seems all is lost, dangle the promise of success just beyond a protagonist's reach. Make her struggle to attain her final goal harder than ever.

Add a twist that unexpectedly increases the goal's value. Perhaps someone the heroine believed had escaped or been moved to safety is still in danger.

Maybe the path to victory has been mined or the just-captured villain has a concealed weapon.

Good pacing involves logical surprise. The effects of one crisis or failed attempt to reach a goal should resonate through later crises.

My heroine in *Someone to Watch Over* has a serious problem with heights. I establish this fact during a minor crisis scene that requires Kate to climb a ladder in a failed attempt to change the lightbulb in her stairwell.

The emphasis of the scene is that being a widow involves a series of unexpected daily challenges. A second scene midway through the novel touches briefly again on her problem. Only during the book's climax is the true danger of Kate's weakness revealed.

In a thriller, each crisis is an unspoken promise that things are going to get worse. Each narrative reflection or resolution is the reassurance that the protagonist has not given up—and neither should the reader.

Avoiding Potholes on the Road to Good Pacing

Often it's not until a book is completed that a writer realizes an overall pacing problem exists. When that happens, major revisions become necessary. Knowing what to watch for may help you avoid extensive rewriting. Later, in chapter fifteen—"Words on a Page"—I'll talk about the fine-tuning revision every manuscript must go through.

START OFF STRONG

The most obvious pacing snag is a slow beginning. Chapter four discussed ways to avoid this. Remember that readers of a thriller open its cover anticipating conflict, action and danger. Give them what they expect from the start and this pacing concern disappears.

KEEP 'EM GUESSING . . . UP TO A POINT

Another common mistake is revealing too much too soon.

Even in suspense novels in which the villain is identified from page one, readers crave the thrill of the chase. Why keep reading if the trip and its destination are obvious? When nothing is held back, pacing is destroyed.

Withholding key information in a thriller is de rigueur. As long as you slowly reveal such data, much like a fisherman plays out his line, readers will continue to be strung along. The trick is to offer enough tempting bait that they keep nibbling the hook.

One successful method is to practice the art of deception. Bury new information in a scene that reveals something previously hidden. The "aha" of the moment distracts the reader but still plays fair. Let's look at two scenes from Michael Connelly's *The Poet*.

Jack McEvoy is a crime reporter who's trying to make sense of his brother's suicide. Sean McEvoy was a homicide cop. Initial indications are that his despair over his inability to solve a particularly grisly killing drove him to take his life. But Jack cannot accept the obvious. In the first of our two scenes, Jack has badgered one of Sean's fellow cops into letting him see the file on the unsolved Theresa Lofton murder case.

> *The last entry in the chronological record was made on the day he died. It was just one line: "Mar. 13—RUSHER at Stanley. P/R info on Terri."*
>
> *"Time."*
>
> *I looked up and Wexler was pointing to his watch. I closed the file without protest.*
>
> *"What's P-slash-R mean?"*
>
> *"Person reporting. It meant he got a call."*
>
> *"Who is Rusher?"*
>
> *"We don't know. . . ."*
>
> *"Why would he go meet this person without telling you or leaving some kind of record about who it was?"*

Jack, as well as the reader, is stumped by this information. But as he digs deeper, pieces of the puzzle begin to fall into place. Soon, Jack has begun to research articles on other suicides supposedly triggered by what a *New York Times* article calls "police blues." Here, in the *Times's* report on the suicide of another investigator, the real significance of "RUSHER" falls into place. The first two paragraphs recreate an excerpt from the article Jack McEvoy is reading. Portions of his first-person narrative follow that.

> *. . . Mr. Brooks and whatever it was that haunted him remain an enigma. Even his last message is a puzzle. The line he wrote on the pad offered little in the way of insight into what caused him to turn his gun on himself.*
>
> *"Through the pale door," were his last written words. The line was not original. Mr. Brooks borrowed it from Edgar Allan Poe's poem "The Haunted Palace" which originally appeared in one of Poe's best-known stories, "The Fall of the House of Usher." . . .*
>
> *. . . I could hear my heart beating, my guts being taken in a cold and crushing grip. I couldn't read anything else but the name of the story. Usher. I had read it in high school and again in college. I knew the story. And I knew the character of the title. Roderick Usher. I opened my notebook and looked at the few notes I had jotted down the day before. The name was there. Sean had written it in the chronological record. It was his last entry.*
>
> RUSHER

The "aha" is the discovery that the Rusher Sean supposedly met is not a real person. But buried within the moment is the more important information that the reference came from a work by Poe. As Jack soon learns, Poe quotations are the link between a series of policemen's murders staged to look like suicides. Key information, revealed at the right time, heightens the suspense and keeps the reader involved in the story.

The Other Side of the Equation

The reverse of the "too much too soon" problem—revealing too little too late—usually involves a sudden dump of critical information near the end of the book or a villain who makes an appearance much later than he should.

All characters who are to become suspects of the evil you've plotted should be introduced within the novel's first three chapters. If they don't make physical appearances, other characters should at least discuss or refer to them until you can actually bring them onstage.

This means you must also introduce red herring characters within the same number of pages.

In an especially long novel the chapter rule might be stretched a little. But the sooner all players are in the spotlight, the sooner you can get to the meat of the story.

Revealed villains, such as Jessie Hunter's Chocolate Man, don't have to be identified until the book's climax, of course. They should, however, make their first appearances during the early pages. And planting clues as to their real identifies when they also appear as their true selves is always expected.

MAKE IT CLEAR

Pacing can also be destroyed when you don't give readers enough information to follow what's happening, or provide so much data that they are constantly confused.

The best way to avoid this problem is to find an unbiased reader to preview your work. A few authors use family members, but often a parent or spouse may hold back in fear of wounding your ego with the truth.

Some writers establish a rapport with an active or retired English teacher or librarian. You might be surprised to discover how many people who choose those professions love good suspense novels. Another solution is to find other writers who understand what's needed and are looking for such criticism themselves.

Critique groups and writers clubs can be wonderful. Unfortunately many such organizations evolve into social societies. If you find one than isn't, stick with it and be thankful.

KEEP IT SIMPLE

Other things to watch for are literary tangents or flights of fancy that produce beautiful prose or scenes and images that go on for pages. These can kill a thriller's pacing faster than Hannibal Lecter can dissect a victim.

Save those long thoughtful passages for slower-paced stories that are slanted for a literary market. Cut the lengthy scene. Find one vivid image and make it count. The perfect simile or metaphor is worth a dozen pages of rambling description.

Listen to Mary Willis Walker describe an old friend of her protagonist Molly Cates in *All the Dead Lie Down*.

> *The old senator's bald pate gleaming in the lights looked vulnerable as a bird's egg, and his doleful mud slide of a face droopier and more creased than usual, as if it were threatening to slip right off his skull.*

A vivid portrait, painted in just one sentence.

Other Pacing Tips

SHOWING VS. TELLING

Contrary to what you might have read, telling is not a sin. Showing *is* preferred, but telling has its place as well.

Tom Clancy used a quick telling sketch to introduce Jack Ryan to the readers of *The Hunt for Red October*. As noted before, this made sense because so much action was taking place in multiple locations. In that case telling fit the situation.

Still, an imbalance in either telling or showing can affect a novel's pacing. The best rule for suspense is this: When showing will enrich narrative, nourish a suspenseful atmosphere or paint a vivid portrait for the reader, that's your best choice. But if at some infrequent points in the story, telling better sustains tension or prevents a weakening of the action, by all means use it. Just keep it short.

TRANSITIONS

Pacing can also be compromised if you put things in the wrong order. This can be especially tough to control when trying to write scenes of simultaneous action taking place in multiple locations.

The solution here is to include a transitional phrase or paragraph at the beginning and/or the end of each scene. Smooth transitions involve more than the "meanwhile, back at the ranch" voice-overs from yesterday's B westerns.

One way to transition from one action scene to another is with time or distance references.

Suppose you open your multiple-viewpoint thriller like this.

> *Ted Basinger entered Nick's Wine Seller with one object in mind—find a vintage Bordeaux worthy enough that Karen's father would forget last night's fiasco with the domestic Chablis.*
>
> *To hell with the SOB snob, Ted decided moments later. To hell with Karen for that matter.*
>
> *Funny how a couple of guys with ski masks and semiautomatics could alter your priorities so quickly.*

The scene might go on to detail what happens when the store's owner sets off the alarm and end with Ted's subsequent reactions. Your second scene might then introduce your protagonist in this way.

> *Twenty minutes earlier, Walt Pardo had just felt himself begin to relax. The quiet anniversary dinner at the city's toniest restaurant was going pretty well. Too bad it was costing him two days' pay. Evenings like this were what made some guys on the force consider soliciting a little graft.*
>
> *At least Nan was speaking to him tonight. And she hadn't mentioned his "stupid macho job" even once. Of course, at this point, she'd only had one gin and tonic. That he knew about.*

The scene might go on another half page or so with Walt and his wife circling the wagons for another fight before continuing.

> *It was her fourth drink that screwed up the evening.*
>
> *The father of the well-behaved family at the next table was scowling in Nan's direction. Not that Walt blamed him. People who came to places like this didn't expect their six-year-old's ice cream to be served to the drunken accompaniment of "F—— you and all those f——ing hostage negotiation buddies of yours."*

> *Rescue from the grim-faced headwaiter bearing down on their table*
> *came in the form of Walt's vibrating pager. He hated to admit how*
> *much he'd been willing the damn thing to go off.*

Because of the transitional sentence at the beginning of Walt's scene, readers will have no trouble understanding that the time frames for both scenes overlap. The last two sentences relating to the pager then transition into the next scene when Walt arrives at the wine shop.

A story like this, in which intense, possibly volatile action alternates between two locations, will call for many transitions. They might be as simple as following a "Walt" scene with one that begins "Inside the store, Ted watched the second gunman's eyes."

The lack of proper transitions in single-viewpoint novels can also result in uneven pacing. Readers need triggers to alert them to time and place as the story moves along. These can be as basic as "By the time he'd finished cleaning the gun, Larry had worked out the details for disposing of Frank's body."

UNNECESSARY SCENES

Two other pacing problems are scenes that do nothing to advance the plot and scenes that don't work. The solution to the first is to cut the scene entirely. If a nugget of information must be retained, rework it until it fits into some other scene.

For scenes that don't seem to work, you have three choices.

1. Rewrite the scene until it does what you intended it to do.

2. Reposition the material to some other spot where it *will* work.

3. Eliminate those sections that slow the plot, then incorporate the remaining information within another scene.

If none of these solve the problem, the scene isn't needed.

The Final Four Hurdles to Strong Pacing
THE MIDNOVEL SLUMP

The first of the final four is called midnovel slump. It's that place halfway through a book when things seem to move in slow motion. Sustaining suspense for three hundred and some pages is hard work. Writers whose thrillers run four hundred pages and up must really have problems. Right?

Actually, the longer thrillers usually wind up that length because they take place over an extended period, contain multiple subplots, have a very broad scope or some combination of all these. In many cases the published work may have already been pared down from a far longer manuscript during author revisions or the editing process.

But no thriller, no book of any genre is immune to the pacing nightmare of midnovel slump. If yours is keeping you awake nights, the problem is most likely one of plot. Several remedies are available.

Every novel needs subplots. These are the threads that can make things more complicated or lead a hero astray. Some will be minor. Some will consume more of a character's attention.

The more subplots, the more dilemmas a protagonist faces. The more dilemmas, the more obstacles crop up along the way to reaching her goal.

Your story may not have enough subplots. Or some of the ones you've created may not be fully developed.

I'm not talking here about padding. Such attempts *never* work. Subplots must grow out of a protagonist's life, the unique situation she finds herself in or some inner conflict she's facing because of what's happening to her.

If your thriller is suffering a midnovel slump, examine your subplots. Perhaps one has an unexplored avenue that could logically be investigated at that point in the book. Maybe a secondary subplot to one you've already created can become another obstacle for your protagonist. Just don't try to invent a new subplot in midstream. Choose one that can grow out of an existing problem.

Say your hero is an attorney, a single parent who's having trouble communicating with his teenage son because of the current crisis. If the father finds marijuana in the boy's jacket, he may have a bigger worry than the high-profile case he's facing.

A confrontation with the son. The boy's anger because he wasn't given a chance to explain that he picked up a teammate's jacket by mistake. Dad's sleepless night when his son doesn't come home after storming out of the house. The uneasy silence that follows the situation's resolution.

These are the type of scenes of conflict and tension that can provide support for a plot with a sagging middle.

INCONSISTENCY

The second of pacing's final four is inconsistency, and again subplots play a part. Subplots that never conclude or are wrapped up in unnecessary chapters or extra long passages that take place after the main story's climax. Too much time spent on subplots in relation to the primary plot.

One definition of the prefix *sub* is secondary. A subplot should never overshadow the book's original plotline.

Untied loose ends and unexplained references are also included under inconsistency. If you've mentioned an ankle bracelet that's missing from a murder victim's body, readers will expect the item to turn up by the end of the book. Probably among the killer's possessions. If it's not there, it better turn up somewhere else.

TIMIDITY

The final four's number three is backing away from painful scenes. Violence, whether physical or mental, is neither pretty nor kind. If you fail to show that in some way, readers will see such action as gratuitous and will feel uninvolved with what's happening to the characters. This in turn endangers pace.

Books about serial killers or those that involve autopsies traditionally hold nothing back. But maybe that's not the kind of book you want to write. Relax. It's not always necessary to provide graphic details to convey the pain that surrounds the characters in a thriller.

The changing sound of a heart monitor as another victim of a deadly virus dies can cause extreme internal anguish for the researcher whose latest attempt at finding an antitoxin has failed. Make that victim a friend and the pain goes even deeper.

Go inside the thoughts of the innocent condemned man. Listen, as he does, to the nervous pacing or quiet sobbing of the prisoner at the end of the hall whose scheduled execution is tomorrow, forty-eight hours prior to his own.

Show readers the emotional turmoil within a detective whose thoughts keep returning to the abandoned doll found beside the body of a pedophile's last victim. And something as subtle as a crazed fly hammering the wall at an indoor murder scene lets readers use their own imaginations about the carnage in the room.

INAPPROPRIATE ENDINGS

Inappropriate endings are the final pacing problem. Readers expect the climax of a thriller to be the high point of all the action that has gone before it. A too pat or uneventful ending is sure to disappoint them. One in which either the protagonist or villain reacts against the characterization you've established throughout the book can be just as bad.

A satisfying ending is vital to the success of your thriller. In fact, appropriate endings are so critical to a suspense novel's pacing they get chapter thirteen all to themselves.

But first we're going to talk about theme.

CHAPTER 12

Theme

B efore we can talk about theme and its place in today's thriller, we should know exactly what it is we're discussing.

Ronald B. Tobias, author of *Theme & Strategy*, defines theme as "the central concern around which a story is constructed."

He goes on to point out that this concern may be the action, the emotional effect on the reader, an author's style, an exploration of character or an idea.

In this chapter we'll deal primarily with the question, Can ideas be used successfully as the theme in a suspense novel? And if so, how?

Tobias lists six universal ideas that appear as themes in novels.

1. The moral statement
2. The struggle for human dignity
3. Social commentary
4. Commentary on human nature
5. Commentary on human relations
6. The journey from innocence to experience

Novels that become literary classics are often heralded as such due to the strong presence of one of the above themes. The work of Charles Dickens comes most quickly to mind. Many of us first learned about the life and mores of nineteenth-century England through Dickens's social commentaries we were assigned in school.

Thrillers are considered commercial fiction. As such, they are first and foremost entertainment. For that reason the *central* concern of the novel is rarely an idea-based theme. This does not mean that such themes cannot be addressed at some other level within the book.

Most people read commercial fiction to be entertained. They want to escape the pressures of daily life. The last thing they want is to be hit over the head with someone else's idea of what they should think or believe about that life.

The trick is to create such a seamless blend of theme and entertainment that the reader doesn't realize his consciousness has been challenged until the experience is over.

How To Identify Your *Book's Theme*

Regardless of category, plot or characters, you chose to write your thriller for a reason. Your number one reason may be just to entertain. And, yes, you hope to make a few dollars from the process.

But what I'm talking about is why you chose to write a *particular* book.

• If your aim is to weave a great action yarn, then **action** is your theme.

• Want to expose your reader to the internal torment that consumes a homicide detective charged with stopping an especially brutal serial killer? Your theme is **emotional effect**.

• Planning to write a thriller that explores what makes a protagonist tick and how she'll react to and be changed by a forced encounter with her own mortality? Your theme is **characterization**.

Wonderful suspense novels have been and will continue to be written using these three themes. They are the books readers reach for when they want a great read. As long as they continue to do so, authors will continue to write them.

And unfortunately many critics will continue to insist that thrillers are not true "literature." Poe's work may qualify, but every rule has an exception. After all, everyone knows classic literature must be about ideas.

Which brings us to the six idea-related themes mentioned above. These are serious issues. To examine them in depth does call for a literary approach. Still, most, if not all six, can be addressed in a valid way within the pages of a suspense novel.

If you think the thriller you envision might be fertile ground for exploring one of these themes, by all means go for it. But before you begin, there are things you should understand.

Getting It Wrong

Subtlety is imperative.

I once heard someone read from the manuscript of a potential thriller during an open critique session. The writer had lived for some time in Japan. The premise of the book was that certain factions within the Japanese government had never really given up after World War II and had manipulated the next generation into plotting America's destruction. This new attack was to come from within, targeting weaknesses within America's infrastructure.

The basic story showed promise. Culturally, the overall characterizations sounded accurate. A suggested romantic entanglement for the U.S. government-employed hero and heroine fit the action-adventure scenario as well.

The book's fatal malady was author bias.

Unfortunately, the writer had a personal hostility toward the chosen villains of the piece. This animosity came through in long narrative passages and forced dialogue that bombarded the intended audience at every turn.

Despite carefully worded criticism from both experienced and novice writers during the session, the author refused to consider changes to the manuscript.

When readers want to learn an author's personal opinions on politics, religion or why humankind is going to hell in a Ferrari, they head for a bookstore's nonfiction section. They may be willing, however, to hear a less biased version of those same views voiced by a fictional protagonist. *As long as such views are woven into and have direct bearing on an interesting plot.*

If either the hero or the heroine in the book I just outlined had sounded a warning or suggested caution to superiors based on his or her own reservations, readers would have accepted that subtle version of the author's voice. A belligerent secondary character who shared the writer's strong opinions might even have gotten the point across.

Instead, a potentially interesting thriller that might have included commentary on human nature and relations—two nations' tendencies to forget the lessons of their pasts, for instance—succumbed to an agenda.

Getting It Right

Theme can not operate independently within a thriller. It must be an integral part of what's happening.

Raise questions about theme rather than lecture readers. Let these questions arise from characterization and plot. Melding theme with characters' goals and motivations is one way to create this seamless bond.

A book's main character must have an opinion on the issue at hand. It may be pro or con or wavering between the two, but it can never be neutral. Most readers will accept that a character's viewpoint differs with their own as long as the writer makes them privy to that character's reasoning process.

In recent years two authors of suspense novels have successfully tackled the moral statement theme surrounding the death penalty—John Grisham in *The Chamber* and Mary Willis Walker in *The Red Scream.*

Both novels involve convicted antagonists awaiting state-ordered justice for horrendous crimes, and protagonists who oppose (or believe they oppose) that solution.

Grisham chose to address the subject via an examination of the appeals process. Rather than simply give his attorney hero moral reasons for his anti-death penalty stand, Grisham made the condemned prisoner the lawyer's recently discovered grandfather, a despicable man who readily admits his guilt.

Stirred into this mix are civil rights, dead children, bigotry and a death threat against the condemned man's family from an unidentified coconspirator. With all that on their plate, readers barely register as they read that the book has a theme. Yet the issues—the questions Grisham raises about the morality of the death penalty—stay with the readers well beyond the novel's final page.

Mary Willis Walker's protagonist Molly Cates also begins and ends her exploration into the morality of the death penalty on the opposition side of the issue. Unlike Grisham's hero, however, her conviction wavers during the story. Readers are witnesses to her inner conflict.

The condemned man in this instance is a confessed serial killer convicted of multiple murders but sentenced to die only for the one of which Molly believes he's innocent.

Because of reporter Molly's interviews with this murderer, she knows how vile and unrepentant he is. This knowledge battles with her stance when she uncovers what may be the evidence that can commute his sentence.

In the case of *The Red Scream*, the focus appears to be Molly's quest to discover the truth about who committed the murder in question. Readers are aware even as they turn the pages that more than one conviction is being questioned. Yet, because of the book's pacing, not until they close the back cover will they have time to focus completely on the moral question.

That is theme integration at its best.

The theme should always be involved in some way in the resolution of the story. This resolution may not entirely lay to rest the issue itself. Even after "The End," questions may remain to nag the protagonist—and the reader. But the issue as it pertains to the book will have reached a point of closure.

The best-themed books are those in which the author distracts the reader by suggesting the actual story is about something else entirely. If, at the end of the novel, readers come away with the theme's questions resonating in their thoughts, such a book has succeeded.

How to Make a Point Without Using a Club

For readers to stick with a story with whose theme they disagree, they must be captivated by the characters and the struggle those characters experience because of their views.

Using major characters' interactions with others is one of the easiest ways to introduce a theme, especially one that addresses moral or social issues.

An antagonist's passing encounter with another character can show a reader volumes. That reaction can then be contrasted by allowing the book's protagonist a similar confrontation.

Take a serial killer who disdains and avoids a guy with a swastika tattoo and burr haircut at the end of the bar. Perhaps internal dialogue reveals that, despite his own evil acts, the protagonist considers himself above those who hate other races or religions.

If it's then later revealed that this killer targets gay men, it's clear that he's as bigoted in a similar way as the white supremacist. Even murderers lie to themselves.

Now look at the protagonist, a tough-as-nails cop being ribbed by his colleagues for catching the investigation of the "fag" killings. Does the hero agree with his buddies' opinion of gays, even to the point of making a joke about one of the victims? Or does he feel uncomfortable because he doesn't share their views? Perhaps he witnessed a childhood friend's struggle with his sexuality. A friend so tormented he ended his life rather than face a lifetime of derision.

Maybe it wasn't a friend, but an adored older brother who now accepts his homosexuality but stays away because he knows his presence would cause problems for his brother the cop.

How the detective handles the situation with his co-workers and faces his own prejudices as he investigates the case could provide an ongoing commentary on human relations, moral judgments and human dignity. For good measure, let's toss in social commentary as well.

Whether or not you choose to work an idea-based theme into your suspense novel, being aware of the potential to do so can only broaden your approach to your writing. The examples by John Grisham and Mary Willis Walker enrich the genre and add multilevel depths to their work. Both are goals to which we all can aspire.

⤛ CHAPTER 13 ⤜

Endings

All things eventually end. But a novel experiences dozens of deaths and rebirths before its author types "The End." This is because books have many endings—scene endings, chapter endings and that ultimate ending, the climax.

Multiple endings lead to multiple beginnings. In a suspense novel, scene endings sound an alarm, send shivers down readers' spines or in some other way cause them unease. Subsequent scene beginnings reassure them things are not over yet. As each scene or chapter closes, it prepares readers for the genesis of the story's next reincarnation.

Let's examine a mythical women-in-jeopardy gothic suspense plot to see how this works.

THE JOB

A young woman we'll call Lanore is in desperate need of cash. She answers an ad for a position as assistant to a wealthy invalid who wants to dictate his memoirs before his death. The requirements listed are the usual secretarial skills, an ability to spend at least three concurrent months at the man's remote estate and a courageous nature.

While the last item seems bizarre, the salary is more than Lanore hoped for, so she readily accepts the offer of employment.

She's flown by private jet to a rural airport where she's met by a limo. When she asks about her employer, the driver says she'll learn all she needs to know in due time. He then closes the partition.

On the way to their destination, the backseat of the vehicle fills with fumes. Unable to open the doors or roll down a window, Lanore passes out.

The ending of this opening action scene leaves plenty of questions for the reader. The protagonist should echo these questions in a resolution scene in which she examines what happened and rethinks her situation.

THE DILEMMA

Lanore awakens from her drug-induced sleep to find herself locked in a third-floor room. The windows are barred. Finding no way out, she tries to control her terror as she contemplates why someone might have lured her into such a nightmare.

Suddenly she hears a sound and discovers someone has slipped a key under the door. When she tries it, the key turns in the lock. All that remains for her to do is open the door, locate the stairs and make a cautious escape. Except . . .

What will she find when she opens that door? Who provided the key? Is whoever it was still lurking in the shadows beyond the threshold, waiting to see what she'll do? She's not certain where she is. Where will she go if she finds her way out?

Perhaps the key is a trick—a test in some weird game, or part of the "courageous nature" requirement of the job. Maybe even greater danger lies in wait outside the door.

This scene ends when the heroine decides that game or no game she must take the chance. She reaches for the doorknob. And the chapter ends.

→-◄

Scene one introduced the main character, established her situation and ended in suspense. The questions it raised were acknowledged at the beginning of scene two. That those questions have not been laid to rest as the second scene ended does not matter. The heroine confronted them and speculated on possible answers. For now, that's enough.

A response to the new questions raised in the second scene will be answered in chapter two when Lanore opens the door.

Endings That Set Up Beginnings— But Allow Readers to Breathe

Not every scene or chapter has to leave readers with their hearts in their throats. Part of the rhythm of suspense includes time in those valleys I talked about in the chapter on pacing.

As an example, we might extend the second scene of our gothic suspense and end the first chapter in a different way.

THE DECISION

Lanore overcomes her fear about what awaits outside the room, opens the door and finds herself in a short hallway. Three other doors open off this corridor, and each one is locked. Her key opens none of them. Now she has several new options.

She could burst into tears. She could go back to the room she just came from. Or she could beat on each of the three doors and demand her freedom. The last choice would repeat her initial response when she awoke, but that had gotten her nowhere.

Or had it?

Methodically she knocks loudly on each door and asks to be let out. Again, nothing happens. She decides that perhaps it's too soon. Quite a bit of time elapsed between her pounding and the appearance of a key the last time. Still wary, she settles down in the hallway to wait.

+>-<+

Readers can breathe a little easier with this ending. The original questions still remain, but some they may not have voiced have been answered.

Their initial impression might have been that Lanore was pretty stupid for putting herself in jeopardy by accepting a position she knew so little about. Now they suspect it was the job's last requirement that most intrigued her—

a courageous nature often goes hand in hand with a love of adventure. They've also learned that Lanore is patient and able to reason. Rather than panic in the midst of a frightening dilemma, she's calmly made the connection between her past actions and her current situation.

This ending suggests a variety of beginnings for the second chapter. Another key may be slipped under one of the doors. Three such keys may appear. One of the doors may swing silently open to reveal the stairs or someone who leads her to her new employer.

Even as they raise new questions, the possibilities assure readers that the questions left unanswered will eventually be laid to rest.

Personally, I vote for the three keys. Lanore's reasoning on which to try first can show the readers something new about her. And perhaps if she makes the right decision, they and she will learn that all this *has* been a test.

Perhaps the old man wanted to see how she'd react to being confronted by danger. Why? Because knowledge of the information she'll be transcribing could put her in an even more hazardous situation once she's completed her work.

The Ultimate Ending

What do you want your readers to feel when they close the back cover on your thriller? Relief? Satisfaction? Unease? Anticipation?

Good suspense novels seize the readers' imaginations, convey them on a twisting turning journey, then drop them off at the end of the story only to stun them yet again with the unexpected.

Two things to consider when planning the climax of your thriller are appropriateness and timing.

SLAMMING ON THE BRAKES BEFORE THE LIGHT TURNS RED

End a book too soon and readers will feel cheated.

The villain has put your hero Dave through hell. Sent his BMW over a cliff. Planted a bomb in his briefcase. Kidnapped his wife. Shot his dog, for heaven's sake.

Still, do you really believe readers will rejoice if Dave turns the corner one morning, sees his nemesis casually strolling toward him with a smirk on his face, and calmly blows the creep away with the .45 he just happens to be carrying in his raincoat pocket?

Sure, the guy might have deserved being blasted into next Tuesday. And Dave may have been pushed to the limit. (Although the police and the district attorney might challenge that contention.) But unless Dave has a background as a cold-blooded killer himself, your climax will ring false.

Were readers privy to Dave's momentous decision to *murder* his enemy? Did you show him buying the gun? Agonizing over his proposed solution? Weighing pros and cons, considering the consequences to himself and his family? Have you made it clear he has no other options?

Even if Dave has shared his angst in the scenes leading up to his moment of truth, the ending is still too detached and abrupt. The guy needs killing, so Dave shoots him? What does that make Dave?

Suppose, instead of a casual confrontation, Dave is meeting the villain in the hope of getting his wife back. Show him driving to the rendezvous. His hand keeps straying to the gun. Internal dialogue shows that he's worried, unsure if he'll be able to use it.

When he gets to the meeting spot, no one is there. Panic. Is he on another wild-goose chase? Then an apparently unarmed man steps from a clump of trees. He's dragging Dave's wife by the arm.

She stares vacantly into the distance. Her face and arms are bruised; her clothing torn and ragged. The villain shoves her ahead of him, and she stumbles and falls. He makes a crude sexual remark. And then he smirks.

Now if Dave guns the guy down in cold blood, readers will cheer. They can understand the emotions that pushed him over the edge.

If it later turns out in a wrap-up scene that his wife was injured in an escape attempt rather than raped and abused, Dave can suffer a tortured moment of self-doubt before accepting his action as justified for the situation.

To account for the villain's bravado and lack of a visible weapon, it would be best if Dave's aversion to guns had been established earlier in the story. Perhaps it was well known that he refused to go hunting as a boy. This makes his ultimate action both dramatic and unpredictable.

KNOWING WHEN TO STEP ON THE PEDAL

Just as disappointing for readers as an ending that happens too quickly is a climax that goes on too long.

Suspense strings readers along. Confrontations should not. Once the two main characters come face-to-face for the climax, the action should move swiftly and surely to a close.

This does not mean their conflict cannot break off and then begin again a few times. But chapters and chapters of near misses only dilute the suspense and endanger the pacing.

If a character has lost everything, he might be distraught enough to begin stalking his enemy. Unless the book's main plot is about that pursuit, however, the chase should be relatively short. Two or three near confrontations would probably be enough. Any more and you risk trying the reader's patience.

Ambiguous endings are acceptable as long as they answer all the other questions raised by the plot.

A killer might fall off a cliff into the ocean during a raging storm. If it's noted that his body was never recovered, readers are left wondering. But the ending is still satisfying.

Readers who like things neat and tidy can rationalize that the body washed out to sea or was eaten by sharks. Those who prefer to be left with a final shiver will savor the uncertainty. Others will be certain a sequel must be in the works.

Several authors have added another dimension to the ambiguous ending. Their plots about cunning serial killers who appear to have died have concluded with postscripts that report that new strings of deaths with the murderers' signature have occurred in some other parts of the country.

Copycat or evil Lazarus? Readers love the possibilities.

Postscripts

While we're on the subject of postscripts, short ones are OK, but extended explanations can ruin an ending's pacing. Tom Clancy knew this when he wrapped up the loose ends in *The Hunt for Red October.*

Because the book involved several different locations, the final, postclimax chapter takes eight-and-a-half pages. The longest scene uses three of those; the shortest only five lines.

Those five lines show Jack Ryan on a plane home. A single line in one of the chapter's earlier scenes noted that his daughter's hoped-for Christmas present would be going with him. Clancy could have followed Ryan home for a tender reunion with his family. That he didn't proves he understood the value of a perfectly timed ending.

Author John Gilstrap wrestled with the problem of adding a postscript during the creation of *Nathan's Run.* "It's important to end a suspense novel at the right moment. In *Nathan's Run* I originally had a wrap-up chapter. But Nathan's problems were so huge, and there were so many things that couldn't be resolved in a day or two or four. The chapter was set six months later. That didn't feel right, so I cut it.

"We'd been living very intensely over the course of the two or three days that Nathan runs. Then to just have this summary chapter felt like the old Quinn Martin-produced TV shows where you came back after the last commercial and you had an epilogue. I thought there was some merit to leaving the question open."

Sometimes eager fans want even more information about the characters they've come to care about. "A lot of people *say* they want a sequel to *Nathan's Run,*" says Gilstrap, "when in fact they *really* want another chapter. I thought the outcome was pretty obvious. Why not leave on the emotional moment?"

One more thing to remember: Beware of creating an ending so lacking in hope that readers are left with nothing but depression. If a hero or heroine has to die at the end of a thriller, something positive or noble must remain for readers to cling to—some sign that life will go on.

The fireman who dies rescuing trapped children from a building torched by an arsonist is allowed a poignant last scene. But after that moment the writer should pull back from the anguish with one final scene.

Such a scene might show the reunion between the kids he saved and their parents. Perhaps a line or two—gruff, not sappy—from the hero's captain about the void that the hero's death has left. Or the scene could jump ahead to show a ceremony that adds his name to a memorial for fallen firefighters, or his own son's graduation from the fire academy.

Tapping Into Readers' Emotions

Bringing a villain to justice can take many forms beyond the classic arrest and conviction. In the earlier scenario with Dave, the situation seemed to leave the protagonist little choice but to destroy his enemy.

Fate can play a part, as with the killer who falls into a raging sea. However, that ending must grow out of characterization and plot circumstances. If a novel's climax seems contrived in any way, readers are sure to cry foul.

Sometimes letting a villain live is the greatest revenge.

Suppose you've established an antagonist who's clinically claustrophobic or obsessive-compulsive. Living inside a $6' \times 9'$ cell, prevented from observing his rituals could translate into the ultimate punishment. And a sex offender who targets children knows he won't survive long in the general prison population.

All's Well That Ends Well

Choosing the proper ending for a thriller is sometimes easier than you think. Many authors know the way their books are going to end before they start writing.

Some writers, and I'm among them, find they have to know the endings before they can begin plotting their stories. This is not to say that a final outcome won't evolve or mutate in some way. Quite often it does. Now and then it even metamorphoses into something else completely.

Whether you share this experience or not, be aware that getting from point A to point Z involves *some* knowledge of direction. Don't wander all over the alphabetical map without occasionally checking a compass.

Remember, too, to consider the suggestions I outlined in chapter eleven about pacing a book's climax.

Shorten the length of chapters slightly as you begin to wind up the story. Do the same for scenes that build to the climax. Write shorter sentences and choose simpler words to add to the feeling of impending disaster.

Any and all of these things can make readers feel that time is running out. And after all, isn't that exactly what's going to happen when your novel reaches its explosive conclusion?

CHAPTER 14

Style

Searching for reference material for this chapter proved to be a challenge. Among my files are the contents pages from the last fifteen years of *Writer's Digest* magazine. During that period, various writers discussed fiction-writing topics such as plotting, dialogue, character and pacing in hundreds of articles. Each writer's approach differed from the others.

Only two articles addressed matters of style.

My personal library contains over two dozen books on the subject of writing. In only one of these, *Writing the Novel* by Lawrence Block, is style given a chapter of its own.

Then there is the slender text entitled *The Elements of Style* by William Strunk Jr. and E.B. White. This volume from my shelves is notable for several reasons.

1. *The Elements of Style* contains only eighty-five pages.
2. It began as a textbook privately printed in the early twentieth century by Strunk during his tenure as professor of English at Cornell University.
3. Although revised several times since its first commercial printing, it has never been out of print.
4. Most bookstores stock at least one copy at all times.
5. Many writing teachers consider it a required text.
6. As we enter the twenty-first century, almost a hundred years after its inception, *The Elements of Style* is still the definitive work on its title subject.

Obviously, there is little I can add to the information contained within those eighty-five pages. I can, however, discuss style as it pertains to the writing of commercial fiction, with an emphasis on style's relationship to the various categories of suspense.

What Style Is

Mention style to a journalist and she'll probably ask whether you're referring to *The Associated Press Stylebook and Libel Manual* or *The Chicago Manual of Style*. Ask a grammarian and he'll launch into a discussion on the use of language. A literary scholar deposed on the same subject will immediately think of Hemingway and Fitzgerald or Faulkner or Updike. Each of the three queried will talk about the same things.

Style is composed of many components. Among these are a writer's choice of tense and viewpoint; the sound and cadence of sentences (determined by words, their arrangement and punctuation choices); the length and flow of sentences, paragraphs and chapters; and the sound and placement of dialogue within those sentences and paragraphs.

Do You Hear What I Hear?

> *When we speak of Fitzgerald's style, we don't mean his command of the relative pronoun, we mean the sound his words make on paper.*

The above excerpt from *The Elements of Style* best describes what is meant by the sound and cadence of a writer's sentences. Not only are the word choices themselves a factor of style, their placement within those sentences is important.

Think of two or three great quotes that have affected your life. Write them in another form. Would they have impacted your life or stayed in your thoughts if you'd first encountered them in these rewritten versions?

How much patriotic fervor do you think this sentence might have generated?

Instead of wondering what's in it for you, you should consider what you might do about the things that you think are wrong with the United States.

JFK and his speechwriters clearly understood the power of word choice and placement. As did Abraham Lincoln when he rejected the simple "Eighty-seven years ago" for the cadence of "Four score and seven years ago."

Such eloquence would seem out of place in a thriller. Unless, of course, you're portraying a political figure in a historical setting. Still, there are ways to give your prose a richness that today's readers will not only accept but admire.

We'll explore some of them in chapter fifteen, "Words on a Page."

The Long and Short of Things

If you study a random sampling of ten or twelve writers, you'll find a wide range of styles regarding sentence, paragraph and chapter lengths.

Some authors prefer short uniform chapters. Action in such books often moves very swiftly. A majority of sentences may be simple rather than compound. The longest paragraph might take up, at best, four or five printed lines. Dialogue—crisp exchanges with few tag lines and minimal stage directions—will usually dominate over descriptive and narrative passages.

You'll find other books whose authors vary chapter lengths, basing each segment on what is taking place. Crises may take several pages; resolutions only a few.

John Gilstrap, author of *Nathan's Run* and *At All Costs*, likes consistent chapter lengths: "Truthfully, chaptering has always been a mystery to me. I make a chapter break where I think one belongs, not necessarily as an effort to provide pacing, but because there is either a major point of view shift or passage of time. I start to get kind of antsy if my chapters run much longer than fifteen manuscript pages. Having a one-page chapter is not a problem, but I prefer uniformity. I guess I'm a symmetrical person."

That said, it's worth noting that any length that works is correct. Pacing and rhythm are what count, and good writing is good writing.

Where Things Belong

The positioning of dialogue is part of a writer's style. Some authors prefer to isolate exchanges by giving them their own paragraphs. Tag lines or a character's physical actions while speaking may appear as well, but other narrative will be restricted to separate paragraphs,as in this example.

> *"Things aren't getting any better," Mason said. He toyed with the letter opener on his desk. "I think it's time to end this thing once and for all."*
>
> *For a moment no one dared speak. Steve shifted uneasily in his chair. Rafe opened his mouth, then closed it again, shaking his head. Finally Natalie said what was on everyone's mind.*
>
> *"Are you suggesting we kill them?"*

Other writers may begin a paragraph with a line of prose then switch to dialogue. Depending on the situation, they may revert to prose again before ending the paragraph.

> *Natalie knew everyone was thinking the same thing. After a moment she decided if no one else would say it, she would. "I guess that means you're willing to pay for a hit?" Mason's expression was the only answer she needed.*

Neither format is better than the other. The decision is simply part of a particular author's style.

Every writer also has strengths and weaknesses.

A natural ability to "hear" dialogue is a blessing that translates into realistic exchanges between an author's characters. This then, becomes a part of that writer's style.

Stilted dialogue can ring a death knoll for an otherwise competent novel. Writers who lack an intuitive affinity for the spoken word must consciously work on the rhythm and content of their characters' speech.

Those writers who are masters of the simile or metaphor are able to create rich description and vivid images with a minimum of words. Certain authors find that depicting realistic action comes easily, while others are forced to rewrite such scenes again and again. Each of these assets and liabilities is reflected in a particular writer's style.

Other Things to Consider

Style is best when it's invisible. I discussed in chapter seven how the use of second-person POV or present tense can call attention to a writer's style. Readers cannot continue to care about what happens to the characters in a story when there are constant reminders that it *is* a story.

If readers of a thriller become aware of an author's style, reality intervenes. Pacing is destroyed. And suspense evaporates.

But other aspects of style beyond tense and POV can also affect suspense. Clarity of writing is one. Style should never confuse or lead readers astray.

I talked about author bias in the chapter on theme, but it's important enough to mention again. If you feel a strong need to openly voice your editorial opinion on a subject, consider switching from novels to nonfiction.

No style may be as bad as *too much* style. Books with sentence after sentence using a subject, predicate, object structure with a sprinkling of adjectives and adverbs quickly begin to sound like grade school Jane, Dick and Spot stories. The next chapter offers suggestions for avoiding such problems.

Identifying Your Own Style

Some writers have an instinct for style. If you're not one of them, there are things you can do to help yourself develop a style of your own.

• Identify an author or two whose styles you like. Study them to see what makes them unique. Compare your own writing to their work. Pinpoint areas where your writing seems somewhat similar to that of the writers you admire.

Now forget about those authors. Concentrate on strengthening the areas where you feel your own style could use improvement. Don't copy what you found. You're not trying to become a clone of another author.

• If dialogue is a problem for you, use the taping technique I suggested in chapter ten. Uneven pacing calls for attention to transitions and a review of chapter eleven. Other difficulties may mean you need to "read like a writer" and take apart a few more thrillers to understand how things are done.

• Never force your style into a preconceived pattern. Write in a way that seems natural. Note that many writers feel more comfortable writing in the tense and POV they most enjoy reading.

• While it's not necessary to restrict your writing vocabulary to five and ten cent words, twelve dollar words sound pretentious in commercial fiction. Choose carefully those instances where an obscure word is the only one that will do.

This doesn't mean that writers of suspense can't let their prose shine. It's the way words are combined that make an author's writing memorable.

It has been said of Michael Connelly that he writes with a poet's eye. The following is just one of many sentences from *The Poet* that would seem to confirm this.

> *I gingerly stepped out of the car and walked to the edge of the asphalt where the light from the passing cars reflected in moving rainbows on the petroleum-exhaust glaze on the February snow.*

No twelve dollar words, just several strategically placed and visually expressive six and eight dollar ones.

A word of caution to those who may be drawn to an unusual or flamboyant style: Unless you're able to adapt that style to the needs of suspense, you may find that literary novels are a better vehicle for your writing.

Matching Style to Category

Knowing your own style may help you decide which category of suspense best fits your writing.

A spare writing style works especially well with action-adventure. So does one that assumes a light touch. James Bond's droll remarks and witty repartee come most immediately to mind.

A light touch can be a plus as well when it comes to dialogue in categories in which characters traditionally banter or use sarcasm with one another. Law enforcement officers often do this to break tension or to avoid dwelling on the misery they witness.

If you like to examine your characters' personalities through rich narrative passages, your writing style will probably work well with psychological, romantic relationship or women-in-jeopardy suspense. Writers of categories that deal with emotions usually use lengthier sentences, paragraphs and chapters.

First person also works well in these categories because it provides the opportunity for a writer to express her own thoughts through one central character.

A style that lends itself to order and detail meshes well with legal and medical thrillers. Clarity is important in techno-thrillers, in which a lean, crisp style echoes the technical nature of the subject matter.

Political thrillers offer a chance for keen observation and cutting dialogue with hints of double meaning. A style that's strong on these elements will shine in this category.

All of this said, in the final analysis, an accomplished writer can create a thriller in the any of the eight categories regardless of style. The best advice I ever heard on the subject was to write without thinking about style. Tell the best story you can using the choices that feel most comfortable. Then, when you least expect it, you'll discover you've developed a style all your own.

CHAPTER 15

Words on a Page

Words are writers' tools. We twist them and turn them until we discover the best combinations for each individual endeavor. But the language we choose for our thriller should be more than simply a reflection of our writing styles. Each phrase should become a strand in the webs of suspense we weave to ensnare the unsuspecting reader.

The Name Game

The first words that a reader sees will be your book's title. Yet many writers confess they dread the process of naming their pride and joy. Others find they can't get started on novels until they're satisfied with their working titles.

Many times the decision about a novel's ultimate title will be made by someone other than the author. Publishers' marketing divisions have access to historical sales data a writer never sees. Often, they can tell when a title won't do its intended job of catching readers' attention and giving a hint what lies within.

Mary Willis Walker had to deal with a new title for one of her books: "An excerpt from *All the Dead Lie Down* had already appeared at the end of the paperback edition of *The Red Scream* [another book by Walker] under the title *Midnight Hags*. I thought *Midnight Hags* fit perfectly with the book's subplot about the homeless women story Molly was working on. But when I finally turned the manuscript in, the publisher said they couldn't live with the original title. They were convinced that the book wouldn't sell and they talked me into changing it. . . . So I bowed to the marketing department's expertise. But I still always think of the book as *Midnight Hags*."

Titles cannot be copyrighted. This is why you may see a familiar title by a different author on a bookseller's shelf. Marketing representatives thus have to be alert to the titles recently or about to be published by other houses. Nothing kills a new book's sales faster than an appearance under a title that is too similar to last season's best-seller.

Still, an intriguing, on-the-money title can aid in catching an editor's eye. While the following titles may or may not have been their authors' original choices, consider the intriguing questions they might have raised in their editors' minds.

The Hunt for Red October (Tom Clancy). What's a red October? Who's hunting for it and why? What will happen if they find it?

Lost Angel (Marilyn Wallace). A child must be missing. Who took her? Will the parents get her back?

Blood Work (Michael Connelly). This one must involve murder. By whom? A hit man? A serial killer? Or someone else?

At All Costs (John Gilstrap). What's so important that someone is willing to do anything to protect or preserve it?

Stillwatch (Mary Higgins Clark). What is a stillwatch? Who or what is watching whom? The word itself sounds forbidding.

A Time to Kill (John Grisham). How would someone identify or justify such a time? What happens once the killing is done?

The Red Scream (Mary Willis Walker). What is a red scream? What would cause one?

Each of these titles suggests that the book will contain the element of suspense. Each evokes fear or concern or a sense of unease—exactly what the fans of thrillers look for in a book.

A good title may catch the eye, but it's only a small part of the presentation. What follows are suggestions that can help make your *manuscript* capture that all-important audience of one—an agent or editor.

Revision—Your Ultimate Tool

Many approaches to the art of revision exist.

Some authors prefer multiple drafts, rewriting an entire book anywhere from two to twenty-plus times. Others are more comfortable revising as they go, usually by scene or by chapter.

I fall into this second category. The content and structure of the chapters you've been reading were first revised as each one was completed. Ironically, this one required the most rearranging.

After the book was complete, I reread the entire manuscript several times, doing a series of detailed edits and making additional corrections. All this preceded any final revisions suggested by my editor.

My approach to the revision of my fiction differs somewhat. There I am more concerned with pacing and the rhythm of suspense during my in-progress editing.

At various times I've tried waiting for a complete manuscript before beginning the revision process. Experience has taught me that the material I produce beyond a few unedited chapters is rarely as strong as what winds up on paper when I stick to my normal method.

Regardless of how *you* choose to revise, the process itself is essential to producing a professional manuscript.

Many books are available that address what to look for during revision. My favorite is *Getting the Words Right* by Theodore A. Rees Cheney.

It would be impossible to condense the knowledge contained in an entire reference text into a few pages. The sections that follow, however, outline areas that require special attention when revising a thriller. Also included is an abbreviated course on manuscript preparation.

Content and Structure

These are some of the things you should consider first when revising your work.

• Does your opening raise an alarm, identify a threat or place one or more characters in danger?

• Has your POV remained consistent within every scene?

• Are your characterization and dialogue also consistent?

- Examine the way characters respond at critical moments. Have you previously established a background or character traits that support such reactions? If not, either change their responses or add a scene or exchange of dialogue that justifies whatever it is you need them to do.
- Tape or ask a friend to read passages of dialogue aloud. Do the speech patterns of major characters sound natural or stilted? Is each voice distinctive, or are the words of one interchangeable with several others?
- If your villain's identity is withheld until the end of the book, will things he said earlier spoil that surprise?
- Have you maintained the edge-of-the-seat pacing necessary to the category of suspense you've chosen?
- Are there words or sentences or scenes or chapters that should be cut, revised or rearranged because they don't move the story forward or do so only at the expense of suspense? The worst offenders here are passages of telling.
- Do events transpire in chronological order, or are there scenes out of place that need to be rearranged?
- Is the manuscript a victim of midnovel slump?
- Are there areas that might confuse or mislead the reader, or vague passages that need clarification?
- Does each scene and chapter transition smoothly into the next? Do these transitions promise greater danger, hint that a solution to a problem is at hand or otherwise raise the level of suspense for your reader?
- Have you introduced sufficient subplot threads for the scope of the novel and provided resolutions for each one before the book's climax?
- Did those subplots remain secondary to the main story line throughout the book?
- Has your protagonist achieved her original goal or accepted a logical substitution?
- Will the ending you've chosen satisfy, intrigue or otherwise be accepted by your readers?
- Consider the overall tone of your work. Is it consistent? Or does the book begin with an atmosphere of dark noir, mellow out in the middle, then end with a climax more suited to another category of suspense?

Word Choice

Just as cream rises to the top of a bottle of milk, good writing leaps on the stage and shouts, "Hey! Look at me!"

Avoid clichés and mixed metaphors—such as the ones I just used to open this section. Try to identify words that connect to the setting or a plot element when providing illustrations or making comparisons; for example, a novel with a connection to the water might use the image of the ocean on a moonless night to enhance its atmosphere of suspense.

> *Adam swam steadily against an aggressive current toward the yacht. Pausing to wipe saltwater from his eyes, he treaded water for a moment as he peered into the darkness and listened. If Deaver had posted sentries, Adam couldn't see them. Couldn't hear them either, for that matter. He smiled at the irony.*
>
> *Deaver's thugs weren't the only ones muffled and hidden from view. The ominous clouds that had crowded the horizon at sunset now blacked out the moon and the stars. Rumbles of distant thunder drowned out any sounds from the water.*
>
> *A piece of flotsam surfing on the relentless sea that pounded the shoreline couldn't have been more invisible.*

Readers want to share a character's experiences. Appeal to their senses of taste, touch, smell, sight and hearing whenever possible.

In addition to the images conjured in the above passage—comparing Adam to a bit of debris in the vast ocean—other word choices add to the aura of suspense and conflict and tension.

VERBS

The use of visual, active verbs places readers in the water with Adam. *Muffled and hidden* speak of secrecy. Clouds that *crowded* the horizon suggest a stifling closeness and tension. A moon and stars *blacked out* play on people's fear of blindness and losing their way.

Drowned out echoes the danger inherent in swimming alone on a stormy night. *Surfing* a sea that *pounded* the shore supplies the motion and sound usually experienced in film.

Such verbs also allow readers to share Adam's emotions.

NOUNS

In the same vein, nouns should be concrete, never vague. They should also provide vivid images that flit through readers' minds like frames from a film on the screen.

Yacht brings to mind a level of wealth one doesn't envision with the more generic *boat*. *Saltwater* alerts readers that we're dealing with the sea rather than a river or large lake. It also provides a sensory flavor. *Sentries*, a stronger choice than the mundane *guards*, suggests an intellectual protagonist. *Irony* is a different context than simple amusement.

Deaver's *thugs* sounds more threatening than Deaver's *men* or *hired guns*. *Rumbles of distant thunder* add to the auditory perception achieved by the verbs. *Flotsam*, rather than a specific like *discarded milk jug*, evokes the unknown. The use of *sea* instead of *ocean* adds a touch of the exotic.

If a word choice can do double duty by adding to the atmosphere of suspense or by pinpointing a character's features or personality, so much the better. The fact that Adam can smile and identify an irony within a tense situation speaks volumes about his approach to a challenge. Or to life in general for that matter.

ADJECTIVES

One way to avoid the overuse of adjectives is to make each one as concrete as your nouns and as visual as your verbs.

Aggressive current brings an image not just of motion but of conflict and struggle. *Ominous* clouds underscore the threatening atmosphere. The *relentless* sea emphasizes the tension already present in the situation itself.

ADVERBS

Be stingy with adverbs so the ones you do use can be savored. Swimming *steadily* infers determination, which adds to the reader's understanding of Adam's character.

Avoid adding adverbial tag lines to a character's dialogue. If someone says something angrily or disgustedly, that emotion should be clear to readers in the speaker's choice of words, not in the author's usage of a part of speech.

"You want me to empty my suitcase?" Sadie asked warily.

The next line conveys wariness without the adverbial tag and offers a glimpse of the character's personality as well.

"You don't really expect me to empty my suitcase right here in front of God and everybody, do you?" Sadie asked.

ACRONYMS

Another thing to watch for is the use of acronyms. Readers should have no problem with FBI. But an initial reference to that agency's VICAP unit might momentarily jar some from the story.

Better to refer in narrative to the Violent Criminal Apprehension Program and give a brief description of its duties—the comparison of murder data to identify patterns of serial killings—the first time you use it. After that you can refer to it as VICAP.

Every word in your manuscript has a job to do. Your job is to make sure each one does its best.

Because being conscious of the words they put on the page means reduced time spent on revision, many authors condition themselves to think in strong verbs and concrete nouns as they write.

You can do this as well. The images are already waiting there in your mind. All that's required is a good vocabulary and concentration. After a while the process becomes second nature.

Sentence Structure and Word and Sentence Placement

Sentence structure is another tool a writer can use to create compelling work.

During the revision process check both your narrative and your dialogue closely. Do the majority of your sentences begin with *he, she, it, a, the* or *there?*

Do characters always speak in complete sentences? Is your favorite structure a simple sentence of subject, predicate, object?

If your response is yes, you have your work cut out for you.

In listening to dozens of agents and editors at writers conferences over the years, I've picked up on a common theme. When asked what first caught their attention about a particular author's submission, many give the same response.

"I loved his/her writing."

Publishing is a business. Writers are vendors offering the raw material that will eventually become the product (a book) for a publishing house. Cover artists, copy editors and print designers will mold and shape the final commodity. Marketing people will do their best to get it to the buying public.

But only the writer can influence the acquisition editor's or editorial board's decision to begin production.

Strong plotting and characterization may sway that decision, but it's the words she chooses and the way they're presented that let a writer wedge a foot in the door. If the majority of the writing is lifeless or weak, the other elements may never get the chance to shine.

Good writing has a rhythm all its own. So what can you do beyond careful word choice, vivid characterization and sound plotting to strengthen your writing?

- Find a good book on English grammar and review the basics.
- Vary the length and structure of your sentences. Begin some with an adverbial or prepositional phrase. Break unusually long sentences into two separate ones.
- Reveal strong emotion and fast-paced action in short sentences for maximum impact. These are at their most powerful when used as one-sentence paragraphs.
- Make use of compound sentences and subjects. Begin with a verb or verb phrase now and then.
- Start several sentences in a row with the same forceful word or phrase for emphasis. For example: Nothing had prepared her for this nightmare. Nothing her momma warned her about even came close. Nothing they threw at her during her academy training had covered being buried alive. Nothing at all.

- Include an occasional string of descriptive words, phrases or sentences. For example: The blond cop was tearing the sheets from one of the twin beds—Lexie's bed—prodding bulges in the mattress, poking his fingers through the worn spots in her stuffed animals, squeezing their insides, then tossing them onto the floor.

- Search for passages where calculated placement of the word choices discussed in the previous section can reinforce or enhance the suspense in your manuscript.

- Emphasize what's important by placing a key word at or near the end of a sentence. Compare the difference between the following two sentence constructions.

> *If everyone in the small town already believed Casey was capable of murder, how would her lawyer find an impartial juror?*

> *How would Casey's lawyer find an impartial juror if everyone in the small town already believed Casey was capable of murder?*

Casey is obviously the heroine of the piece. While her trial may be at the heart of the plot, the emphasis at this point should be on the accusation against her. Thus the question of her character, not jury selection, should be the focal point of the sentence.

- Placement considerations also apply to sentences within paragraphs. Foreshadowing would normally be buried among other information. A fact that requires a reader's attention works best at either the beginning or the end. Startling revelations usually call for emphasis and thus should be the last sentence in a paragraph.

- A paragraph that consists of a single sentence at the beginning or ending of a chapter can make a powerful statement.

Opening chapter paragraph:

> *Erin Welch waited until her husband stopped struggling, then removed the plastic bread bag from his face and made herself a peanut butter and banana sandwich.*

Ending chapter paragraph:

The man in the ski mask levered the lid of the old cistern into place, plunging her damp and frightening world into darkness.

Nitty-Gritty Details

Often it's the little things that cause a manuscript to look less than professional and label its author an amateur. What follows is a checklist of the things that should be reviewed as part of your final revision.

Spelling. Take nothing for granted. Don't rely on spell check. Computers can't always catch proper usage and can't tell the difference between similar words such as *to, too* and *two* or *rain, rein* and *reign.*

Punctuation. This can be tricky because the rules for some situations (such as the use of commas in series) have evolved over the past few decades. Rules can also vary between publishing houses. Your best bet? Choose a stylebook, such as *The Chicago Manual of Style,* and then be consistent.

Pronoun antecedents. If there's any chance that readers might confuse whom a *he, she, his* or *hers* refers to, repeat the character's name. Even if you just used it in the previous sentence. Or restructure the sentence to clarify the antecedent.

Misplaced modifiers. A misplaced modifier is a word or phrase whose placement in a sentence results in an ambiguity. For example, "The villain was described as a bald man with a pock-marked face weighing a hundred and ninety pounds." (Surprising he could carry out a crime with that much weight on his shoulders, isn't it?)

Some writers have a blind spot about misplaced modifiers. I have a friend who begins every critique session with a plea to watch for the darn things. She definitely knows her own weakness. We always find at least one. If you're dyslexic, as she is, you too might need someone else's help.

Correct and consistent verb tenses. Be especially alert to abuses of tense in connection with flashbacks.

Remember, the general rule is to switch to the past perfect tense to signal the *beginning* of a flashback. Use past tense while *in* the flashback. Then use the past perfect tense to alert readers that the flashback is *ending* before switching to the tense you've chosen for the story in progress.

> *It was happening the same way it had five weeks ago, Jonah thought. Except then the man had worn a Phillies ball cap. This one had a tiger on it. Probably Detroit.*
>
> *The last time, Jonah* had thought *at first that the man was the same guy Mom* had talked *to on parents night at school. Especially after the man asked how she was.*
>
> *The man knew about Jonah's dog and about the rosebush at the end of the porch that Aunt Jen had run over when she backed up the car. He knew about a lot of things, and he had a nice laugh. At least he did until Jonah said he didn't want to get into the man's truck to look at some special pictures. That's when the man* had stopped *laughing.*
>
> *He wasn't laughing now, either. And Jonah was more scared than he'd ever been in all his seven years.*

The unitalicized verbs in the above passage indicate the tense changes going into and out of the flashback.

Tricky verbs. Watch, too, for the incorrect usage of words such as *lie* and *lay*; *put* and *place*; or *affect* and *effect*.

Who Said Looks Don't Count?

Some things should go without saying. They should, but they can't. You might be shocked by some of the submissions agents and editors receive every week.

Handwritten manuscripts on ruled paper. Lavender cover letters doused in White Diamonds. Quarter-inch margins. Single spacing. Ornate fonts in fourteen or, worse, in five-point type. Stream-of-consciousness ramblings. Typeovers. Passages crossed out by hand or deleted with correction fluid.

Must I go on?

Experienced authors will be familiar with the following manuscript preparation guidelines. For novice writers and those who need a review, here are the basics.

- Double-space text using twelve-point courier type on twenty-pound white bond paper. Leave one- or one-and-one-quarter-inch margins at top, at bottom and on each side. Do not right-justify text.

- Use black toner in your ink-jet or laser printer, and reprint any pages that contain smudges. Dot matrix submissions are acceptable only if produced by a letter-quality machine. If you use a typewriter, begin with a new ribbon and replace it at the first sign that the ink is fading.

- Except for the manuscript's first page, a header consisting of the book's title in caps followed by your last name (e.g., THE POET/Connelly) should appear in the upper left-hand corner of each page. Your top margin should be measured from this header.

- Pages should be numbered consecutively in the upper right-hand corner on the same line as the header. Do not number the title page or the first page of the first chapter.

- Chapter one should begin one-third of the way down from the top of the page. Subsequent chapters should begin four to six lines from the top. Each chapter should begin on a new page.

For a more detailed look at manuscript preparation, I recommend *Formatting and Submitting Your Manuscript* by Jack and Glenda Neff, Don Prues and the editors of *Writer's Market*.

After you complete the revision routines, put the manuscript aside. Work on another project. Remind your significant other that he's the most important person in your life. Take the kids to the park. Plan next year's vacation. Go to a movie.

At the end of a week or ten days, reread your thriller with a critical eye to all the things I've discussed in this chapter. Then, if—and only if—you still believe the book is your very best effort, it's time to plot your submission strategy.

CHAPTER 16

The Mechanics of Submission

N ow that you have a completed, heart-stopping, letter-perfect manuscript on your desk, what's your next step?

You have an important choice to make. Consider the options carefully. You've waited a long time for this moment. Don't rush things now.

Whom should you approach first, an agent or an editor? And once you've settled that issue, where do you find the right one for both you *and* your thriller?

David vs. Goliath

The reference books writers most often consult for information about literary agents and publishing houses are *Literary Market Place* (*LMP*) and *Writer's Market*. Both the *Guide to Literary Agents* and *Novel & Short Story Writer's Market* can also be helpful.

You should be able to find the annual *LMP* in the reference section of your library. Availability of the other three may vary, although most libraries also carry the annual *Writer's Market*. And, while the cost of owning your own copy of *LMP* may be prohibitive (over three hundred dollars retail), copies of the other books are reasonably priced.

Scan the "Book Publishers" section of any of these works and you quickly notice one thing: Most of the entries contain the notation "no unsolicited mss" or "agented material only." A few even state "no unsolicited queries."

Unfortunately, the days of "over-the-transom" or "slush pile" sales have become as obsolete as manual typewriters. You may use a typewriter, but locating a replacement for a broken platen or key and a repairman to install it could mean hours away from your writing. Multiply that by about one hundred and you'll have some idea of what you face if you choose to submit directly to publishers without an agent.

The reasons for this are many, but one is that the number of submissions has increased dramatically in recent years. And sadly, poorly written manuscripts far exceed quality material.

The bottom line—in the literal sense—is that publishers can't afford to mine all those lumps of coal in the hope of unearthing a single diamond.

Editors are extremely busy people. Contrary to what you might think, editing is only a small portion of their duties. Shepherding purchased properties through the production process takes up most of an editor's day. Editorial and sales meetings. Cover art and typestyle discussions. Phone negotiations with agents. Calls from authors who need to discuss editorial comments. The list goes on and on.

Editors skip lunches, work late and often take their work home. The only time most of them have to look at unsolicited material is on the ride home or during the few moments before they fall exhausted into their beds.

Those who stick with the job do so because they love what they do. An editor loves discovering a manuscript that might become the company's next best-seller. But the fastest route to that discovery is via agented manuscripts. Literary agents act as a filter. In truth, until a contract has been signed, many editors prefer to work directly with agents.

The People Who Work the Mines: Agents

One of the first requirements for becoming an agent is an ability to identify that sparkling gem among the lumps of coal. Another is knowledge of the various publishing houses and which editor within each of those houses is looking for what. A third qualification is savvy negotiating skills.

An agent who consistently touted the work of unskilled or unprepared writers would soon find his phone calls were not being returned.

Just as editors are busy people, however, so are agents.

This may sound as if the major characters in this drama that controls your career aren't looking for new players. If you think that, you're wrong. Getting an agent to look at your work is not mission impossible. Some editors do occasionally look at unsolicited manuscripts. Most still accept unsolicited queries, although an assistant almost always screens these.

Still, your best bet is to interest an agent in your work.

Agents do the marketing so you can keep writing. They brave the minefield of contract negotiation. They handle or can arrange for subsidiary rights, such as magazine serialization, foreign-language translations and the sale of movie or TV rights.

An agent also acts as a buffer between you and the publishing world, in which editors are apt to play musical desks between houses. Having to deal with a different teller at your bank every few months may be annoying. Changing editors in the midst of the publication process is a bit more unsettling. (I went through three with my first book.)

The key is getting the right agent to look at your work.

You have three choices.

1. Meet and talk with agents in person.

2. Be introduced to agents by someone whose judgment they trust.

3. Submit queries to agents who are actively seeking clients *who write what you write.*

Those last five words are important. An agent who is not well versed in a particular genre will have a harder time selling that type of work.

Some agents deal with nonfiction or literary novels only. Others may exclude specialized genres, such as science fiction and fantasy. Most of those who handle commercial fiction, however, are familiar with a variety of genres. Large agencies may have several agents whose clients write within the same genre.

Still, agents' best publishing contacts will be in their areas of interest. While someone who handles primarily romance novels and women's fiction will know editors who work exclusively with true crime and hard-boiled detective fiction, such connections will probably not be as wide ranging.

Submitting a *good* query, as opposed to a bad or even mediocre one, can mean the difference between achieving your goal of representation and struggling on in your search. John Gilstrap can speak to this from experience: "My first novel, *Nathan's Run*, wasn't a terribly hard sell once I found an agent, but I'd previously been rejected by twenty-seven agents. My problem was in writing bad query letters. Once I finally got the synopsis and the rest of the package right, I got interest from four agents at once. I went with the one that I perceived to be the most powerful, and she sold it the first time out. I had a book deal, the first foreign deal and a movie deal all within six days of finding an agent."

A Match Made in Heaven

No matter how experienced an agent is with suspense, she still may not be the right person to handle your book.

The relationship between author and agent is in many ways similar to a marriage. Just as a chain-smoking lug who lives for the next telecast of World Wide Wrestling would be a dubious match for a teetotaling cat lover who enjoys ballet and the opera, the compatibility of your agent's personality and your own is important.

Every agent has her own style. Some prefer to keep things on a business level. Others foster a closer relationship, suggesting story lines or asking for specific revisions before marketing a particular book.

I have a friend whose agent insisted her romance manuscript be cut by over a hundred pages before submission. Discussions about which characters and scenes or minor subplots might best be eliminated ensued. Although certain she was making a mistake, my friend complied with her agent's request. Soon after the revised book was submitted, she signed a multibook contract.

The original work was perfectly paced. It contained colorful characters, a historically authentic setting and rich dialogue that read as if the speakers had stepped out of the period in question. None of this was harmed by the revisions.

Why was the agent so adamant about the book's length?

She knew that the highly specialized subgenre of romance my friend was writing for targets a specific word count. Books in that subgenre are also never considered candidates for "breakout" status to a longer mainstream novel.

Another agent, though equally competent, might not have taken such a hands-on approach to that particular problem.

Regardless of how you've chosen an agent to approach, never submit a complete manuscript unless you have been told to do so, either by the agent himself or through his listing in one of the books I mentioned above. Even in the second situation, querying first is often your best bet.

Up Close and Personal

The best way to meet and talk with an agent in person is to attend a writers conference or workshop. *Writer's Digest* magazine prints a by-state listing of such events in its May issue every year. The annual *Guide to Literary Agents* also lists conferences. Local colleges and universities can be a good source of information as well.

Another helpful on-line resource is the ShawGuides, located at www.shaw guides.com. This site allows you to search conferences by state, type or date. Links to each listing provide basic information and often E-mail addresses for requesting brochures.

Look for conference formats that focus on commercial fiction. Most conference workshops offer tips for improving writing skills; those focusing on literary fiction may not address marketing and publication issues.

Study the theme of the event. Conferences often emphasize different genres from year to year, romance or children's writing this year, nonfiction or mystery/suspense the next. Verify which, if any, attending agents handle suspense.

Don't let cost be your only determining factor. This is an investment in your writing career. Ask another writer to share travel expenses or the cost of a room. Sometimes organizers can put attendees in touch with others looking for roommates.

Even if you don't meet the right agent at the first conference you attend, you'll learn a lot about your craft. You'll also make contact with people who might help you in the future. When they do, be sure to return the favor or pass it on to another beginner.

Many conferences provide limited one-on-one time with attending agents. Even when they don't, participants are encouraged to visit between sessions and share luncheon or dinner tables. Asking who is writing what is a common opening for mealtime conversation.

Assert yourself, but don't be *too* aggressive. Offering to buy an agent a cup of coffee or a drink in the bar is OK. So is politely asking if they might have a moment before or after the day's sessions to discuss your work. Cornering one in the bathroom will make an impression, but not the one you want.

If the agent doesn't have time to talk to you, thank them politely, then ask if they would be open to a query. Exchange business cards. A mention in your query letter that you talked briefly at the XYZ conference probably won't jog their memory. It *might* result in a request to see a synopsis or opening chapters, however.

Not sure what else a query letter should include? Many books on writing, including *Formatting and Submitting Your Manuscript* which I mentioned in chapter fifteen, provide instructions and examples of query letters. An excellent source for instruction on writing a synopsis is contained in Evan Marshall's *The Marshall Plan for Novel Writing*.

Have a sample of your work available in case you manage to arrange an impromptu meeting with an agent. *Don't take it out unless the agent asks if you have something with you.* And never suggest they might like to read it in their room or on the plane home. They'll be reading all right, but it will be work they brought with them.

Aggressiveness is out, but this isn't the time for shrinking violets either. I speak from experience.

A Case History

I was still unpublished in 1990 when I attended a conference in Dallas that featured open critique sessions. This was my second time at the event, but reading aloud to a room full of strangers proved no easier than the previous year.

Nevertheless, when the session ended, the published author who had acted as moderator called me over. She asked if I'd spoken to any agents or editors about what I'd just read. When I admitted I was too unsure of myself to approach anyone, she offered the most encouraging words I'd heard up to that moment.

"Trish, I think your work is marketable."

Then she introduced me to the agent she was hosting as part of her conference duties and told him he should talk to me about the book I was working on. She also made sure I sat at their lunch table. Luckily our other table mates were good conversationalists. I was too intimidated to say much during the meal.

When the meal was over, my new mentor pointedly mentioned that there was plenty of time before the next session to have that chat. Thankfully, the agent was used to awestruck writers and graciously agreed.

Even though I had been too timid to initiate the meeting, I knew the proper procedure. I was carrying a folder with the first several chapters of my novel. The agent asked if he could flip through a few pages as we talked.

He liked my writing. I liked him. Six months later I sent him a polished version of the manuscript we'd discussed. Three months after that, we signed a representation agreement.

As it turned out, he wasn't able to sell that first book, but the tone of the rejections it received were encouraging. Two books later he did sell *Someone to Watch Over* and an unwritten novel that became *Buried Secrets*—to an editor at Dell who'd written one of those initial rejections.

The agent's name was Evan Marshall and he still represents my work. It was through his recommendation that I submitted the proposal that resulted in the contract for this book. And yes, he's the same Evan Marshall whose own instructional text can teach you how to write a novel as well as a synopsis.

My purpose in sharing this story is not to infer that my work was better than any of the other aspiring writers at that year's conference. Or that I was unusually lucky. I know of at least one other author who met her agent at that same function.

The point is that attending such gatherings and networking with others within the profession is one of the best ways to find representation.

Writers as a whole are a supportive group. Those you meet will know agents. Members of critique groups whose own work has been published will know agents. Workshop presenters often know agents. Contacts you make in business circles outside the writing venue may even know an agent, or someone else who does.

My introduction to my agent might seem serendipitous. But the woman who acted as my mentor, and is now my friend, was a stranger at the time. *She* did not convince my agent that I was worthy of representation. My work did that. She was simply the catalyst that put us together and encouraged me to speak.

Many years, much study and lots of hard work brought me to that point in time. A year earlier my book wasn't finished. The day of that writing conference it was still a diamond in the rough. But six months later, when it reached Evan's desk, it was the best manuscript I could produce at the time.

Both my work and I were ready and I took the right steps. *That* is the reason I found representation.

Learn to write well. Write the best book you possibly can. And be sure it's ready to be seen before seeking representation.

Agents you meet at conferences who express interest in your work simply need to be reminded of where and when you talked. Do this in the opening sentence of your query letter.

Use the same procedure here for identifying an agent who handles suspense as you would for one you might hope to approach at a conference.

Look also for a notation of membership in the Association of Authors' Representatives (AAR). AAR is a self-policing organization that mandates certain professional and ethical standards for its members; for example, charging fees for reading or evaluating material is prohibited.

The lack of a membership in AAR does not mean that an agency is not reputable. It is simply a point to consider as part of your research.

When corresponding with an agent you've never met about representing your work, follow the guidelines provided in her *LMP* or *Guide to Literary Agents* listing. Some request query letters only. Others want a query, a synopsis and the first three chapters.

Once you've chosen the agent you want to approach, it's time to send a query letter.

Querying more than one agent at a time is often OK. But be sure to state that you are doing so in each query letter. You should also check the listing for each agency to be certain none contain the phrase "no simultaneous queries."

Now what about those editors I mentioned earlier—the ones who still occasionally look at unsolicited material? What are the coordinates for traveling that route?

Doing Whatever It Takes

Editors do sometimes look at unagented material if authors they already publish or friends or other industry professionals recommend the works. Editors also attend writers conferences. Follow the same guidelines for approaching an editor in that setting as you would for an agent.

But while it's nice to be able to meet editors and agents face-to-face, many successful business relationships have been forged through only written correspondence. When this is your only recourse, these are the steps you should follow to submit a query to an editor.

1. Identify listings for those houses that list thrillers or one of our eight categories of suspense among their fiction needs. Eliminate those that contain the notation "no unsolicited mss or queries."

2. Check the "Small Presses" section for the same information. These markets pay less and publish fewer books than the big conglomerates, but they're often more open to new authors. In addition, their editors usually give more personal attention to those writers they do sign. Both Tom Clancy and John Grisham began their careers at small presses.

3. Make a list of the publishers you've identified in steps one and two.

4. Choose the one that looks most promising, and identify the editor who handles the type of book that you've written. If this information doesn't appear in the listing, call the publisher, request the editorial department and ask whoever answers for the name of the suspense editor. *Be sure to ask for the spelling of the editor's name.* Nothing turns an editor off quicker than discovering a writer wasn't professional enough to verify the proper spelling.

5. Prepare a one-page, single-spaced query letter that contains a brief (one-paragraph) description of your book. Also note its length and target audience, for example, fans of Mary Higgins Clark's women-in-jeopardy suspense. Add any credentials that apply, such as publication in a related field or work qualifications, for example, an M.D. or R.N. degree if you've written a medical thriller. *Query only one editor at a time.*

6. Include a self-addressed stamped envelope (SASE) with your query. Many authors now also include self-addressed stamped postcards (SASP) that request acknowledgment of receipt. *Do not use certified or registered mail for your query.* Signing for such mail takes up the staff's valuable time and labels the writer as an amateur.

7. Check the response time listed in your reference material, add two or three weeks to that time and mark your calendar accordingly.

8. If you haven't heard anything by the time the projected date rolls around, send a polite inquiry asking if your previous correspondence was received. If, after another three weeks, you still haven't gotten a response, move on to the next name on your list. (I never said this route was the fastest way to travel.)

Even submissions addressed to the proper editor may be screened by an editorial assistant. Sometimes this can be a blessing. Assistants are editors-in-training. They watch closely for properties that might reflect favorably on their own editorial skills.

Going Back to Square One

Your query or the material an agent or editor has requested is in the mail. What comes next may be the hardest step on the road to publication. The wait for a response is going to seem like the longest wait in the history of humankind. Longer even than the months that lead up to the birth of a child. At least with a pregnancy you have a fairly narrow ETA.

Is there anything you can do while you wait for a response?

Yes, there is. Start another book. Don't tinker with the one you just finished. Move on to something new. Each book is a learning process. The next can only be better than the previous.

And don't despair if the one in the mail isn't the one that eventually sells. I have three on my own shelf that didn't.

A friend has seven manuscripts that never quite made the grade. But the eighth launched a career that has earned her glowing reviews, at least one national award and an option for the film rights to one book from the director of one of the hottest movies of the past decade. Not to mention the kind of income many of us can only daydream about.

Someone with more confidence than I had at that long-ago conference asked Evan about his procedures for responding to requested submissions. He said that if he didn't believe he could sell a manuscript, he sent a letter to that effect. When a novel excited him, he called the author.

Regardless of which path your writing takes you down, I wish you God-speed. I also suggest you keep a chair near your phone at all times.

The reason for this is that a chair makes a better landing pad than does the floor on the day you answer your phone and hear the agent of your choice say, "_____, this is _____ from the XYZ Agency. I'd like to represent your work."

In the meantime, turn to part two of *Writing the Thriller* to hear what some of the experts in the field of suspense have to say about their work.

Part II

Interviews With the Experts

⚜

AUTHOR'S NOTE

Reading the works of authors who write thrillers is one step toward understanding the genre. Speaking directly with such authors provides valuable insight into how an individual writer crafts a suspense novel, how a particular plot is conceived and developed. But opportunities to ask in-depth questions are rare. After all, most of these busy people spend their time actually doing all those things you'd like to ask them about.

In the following interviews, I tried to ask the questions I thought you, as aspiring suspense writers, would ask. Many are questions I wished I had been able to ask on my own way to publication. In an effort to avoid general topics, my queries were constructed around what I perceived as each author's special strengths. Not surprisingly, many responses led to new and even more revealing areas of discussion. I hope you enjoy—and learn from—them all.

For easier reading, the questions themselves have been stripped away.

Writing Crime-Based Psychological Suspense

Lucian Truscott IV in the *Los Angeles Times Review* may have said it most succinctly: "Sheesh! This guy can write a thriller!" He was referring to Michael Connelly's sixth novel, *The Poet*. Such has been the praise for Connelly's work since he began his writing career.

Connelly attended the University of Florida before working as a newspaper reporter in Florida and for the *Los Angeles Times*. While in Florida, he and two co-authors were finalists for a Pulitzer prize for feature writing. His first novel, *The Black Echo*, introduced tormented and complex LAPD detective Hieronymus "Harry" Bosch. It also won the Mystery Writers of America's Edgar Award for best first novel of 1993.

Although generally touted as crime novels, the Bosch series, which now numbers six, reads as much like suspense as Connelly's stand-alone psychological thrillers *The Poet* and the more recent *Blood Work*. Atmosphere and a depth of character account for much of this. As does Connelly's eye for detail and flair for language.

Connelly lives in Los Angeles with his wife and daughter.

Stand-Alone or Series Book?

There are two main factors that influence my decision as to whether a story idea should be a one-shot thriller rather than a series novel. As a writer I'm most fascinated with exploring my Harry Bosch character over a period of many years and in different situations. My goal is to keep him fresh and interesting. To do that I have to step away from him every now and then, so often I'll do a stand-alone based on that.

The second factor has to do with story. When I have an idea for a plot, I look at the main character in that idea and consider what I'm going to put that character through. If the changes or the questions the character will confront are not appropriate for Harry Bosch, the book becomes a stand-alone.

For example, in *Blood Work* the main character is recovering from a heart transplant. The idea for the story came when a friend went through the same process—waiting for the heart, surgery in 1993 and then the recovery. I was with him during all that, and I knew back then that I wanted to write this story.

It took me a while to come up with an idea; and then once I had the plot, I had to decide if this was something I wanted to put Harry through. Would it be a good story for him? I decided it wouldn't because I deal a lot in metaphors in my writing. I felt that in the four Harry Bosch books I had written up to that time, I had created this guy who had a good heart, a noble heart. I didn't like the idea of him having to get a new one.

It's always a challenge to go from Harry Bosch to a new stand-alone character. The book I'm writing now is a double challenge because it's the first time I've written from the feminine point of view. And not only is my protagonist a woman, she's also a criminal. I usually write from the investigator's point of view.

The Writing Environment

I've set myself up for a lot of new things with this book; therefore I wanted a new environment for my writing. A lot of this story takes place in Las Vegas, so I've gone there a few times and holed up in a hotel and written on my laptop. I've also been renting hotel rooms in Los Angeles and just writing. This change in routine has helped break me away from the mind-set of having written Harry Bosch and other male character books.

Research

The FBI gave me almost no cooperation when I was writing *The Poet*. If you read the book, you probably know why. [*The Poet*'s newsman protagonist manages to muscle his way inside a federal investigation. Due to plot considerations, the characterizations of some agents might be described as less than flattering.]

I was allowed to call one person in Quantico and ask him questions, but I wasn't permitted to go there. Most of what I wrote on the subject was drawn from what I would call paper research through databases, libraries and books. Many books about FBI profiling contain sample profiles. What you need in terms of tactics and that kind of thing is always out there. Sometimes it just takes a little digging.

Most of the crimes or the themes or plotlines in my books are really about how cases work on cops as opposed to how cops work on cases; therefore, the cop is more important than the case.

You still have to have some personal contact with some cops to capture their world, even if it's by osmosis. You need to hear how they talk and so forth because the police, especially detectives, are a different breed than most people you know.

Even though I write about LAPD cops and FBI agents, cops from all over the country come to my book signings or E-mail me to say they're willing to help. By and large, law enforcement people, including the FBI, are in a very insular world. They don't think the people outside that world understand it or the pressures they're under or the tactics they have to use; therefore, they're willing to try to help change that.

And it's not like they're saying I got it wrong. A lot of times they're saying, "You got it right, but if you ever need any help, keep my E-mail address." The image of the cop as being some guy who's not interested in helping writers I don't think is really correct. Most writers I know who have sought help from police departments have gotten it.

Characterization

If a character is worthy enough to be at the center of a scene or chapter or a particular plot point in a book, you gotta give him his due. Kurt Vonnegut once said to make sure every character wants something, even if it's only a glass of water, because if somebody wants something you're helping to delineate her character. I try to keep that in my mind when I'm creating characters.

Another thing I try to do is keep the idea that the story is moving forward *and* backward at any given time. It's obviously moving forward because the plot is carrying it forward. But you should always—and this takes a lot of finesse so it doesn't stop that forward movement—be dropping in things about characters that start filling out their back stories. As you're moving forward through the story, you're also learning about this person's life, so in that way you're moving backward.

That's one of the hardest things to do as a writer. You can't suddenly put in two paragraphs about how a character did something growing up, because it stops the forward movement dead.

For example, in *The Black Ice*, one of my Bosch books, Harry is on his back deck and he sees a brush fire on the hill across Topanga Pass. This is setting up the motif of fire that's going to carry on through the story; so we're starting to move forward.

Harry sees the helicopters moving in and dropping water to put out the fire. And he recalls how the helicopters' unsteady flight (because of the weight of the water) reminds him of the helicopters lifting off in Vietnam full of people during the evacuation and how they also flew unsteadily. In the book the memory comes to him very quickly, in one line, and then we go back to the forward movement of the story, the fire.

In that one line you learn this guy was in Vietnam and that he has memories that are still very fresh, but then the narrative goes on and keeps moving forward. Now if I'd said it reminded him of Vietnam and then described the time he got shot and he got the Purple Heart, I would have stopped the story before it even got started.

The Process of Writing

To me, the best part of writing is when I'm not actually at the keyboard but I'm thinking and planning. And a lot of that has to do with the character. This probably sounds weird, but I really like it when I'm going to bed at night, when the light's out and my head's on the pillow and I start thinking about what I want to write the next day and running the characters through my mind. I just really enjoy that aspect of writing.

When I wrote *The Poet*, I wasn't a father. I'm pretty sure I would not want to write from the point of view of a villain like that one now that I am. But my latest Bosch book also deals with pedophilia, not in a large context like *The Poet* but as feed for a crime, and it's probably the darkest book I've ever written. And that puzzles me. I have this wonderful new thing in my life and I think my life has improved so much in the last few years; and yet I've written my darkest book during that time.

So what's going on? I don't really know, but I think maybe in writing, your subliminal fears come out. Or perhaps you excise them by writing about them. I think writing itself is a mystery and if we knew all the answers we wouldn't have to write anymore.

On Outlining a Novel

I've outlined only three of my nine books: my first and *The Poet* and the one I'm working on now. In my mind I knew what the genesis of the other stories would be and where they would end up, and I just let things go to see what happened in between.

That's when you get into subplot lines that sometimes go the wrong way and then fizzle out. In the first draft of *Blood Work*, I went the wrong way at the beginning and ended up throwing out 240 pages and just starting over. That's the price you pay for not carefully outlining a book.

It wasn't as if those pages totally went down the drain. There's usually a lot of stuff that I can use over. Every book is a learning process. The good side is that I enjoy it more when I'm not working off an outline. I think it's a purer sense of writing; therefore it's more fulfilling.

The Thriller's Place in the Scheme of Things

There's a school of thought that says thrillers and crime novels are second-class fiction. That doesn't really bother me because I've been reading crime fiction since I was reading books and I've always found more fulfillment from them than from reading the classics. Especially today, I think that it's in crime novels where you get the most comment on contemporary society. The really good writers of this genre are the ones who are reflecting back contemporary life, and I think that's good. There may always be a bias against crime novels, but as a whole I think the genre is getting more literary.

In *The Last Coyote*, Harry Bosch is trying to make his way in the city after a debilitating earthquake and riots, and I think that I gave an accurate portrait of what Los Angeles was like back then. I believe when people read it, it gave them an understanding of what was going on in this community, whether they lived here or in Kansas.

I think the crime genre can also act as a warning about society's ills, either what is coming up, what is happening now or what we're on the edge of. For example, the organization of pedophile groups through the Internet—you won't read about that in standard fiction.

The Poet was fiction but what happened in that book was stuff that has actually happened. A thriller is obviously meant to entertain, but at the same time it also says to people who read it: Look, this is what's happening out there.

Writing as an Art

In my books there are references to the art of painting, paintings in particular, and painters. Hieronymus "Harry" Bosch is named after a fifteenth-century painter. I often feel sort of painterly when I'm working on my characters. I see the building of character in terms of brushstrokes of nuance and detail, the adding of little strokes here and there.

I love reading about painters and then studying their work, looking at their brushwork. And I feel there is some kinship in the process of building a character in a novel. You add small strokes here and there as you go through the book, and when you get to the end your canvas should be complete. Your character should be recognizable to the reader.

This can extend, of course, past the character to the place you are writing about. One reason I used the name Hieronymus Bosch for the character who moves through most of my books is that I viewed him as the tool with which I would delineate, or "paint," the landscape of contemporary Los Angeles.

Building seems to be in my blood. My grandfather and father were house builders for a time. When I went to the University of Florida, I was actually on a track to get a degree in building construction. Then several things, including the discovery of Raymond Chandler's books, influenced me to switch to journalism. Now I build stories instead of houses.

Writing Action-Adventure

Armchair Detective reviewer Ronald C. Miller once described Dirk Pitt as having "the archeological background of Indiana Jones and the boldness of James Bond." Talking with Pitt's creator Clive Cussler is like chatting with that intrepid hero of fourteen (and still counting) action-adventure novels.

Both men have searched for lost aircraft and led expeditions to find famous shipwrecks. Both are involved with NUMA (National Underwater & Marine Agency). Both collect classic automobiles. In fact, it's sometimes difficult to tell where Cussler ends and his fictional character begins. Cussler's love of the sea and his expensive hobbies provided the catalyst for the creation of alter ego Dirk Pitt.

In novels such as *Raise the Titanic*, the more recent *Flood Tide* and the biographical *The Sea Hunters*, Cussler's style is that of a fun-loving, hard-drinking old salt perched on a stool sharing tall tales with his cronies. Exactly the type of character Pitt might run across in some rundown maritime tavern.

A former award-winning advertising executive, Cussler and his wife, Barbara, divide their time between homes in Colorado and Arizona. Married in 1955, the couple has three grown children.

The Evolution of an Author

I said in a recent book dedication that my children grew up with a father who never grew up. When I think about it, that's a pretty good prerequisite for writing action-adventure novels.

As an only child I was lucky to grow up in a neighborhood with several other boys my age. When the other fellows were around, we'd build tree houses and clubhouses. We'd dig caves and build cities out of mud. We'd build ships in vacant lots and play pirate. We were always busy doing something.

I remember having hay fields behind our houses, which was unusual because we were just six miles from Los Angeles. Even though we were only about ten at the time, we heaved those big bales of hay around and built French Foreign Legion forts and pretended we were in the Sahara. We fought imaginary Indians or Japanese and Germans (this was during the war years).

Plotting novels is just an adult extension of those times.

The Development of a Series Character

My first Dirk Pitt novel was published in 1973. There are fourteen now, all still in print. They've dealt with everything from immigration problems and threats of chemical war to overpopulation and social and political concerns. Many of the books were published several years in advance of those issues becoming hot topics. Even so, each book was set from two to ten years beyond its copyright date.

The primary reason I did that was because I remember rereading some of the early James Bond books by Ian Fleming and finding them terribly dated. So I thought, I'll just put mine a few years into the future. That way, when Pitt uses technology we don't quite have yet but will have some day, nobody will tell me the books are boring.

Technology's Place in Action-Adventure

Pitt's technology is never too far out. He doesn't have gadgets to save his life like secret agents do in the movies. I try to have him be very imaginative in devising things. Once he built a type of ancient catapult. He's made a compass with a silk scarf and a pin out of his cummerbund. In other words, he's resourceful. The only time I get into technical stuff is with something like the iridium satellite phone Pitt used in *Flood Tide*, which Motorola is perfecting and should have very soon.

Because his specialty is underwater recovery, I do stretch the technology that deals with that area a bit. In *Dragon* he was working on an underwater project and they were using these tractors that could move around on the bottom of the ocean. I expect those will be a reality someday.

I explain most of the technology I do use in dialogue rather than go into great detail. Action-adventure readers don't want a technical manual. A lot of people aren't into that. I also have a lot of young readers, and they don't like it either.

Identifying a Readership

I actually get lots of letters from schoolteachers and mothers who like the fact that my books have no sex and no four-letter words. I do have a lot of violence, but they seem to overlook that. I don't see any reason to put in graphic sex. I mean, if Dirk Pitt has his way with a woman, they go into the bedroom. All that action happens offstage like in the old thirties movies.

I never get into religion, but that's a personal preference. And Pitt might say, "Oh, my God," in a crisis, but that's as far as I take it. Other writers go much farther. It comes down to knowing your readership or target audience.

Pitt is really a throwback. He waves the flag. He believes in mothers and apple pie, and he helps little old ladies across the street. And then he blows the villain's head off without blinking an eye. I would say he's kind of an old-fashioned Errol Flynn-type hero. I made him that way on purpose.

Developing a Plot

Often, current events can trigger my imagination. I usually start with a concept, a "what if" concept as most authors do. It could be a newspaper article [that triggers the concept]. I read and get a lot of magazines based on oceanography and underwater technology and so forth. It's usually the factual articles are the most interesting.

I remember I'd just stumbled onto a page about Chinese immigration in some text and then, when my wife and I visited Vancouver, the whole airport was filled with Chinese. Out of that came *Flood Tide.*

My wife and I used to go down to the Tucson Gem Show, and it was always fun to look at all the gemstones. That got me interested in diamonds and reading about what a fraud they basically are. The public and women have been brainwashed by the big mining corporations into thinking diamonds are forever, but an emerald is fifty to seventy-five times more rare than a diamond. So all that became a background for *Shock Wave*.

Restrictions That Apply to a Series Character

Shock Wave was the book where I killed the heroine off. And, oh, I got all kinds of nasty letters on that. But I did it because Pitt's gotta continue on with another love life in the next book. I often get letters from ladies that say, "Why don't you let him marry Lauren Smith [the congresswoman who goes in and out of every other book]?" And I say it wouldn't work. Because can you imagine Al Giordino [Pitt's buddy] coming to Pitt's house and asking his wife if Dirk can come out and play?

There have been a lot of times where it looked like I killed Pitt off, but I always resurrect him. In *Dragon* it wasn't until the last two paragraphs. That time the letters said, "You SOB, I thought for sure you'd were going to do it this time."

Endings and Experimentation

Action-adventure readers really look for that happy ending. Obviously the villains can never get away with it, and you can't have children blown up or anything.

I love to do things other authors don't do; it's just fun to me. I'd heard of a case where an author had his own dialogue with his antagonist, so in *Dragon* I thought it would be fun for Pitt and I to have this brief meeting at a classic car club meet. We have our cars next to each other, and we introduce ourselves. It's a case of "the name's familiar, but I can't place the face."

I did it really as a fun thing, thinking I'd probably catch hell from my editors. They didn't say anything, but I received two or three hundred letters saying how great it was. So I had to put myself in the next one; got more letters; and now it's like a Hitchcock situation. Everybody gets a kick out of it, so now I always show up to kind of steer Pitt in the right direction.

Special Considerations in an Action-Adventure Series

When the publisher wanted me to do a companion book with a concordance about all the books and all the characters and a biography in the front, I wanted to do something a little different. So I wrote in a section where I'm dropped off by this taxicab at one end of the International Airport in Washington where Pitt supposedly lives in a converted hangar. Of course there's no hangar there, and the cabdriver thinks I'm crazy. It's the middle of the night, and there's nothing there. I tell him to just come back and pick me up in about an hour.

He drives off, and as I turn around, this whole thing materializes. I go into the hangar where they're having a big reunion-type party and meet and talk with all of the characters. Three or four beautiful women at the bar are arguing. One says to another, "You know, you're lucky. You got to go off with Pitt to Jamaica in the end of the book. Cussler killed me off."

So they're doing that book and then they're talking a TV series or paperback spin-off from *Flood Tide* that would involve the old tramp freighter that was actually a spy ship with all this armament and run by these mercenaries as a corporation. It seems I've created a cottage industry.

Dirk Pitt is a registered trademark. I was the first to do that. It was basically the agent's idea because people were beginning to infringe upon the character. A comic book came out called *Pitt*, and then somebody came up with a game called Raising the Titanic.

Self-Definition

I know it sounds hokey, but I really consider myself as much an entertainer as a writer. I've always felt that my job is to entertain the readers, my readers, in such a manner that when they reach the end of the book, they'll feel they got their money's worth. I know some writers hate that. They shout blasphemy when I say it. But what I'm really doing is creating a product that goes on the shelf. Marketing is a big part of writing.

Advice for Beginning Writers

At writers conferences I tell beginning writers they should first study an author who is successful, one who writes in the genre they want to write in and then copy that author. Ernest Hemingway made no bones about the fact that he copied the writing style of Dostoyevsky. I used Alistair MacLean when I started up.

Eventually, you drift into your own writing style. People are even copying me now. When he was in the Merchant Marines, Thomas Wolfe bought a used copy in some port of James Joyce's *Ulysses*, which is about the size of a telephone book. During the long hours at sea, he copied it in longhand, word for word.

Finally, when he had a stack of paper about five feet high, he threw it all off the stern of the ship. His shipmates said, "My God, after you copied that book, why did you throw it away?" And Thomas Wolfe said, "Because now I know how to write a book."

So I always tell students to study, not plagiarize, other writers' style, sentence structure, characterization and plotting. Do they write in the first person or third person? Do they have a prologue and an epilogue? Do they use flashback, and so on down the line? You save a lot of time by studying somebody who is successful rather than trying to learn it all on your own.

Writing Women-in-Jeopardy/ Psychological Suspense

Joy Fielding once told an interviewer that writing was like "playing with cutout dolls." Such might be the genesis of her work, but the success of her books proves she wields her pen as expertly as her scissors.

Fielding has a simple recipe for romantic relationship suspense. Take one troubled protagonist, outwardly controlled yet vulnerable to personal demons. Mix with a situation destined to compound her weaknesses. Stir in enough doubt about those around her to keep the heroine off balance. Add a new twist to the mixture whenever she begins to feel safe. Fold into 350 pages. Then bake until readers begin gasping for breath.

These are the literary repasts Fielding serves up in *See Jane Run*, *Missing Pieces* and her nine other suspense novels.

Joy Fielding and her family live in Toronto and Palm Beach.

Opening Lines and Inspiration

The opening sentence of *See Jane Run*—"One afternoon . . . Jane Whittaker went to the store . . . and forgot who she was" came to me out of the blue. I remember asking my husband, "What do you think of this line?" And he said, "Oh, I like that." So now I had this great line but didn't know what to do with it.

About eight years later, I was thinking about the line again—it never really left me—and I thought, *What if not only can Jane not remember who she is, but what if the front of her dress is covered with blood and her pockets are filled with money?*

I wrote the opening chapter by putting myself in that position, wandering around trying to figure out what I would do and then discovering the blood and the money. It took me about a year after that to get the rest of the book because, again, I really didn't know at that point what caused Jane's amnesia.

I spoke to a neurologist who gave me technical information on what tests would be done on a woman who went into a hospital not knowing who she was. A GP gave me all the drug information. Then I looked up amnesia at the medical research library and found the hysterical fugue state, which worked perfectly with what I wanted to do. I was quite thrilled to discover that there was a legitimate medical condition like that.

Internal Dialogue

Much of what you learn about Jane is through her internal dialogue. I tend to be very analytical, and I give my characters a vivid internal life because I am usually writing from the perspective of that one character. Since the reader doesn't know any more than the character does at a given time, it's very important to know what that character is thinking.

Internal dialogue is a way of verbalizing the very altered thoughts these intelligent women have in traumatic situations, a way of creating an immediacy and intimacy between character and reader, joining them and making them almost one person.

Endings That Satisfy

If you're writing suspense, it's important to know the ending, because you have to be building toward something. I'm not always sure exactly *how* that ending is going to happen. I wasn't with *See Jane Run.* In my original outline things were much less optimistic and they ended more abruptly. Jane wound up with her daughter, but Michael was never really punished.

But the editor said, "You have to rethink this ending. There has to be real retribution for readers to be satisfied." He didn't tell me how to do it; he just said it could probably use another chapter. When I reread it, I decided that was true.

At that point in the story, readers already knew what had caused Jane's amnesia. I'd introduced the character of Paula, so they also knew about her child. As the writer, I was the only one who really knew the connection between the two mothers. Having Paula come talk to Jane made the ending more dramatic.

The ending to *Don't Cry Now* was sparked by one of the first movies that really made an impression on me, *The Bad Seed*. I found the idea of a seemingly innocent child being truly evil fascinating. And then, having two teenagers— one's now twenty-two, the other nineteen—certainly there were times. . . .

Researching a Setting

I guess it was naivete really, but for *Tell Me No Secrets* I decided I'd make my protagonist Jess a prosecuting attorney. Had I realized the amount of research and work involved, I never would have done it. I mean, my husband is a lawyer, but he's not a criminal lawyer, and we're Canadian, so the legal system is completely different.

I thought, well, I'll make the setting Chicago, because how difficult could it be? Subsequently I found out that Illinois has the most complicated legal system in the United States.

It was very important to me to make the book accurate so that when a reader who was an attorney picked up the book, she wouldn't say, "No, that would never happen; that's ridiculous." So I had somebody put me in touch with a lawyer in Chicago who is now a defense attorney but used to be with the state attorney's office. I spent twelve hours with him on the phone, an hour or two a night. He essentially gave me a crash course in the Chicago legal system.

I was frantically taking notes, and he would quiz me. I felt like I was back in school. Then he said, "OK, I've done all I can over the phone. You have to come down to Chicago and see all the various people I think you should talk to."

He was absolutely wonderful. I spent three days down there, and he took me all over. I had access to everybody. I had lunch with the twelve judges of the Chicago Supreme Court. They were all very forthcoming, very helpful. I sat in on a murder trial one morning, then spent a few hours talking to the judge. I visited the state attorney's office, met with the chief prosecutor, saw the various offices, learned how they were run.

Then, of course, having been exposed to all that and having all those copious notes, I felt compelled to put it all down in the book. In the end I was able to impart the relevant points to nonattorney readers through the discussions that Jess had with the character Adam, whom she considered a layman.

Really it was a lot of work because I'm not a writer who enjoys research. But I did feel as a result that Chicago really came alive in that book.

In *Don't Cry Now*'s opening chapters, I show my protagonist Bonnie and her husband, Rod, being interrogated by the Boston police. I wanted to portray this accurately, so I had a friend who lived in the area drive me around to point out details and explain what I was seeing. At one point we went to a local police station. I was able to get a feel for the physicality of the place, but the police didn't exactly welcome our visit. In fact, they didn't give me much information. It may just have been a question of time and the fact that they didn't know me.

When I was in Chicago, I was being taken around by an insider, a lawyer with the prosecutor's office. That may have given me a little more cachet than when I went on my own to the police station where I think they thought, *I've never heard of this person. Why should I waste my time talking to her?*

On Writing What You Know

You'll get to know me if you read my books. My characters are all variations on me in one way or another, even though I haven't been though the experiences they're involved in. Jane, for example—all those incidents of her losing her temper were things that I thought, *Wow, I've done all of those.*

Jess got my neuroses and phobias. Although I've rarely had the panic attacks that she had, the year after my father died I was having them a lot. I used all that. Basically I pick a situation, put the character in it, then try to think how

I'd react in that particular circumstance. That way the characters seem real because they are.

Characterization and Theme

One of the best pieces of advice I ever got with regard to writing characters was that character shows itself in behavior. You know—don't tell me she's neurotic; show me what she's doing so I can figure it out for myself.

During the course of *See Jane Run* and *Tell Me No Secrets*, my heroines unknowingly sleep with their antagonists. Although I think it may be true, I'm not sure I would go so far as to say that a protagonist has to confront evil in an intimate way. I think it's more a question of not trusting surfaces and things not always being what they seem to be.

The point I was really making in those books was that ultimately the only person you can really depend on for your sense of self-worth and happiness is yourself. Before you can truly know another human being, you have to know yourself.

These are women who seem to be in idyllic situations. It's only when they start the process of self-examination that they confront their pasts and their presents and then arrive ultimately at a clearer understanding of who they are. And often that involves confronting their demons.

The Evolution of a Plot

Missing Pieces was a very personal book in many respects.

The protagonist Kate is older than my previous heroines, and I wrote the book in first person. I was dealing with all these issues in my own life—getting older; facing menopause; raising growing, difficult daughters; seeing my body change; feeling that whole loss of control. We all like to think we're in control, then suddenly we reach a point where we realize we have no control at all.

I used Kate's sister JoLynn, who's obsessed with and marries a convicted serial killer, to increase conflict and underscore Kate's loss of control. I didn't worry too much about going over the top with the character because I'd read about women like that. What surprised me was how many people I've since met who've said to me that they have sisters like JoLynn.

[Life is, as Kate says in the first chapter, not one thing at a time. *That* you could deal with, but what you get is five things going on at once.] It's not as if when you're having a difficult time in one area, everything else will just sort of sit back. Everything generally happens at once.

I did worry a little about putting in too much when I introduced Kate's relationship with Robert, her old boyfriend. But I actually put him in for two reasons. One, because I wanted to give Kate a story of her own. By that I mean I didn't want her to be the sun that all the other planets revolved around. I wanted her to have her own dilemma rather than simply react to what was going on around her.

The second thing that including Robert accomplished was that it underlined what was happening to JoLynn. Robert mirrored the murderer Colin Friendly. [You have, as Kate says at the end, two sisters pining over undesirable men; and though one of them wasn't a murderer, he was, in his own way, equally destructive.]

I felt that Kate certainly described my friends who are in midlife, who are dealing with teenagers and elderly parents who have Alzheimer's or cancer or whatever. And I took great pains with Larry, Kate's husband, because I wanted him to be a very likable, strong character rather than a wimp. I wanted to talk about some of the temptations women have, especially when their lives get so crowded with difficulties.

Robert was the escape, the symbol of Kate's lost youth. JoLynn was a baroque touch, this kind of woman—and there seems to be no shortage of them—who will put her life on the line for someone who is really despicable. I wanted to explore what that attraction would be and what effect a woman like that would have on the rest of her family.

I wanted to show a family in turmoil. How everybody has their own little turmoil and how, often, the crazy in the family allows the others to be sane. As Kate says at one point, JoLynn was that part of her that took risks and did crazy things.

The reason it all works is that the entire story is seen through Kate's perspective. Using JoLynn's or multiple points of view wouldn't have been as effective.

Readers needed to see things through the eyes of the one person with some common sense.

On the Writing Experience

Every book is like starting all over again. It feels like it's the first book I've ever written. I make the same mistakes every time out. It never gets any easier, and when I try to take shortcuts it never works. Generally I find the second half of the book more or less writes itself. The first half, setting everything up, is always difficult.

When I'm actually writing something, I always assume it's good, and sometimes it's really quite awful. I need distance from it, so I have people reading it along the way. I don't like to write too much without some kind of feedback because it's much easier to rewrite three chapters than it is half a book.

I think either you write because you love it or because you have to. I've always loved telling stories, hearing stories and making things up. Each book is a form of self-discovery and a chance to express my views on whatever happens to be important to me at any given time—certain issues, certain things about women's lives. I think realistic women have been under-represented in fiction, especially good commercial fiction, which tends to be very plot oriented, especially if it's written by men. I really enjoy being able to present what I hope are realistic women in exceptional circumstances.

Writing the Medical Thriller

Tony Miksanek, M.D. noted in his *Journal of the American Medical Association* review that Tess Gerritsen's *Harvest* "succeeds not only in entertaining the reader, but also in raising important questions of conscience, corruption, and choices as they relate to health care and the medical profession."

High praise indeed for an author's first medical thriller.

Gerritsen left a successful practice as an internist to raise her children and concentrate on her writing. When she takes her readers inside the exhausting rotation of medical training, they have no choice but to stick with her until they, like her characters, emerge stunned and bleary-eyed inside a medical nightmare.

A Phi Beta Kappa graduate of Stanford, Gerritsen attended the University of California San Francisco's medical school, earning her M.D. in 1979. *Harvest* was published in 1996 and followed by *Life Support* in 1997 and *Bloodstream* in 1998.

Gerritsen lives with her family in Maine, where she enjoys gardening and playing fiddle with her Scottish dance band, The Tattered Tartans.

The Popularity of the Subgenre

Medical fiction has always been popular because of the nature of the profession. A doctor deals with life-and-death issues, with the most intimate details of people's lives. We physicians see people at their most vulnerable—when they're sick, when they're dying, when they're giving birth. We see them in crisis. We see them at what may be the most dramatic points in their lives.

Hospitals are frightening places to most people because they must entrust their lives to others. No wonder medical settings lend themselves so well to fiction, and especially to thrillers—the drama, the fear, is inherent.

Finding the Right Story

I choose issues that frighten or trouble *me*. I try to look into the near future, at what *could* be, not just what's happening at this moment. For instance, *Life Support* was inspired by a news story I'd read about a woman who became pregnant with the intention of aborting her child so that parts of its brain could be used to prolong the life of her ailing father.

That whole idea of "farming" a fetus for another's use troubled me. I wanted to explore the ethical question: Is it right for the old to cannibalize the young in order to live forever?

We often talk about generational wars, about how children are getting so little of the nation's resources. Well, what if the children *were* the resource and adults were using them to their own selfish purposes? It's an ethical nightmare. I couldn't resist writing about it.

In my latest thriller, *Bloodstream*, I write about a bizarre epidemic of childhood violence in a small Maine town.

I'm playing on every parent's fear: What is it like to be afraid of the one person you love most? And what if this small town has had repeated epidemics of violence through the centuries? (Of course, there's a medical explanation.)

I draw many of my ideas from scientific journals. In general, I try to avoid whatever is considered the hot news topic of the day because by the time the book's out, it'll already be old news.

Too often, I'm afraid, medical thrillers use the same tired plots about viruses or bacteria run amok or evil scientists bent on destroying the world. I try my best to do something entirely different.

Writing With an Insider's Knowledge and Understanding

In order to write about medical situations with any sort of authority or accuracy, the writer must know how doctors talk and how they think.

When a doctor tries to diagnose an ill patient, he goes through a mental process that he's learned over the course of four years of medical school and at least three years of postgraduate training. That's seven years of experience. It's hard to portray that believably unless the author understands just what that diagnostic mental process involves.

Also, there are sensory details that add texture to a book, and that only an insider would be aware of. For instance, that satisfying "pop" you feel when you puncture a vein, or the peculiar smell some patients exude when they're close to death. It's possible to learn much of this through interviews with medical professionals, but to sustain that believability through a whole book would require quite a bit of interviewing.

Research Sources

Sometimes you encounter obstacles in researching or interviewing sources because of a book's subject matter.

The transplant community is a very touchy one. When I began interviewing hospital transplant coordinators for *Harvest*, I soon realized I was about to step on some toes. For instance, they were upset that I would dare use that title.

The word *harvest* is considered a "secret" word, never to be used in public. And the premise of the story—that there is a black market for human organs—got some of them so furious with me that one regional organ bank's attorney contacted my publisher, trying to suppress parts of the book, which they felt was dangerous fiction.

They have also written Paramount Pictures in an effort to stop the making of the movie.

As it turned out, much of what I used in *Harvest* was gleaned through organ bank literature and through published journals. And with the latest scandal now surfacing about a black market in Chinese organs, it turns out my premise was not so far-fetched after all.

On the other hand, I have received some wonderful help, especially from other doctors. A neurosurgeon described to me, step-by-step, how to perform pituitary surgery. (I used that information in a scene in *Life Support.*) My local hospital librarian helps track down obscure medical articles for me.

I find that, in general, people are happy to talk to authors, as long as we don't abuse the privilege and keep bothering them. So I try to know ahead of time everything I need to find out, and I read up as much about the topic as I can before I go around asking dumb questions.

Although I base my stories on scientific fact, I am very clearly writing fiction. I don't vilify any real people. Although I may rely on published journal articles, the use of established scientific fact in a work of fiction is not something I can be sued for. I trust in my publisher's attorneys to guide me as to whether I'm wandering into dangerous territory.

Identifying a Story Idea

I used the Russian Mafia as the villain in *Harvest* because of a rumor I'd heard.

I was having dinner with several couples, and the man sitting next to me was an ex-cop who now runs a security firm in Russia, protecting American business travelers. While in Moscow, he'd heard from the Russian police that orphans were vanishing, and that their organs were being sold in the Middle East to wealthy patients. He was absolutely convinced the story was true.

That tale truly upset me. The first thing I did was to call my brother-in-law, a *Newsweek* reporter, to ask if he'd check into it. He never found any concrete evidence, but then, when you're dealing with a foreign country, and the Russian Mafia in particular, evidence would be difficult to track down.

True or not, I could not let go of that terrible story, and that's how *Harvest* was born. I have two sons. All I had to do was imagine their lives in peril, and the plot took off with a life of its own. I changed the setting to the United States, not the Middle East, and I told the story from two points of view: a Russian child and a woman doctor in Boston. But the original kernel of the plot came from a rumor told over dinner.

Using Specialized Terms

If I use medical jargon, I put it in a context that makes its meaning understandable.

For instance, a reader may not know what ventricular fibrillation is. But if the doctors in the scene are getting panicked over it, and are frantically trying to treat it, then the reader gets the idea that this is a life-threatening condition, and that something better happen pretty damn quick or the patient is dead. I do believe that shows like *ER* and *Chicago Hope* have made the public very sophisticated as to medical terms, and I suspect they already understand much of the jargon I write.

Blending Reality With Fiction

When I think of my years of medical training, the number one memory that comes back is fatigue! It's more than just being dog-tired. It's the feeling of being so sleep deprived that your feet are completely numb and you can't talk in whole sentences. It's something I never want to go through again.

Because I write fiction, I sometimes place my heroines in conflict with their superiors, caught between what they know or suspect is right and the risk of losing their careers if they proceed. I myself have never had to deal with that. When a conflict did arise, it was usually because of personality clashes, not ethical issues. And as for sexual harassment or discrimination, I've never experienced it, but I understand, from a recent survey of women doctors, that it's not that uncommon.

Cliff-Hanger Endings

I find that ending each scene with a bit of a cliff-hanger keeps me, as well as the reader, interested in the story. It has always been my goal, as a writer, to write books that keep my readers pinned to the chair. If they can easily set the book aside, then I feel I've failed. So I try to keep escalating the crises, to make the situation more and more perilous for my characters, until their lives are truly at stake.

Because my books involve two or more protagonists, I will often be building toward two climaxes at once, endangering both characters simultaneously.

This allows me to switch back and forth between them. It's a conscious technique on my part, and I think it keeps readers turning the pages.

Personal Observations

Medical thrillers have lost their edge for me as a reader, simply because I'm too busy analyzing how I would have written the story differently. Also, after years working as a doctor, I just don't find hospitals all that scary. (As long as *I'm* not the patient.)

What I love are forensic thrillers, psychological thrillers. Scientific thrillers. I enjoy any thriller where the characters are sympathetic and the premise is believable.

What has surprised me most about the success of my books is the wide range of people who are reading them. I've received fan mail from fourteen-year-old boys who amaze me by their ability to understand medical jargon. I've received fan mail from women in their eighties who wrote to tell me about their medical experiences. And I'm truly surprised by the number of men who are reading my books. I think it indicates that medical thrillers truly have broad appeal.

Writing Issue-Driven Psychological Suspense

John Gilstrap's work with incarcerated children as part of an undergraduate psychology research project served as the starting point for *Nathan's Run*. *Library Journal* said that Gilstrap's "debut work gallops along at breakneck speed to an ending that is guaranteed to evoke a strong emotional response in the reader."

Foreign publishing rights for the book sold for over one million dollars.

In *At All Costs*, Gilstrap used his background as a safety expert and environmental engineer to take readers inside the lives of a family on the run for allegedly causing an eco-disaster of unprecedented proportions.

A native of Pensacola, Florida, Gilstrap received a history degree from The College of William and Mary in Virginia and his master's in Safety from the University of Southern California. He lives with his wife and son in northern Virginia.

Getting Dialogue Right

When it comes to writing dialogue my best advice is to rewrite, rewrite, rewrite. Natural conversation is inefficient, and I tend to write it out the first time *as* natural. Which means I've got twice as many words as I need. When my concentration is high, I'm actually *in* the scene. It's a schizophrenic kind of thing, sort of method writing in the sense of method acting. During the rewrite it's a matter of making sure that it's consistent, while at the same time pithy.

Point of View

For me, telling a story from a single point of view, particularly first person, would be terribly limiting and much tougher to write. And I make a conscious effort to avoid the omniscient or author's voice. The narrative voice is always from the point of view of one of the characters. The use of multiple viewpoints makes it easier to tell the story, easier to build the suspense. Suspense comes largely from the reader knowing things the protagonist doesn't and knowing about impending problems that the protagonist doesn't. Then things come crashing together at the climax.

In my books any character with whom the reader needs to feel emotion will become a viewpoint character. For example, Eddie Bartholomew runs this DC restaurant in *At All Costs*. It's a very high-class place with a very exclusive membership. There are several ways to let the readers know the history of Eddie's place. One is for me to intrude as the narrator and tell them. The other is to do it through a character's eyes, and in the process characterize or fill out that character.

The second choice makes the story flow and kills multiple birds with one stone. I'm providing flesh to what would otherwise be a utility character, somebody who has to be there to make the plot work. As long as he's got to be there, he might as well have some thoughts and the reader might as well bond with him at one point or another as long as it's not an intrusion.

The Use of Foreshadowing in Building Suspense

Like a lawyer laying out a legal argument as he builds a case, you have to lay the foundation before you can build the suspense. It's during that laying down of the foundation that foreshadowing often occurs; although, I quite honestly never think of it as foreshadowing.

It's also important that the readers feel comfortable when they read something that doesn't particularly make sense at the time. They have to be comfortable in a writer's ability to the degree that they're not going to see something as a mistake or an annoyance. They have to be able to figure, *Well, OK, that will make sense to me later on.* Foreshadowing is a promise that readers expect to be fulfilled.

The Validity of Violence

The subject of the violence in *Nathan's Run* often comes up. But despite what readers think they remember, there is no rape scene in the book. I consider such comments a great compliment because apparently people are so intensely into the book that just Nathan's brief comment paints a much larger scene of his experience in juvenile hall. Frankly that's exactly the way I wanted it to work.

There was a point in the rough draft where I got about two paragraphs into a scene that would recount the rape and I thought, *No, I don't want to go here. I'm just not laying this out.* They are images that I don't particularly want to deal with. So in that sense some of the violence that seems very Technicolor to people really isn't. That's theater of the mind stuff.

But having said that, because of my experience in the fire service, the Saturday night knife and gun club violence that I've witnessed has always been very Technicolor, very in your face. I've never seen anybody shot or stabbed, but I've certainly seen the aftermath. Nobody dies who is not somebody's husband or son or brother or sister or wife or grandmother. Therefore I think it's incumbent on a writer who writes the kind of very intense stuff that I do to have a lot of heart.

I think violence must lead to hurt. It needs to have sound and it needs to have texture and it needs to have smell. It needs all the things that real violence has. Which doesn't mean that I'm particularly proviolence. But there are movies, for example, where a thousand people die in these shoot-outs and nobody cares about them. I find that sort of violence offensive.

In *At All Costs*, even where the sadistic Wiggins dies a pretty miserable death, he dies a little bit at a time and he dies with attitude. By making that scene as long and as detailed as it is, we learn a lot about the other characters involved and how the book's events have affected them.

And I don't remember a character quite as reprehensible as Uncle Mark in *Nathan's Run.* But when he's getting his fingers broken and later, at the end of the book, I think there is some level of sympathy for this rotten son of a bitch. Readers have gone through these steps with him and there's a sense of loss even though it's a bad guy who's been killed.

Similarly it provides a backdrop so that when the enforcer Pointer gets his it's a cheering moment. It's, "Yes! He finally got what he deserved!" Which then provides a springboard for the book's climax. We've seen what bullets can do to an adult. Now, when Nathan picks up the gun and becomes the target, we know what's possible. It adds texture to the overall story.

Characterization

Characters carry water for the plot. Without characters there is no plot. If you take a look at Mason and Lauren and Jake and Carolyn and Travis and even Senator Albricht and Irene Rivers in *At All Costs*, these are all people whom I hope you feel you'd like to know. They're people who have their foibles and their fears and their intense feelings that with any luck at all ring a bell with the reader. It's because we identify with their plight and with their fears that there *is* a plot.

That's why one of the questions I hate most is when somebody asks, "What's your book about?" and I say, "Well, *Nathan's Run* is about a twelve-year-old boy who kills a juvenile detention center guard and runs away." Which is true, but that's not what the book is about. Unfortunately in today's commercial market, if you say it's a character-driven thriller, readers think "literary fiction," and the book goes away. I find my work is very difficult to classify for that reason.

Theme

Both my books focus on protagonists running away from the authorities for valid reasons. I think every nightmare I've ever had has had an element of chase in it. There's that person who's trying to get me and I can't run, or I run too slowly. Or there's somebody in the house and I open the door, but they're not in the house; they're actually in the doorway.

Running scenes scare *me*, and I think if you're going to write convincing suspense you ought to be scared of it yourself.

Similarly, I've become fascinated over the years with the notion of prosecutorial misconduct. I frankly think it's very, very easy in this day and age to convict people of things without evidence. The presumption of innocence has become wiggly with time, and there's a growing presumption of guilt. Those two things kind of come together in chase books.

The more universal the fears, the larger the audience. There are certain things of which we are all fearful, and that's critically important to successful suspense fiction. Loss, or the fear of loss, or the loss of moments we've blown and can never get back are universal themes.

Realism and Personal Experience

My background in environmental engineering made the scenes in *At All Costs* in which Jake struggles with his claustrophobia as he dons his protective gear relatively easy to create. There is nothing quite like that feeling when that hood comes over and it's zipped up and there's no way out. I'm not exceptionally claustrophobic myself, but there's something about the inevitability of being in that suit where you can't escape.

Similarly there's a scene where Jake is remembering a Cub Scout tour of a police station where there's a jail cell that you can try on for size. That is absolutely out of my past. I was the scout who thought, *I'm not going in there.* I think it was the thought of not being in control, of knowing that if somebody closes that door I no longer have the option to get out on my own. Which is the same feeling you experience when you're zipped up into that suit. There's no getting out on your own.

As a firefighter for fifteen years, I'd end up in very tight spaces doing work. But I never had a problem with claustrophobia then because I had some level of control. I could always get out. I could always change my location. I could always run away. When I lose that control I begin to feel kind of oogy. That's the feeling I tried to give Jake.

Ending Things at the Proper Moment

When I got to the point in my original draft of *At All Costs* where Jake believes the skeleton in the bunker is the answer to what happened so long ago, I found

I couldn't end things there. I had only plotted out that much in my head, but I realized that solution was too simple.

Then it occurred to me that there's a great deal of irony when you have people who have been deluding themselves all these years discover nothing is as it seems. They had their escape plan, and the plan didn't work. But that's OK. Now they have an answer that will clear their names and solve all their problems. So they bet everything on that roll of the dice. Literally *everything*. And it's wrong. Those are desperate circumstances, and I liked the notion of going there. So Jake's skeleton became a red herring.

In good suspense fiction protagonists have to go through the trials of Job, one thing after another, after another, after another. It should never be easy for them to do anything. If they open the door, the door should stick before it opens. If they go to turn on a light, the bulb should be burned out. That's the way life is. Murphy's rules dominate. And when things go bad they should go really, really bad.

One of my goals in ending a book is that, as they close the page, I want readers to want a moment alone. I want the plot to live on for a while in their heads. And I want them to have a feeling of rejoicing or sadness or whatever. I don't want them closing my book and then turning on *Friends* right away.

By the end of *At All Costs*, Jake and Carolyn have been through a lot. Various agencies have made serious mistakes that have disrupted and endangered their lives and the life of their son. But the government does not apologize. And if it does apologize, it doesn't do it readily and it always leaves a back door for itself.

The thought of Jake and Carolyn becoming these media stars, which is what would be a natural outcome of something like this, didn't sit well with me. That's not who the characters were.

What Jake and Carolyn had, what they'd won at all costs, was the right to be a family. They'd been offered some start-up money, not a huge sum but a good sum. They had their lives back. I didn't want to cloud that with anything else.

↠ JUDITH KELMAN ↞

Writing Issue-Driven Women-in-Jeopardy

What offense could a five-year-old child commit that might generate repeated attempts on his life? This is the question Judith Kelman asks and the boy's mother must answer in *Someone's Watching*, which was adapted as an NBC Movie of the Week.

Heroines in Judith Kelman's women-in-jeopardy novels are strong women who find themselves in unusual circumstances. Adversity may bend them a little, but they never break. On the contrary, these women survive whatever dangers they are confronted with and move on with their lives, stronger than ever.

In *The House on the Hill*, Kelman lets readers explore what could happen if a paroled child killer were allowed to move, unreported, into a small town. Her *If I Should Die* wonders whether confronting our deepest fears can be deadly.

Dean Koontz calls her work "swift, suspenseful and highly entertaining." Mary Higgins Clark notes that "Judith Kelman gets better all the time."

Judith Kelman's work has been translated into nine languages. She lives in New York City, where she is working on her eleventh novel.

Opening the Right Door by Accident

I didn't have a specific genre in mind when I wrote my first novel. I learned that I had penned a novel of "psychological suspense" when I saw the jacket copy.

230

In retrospect, I realize that the woman-in-jeopardy or child-in-jeopardy theme appeals to my concept of dramatic moment. To me, a showdown with evil at the book's climax is far more dramatic than having the heroine divorce the antagonist or drive him off to join the French Foreign Legion.

Research

I do a great deal of research, but typically, it's about the psychological, forensic, medical or technical aspects of the book. When I write from the point of view of a child, old man, criminal, etc., I rely on observation plus imagination.

In *Someone's Watching* for instance, the injured boy's mother has an almost sixth sense that warns her when her child is in danger. I've experienced that sort of intuitive response myself. Several times while my kids were growing up, I somehow sensed that one or the other of them was in some kind of medical, emotional or physical jeopardy.

I majored in psychology, took a graduate degree in the field and continue to be fascinated by the human mind with all its quirks and complexity. *If I Should Die* dealt with phobias, for example, so I interviewed experts, read widely in the field and attended two eight-week phobia clinics.

Characterization

For really dysfunctional antagonists I rely on my warped imagination and the limitless madness reported in the press. In *The House on the Hill*, I created a villain who was a master of illusion and escape. Having him get away at the end seemed the logical, consistent way to affirm his uncanny ability to elude confinement.

While I don't set a bad guy quota, I do believe it's necessary to plant a number of red herrings in order to keep the reader guessing and sustain the suspense.

I try to make all my characters as human as possible. To me, that means flawed. For a jeopardy (or any) novel to work, the reader has to care about and relate to the main characters. It's difficult to believe, much less identify with, people devoid of faults.

I've considered writing series characters many times, and I used one main character twice [in *Where Shadows Fall* and *Hush Little Darlings.*] But so far, I've stayed with the stand-alone novel, which gives me the chance to introduce new players who best suit the situation presented in each book.

Responding to Critics

There are critics for most everything. Some insist jeopardy novels exploit children and create unfounded fear for parents. But the topics addressed in these books are not fictional inventions. I can't imagine that any parent is unaware of child molestation or abduction. When I address such themes, I do so in a way that emphasizes the inner strength and personal resources of parents forced to confront them. I try to empower, certainly not exploit, the characters.

Advice

I enjoy experimenting with voice and viewpoint. First-person narrative allows the reader intimate contact with the thoughts and emotions of the protagonist. Shifting perspectives affords the writer the broadest freedom in telling the story.

If I could give someone who's contemplating writing a jeopardy novel one critical piece of advice, it would be to create vivid, sympathetic characters. Otherwise, the reader won't care what happens to them.

Cutting-Edge Technology and the Techno-Thriller

Shirley Kennett was born and raised in St. Louis, where she grew up in a converted turn-of-the-century funeral home. She has a degree from Washington University School of Engineering and, like her heroine P.J. Gray, is a computer specialist.

P.J., who's also a psychologist, uses the emerging technology of virtual reality (VR) in tandem with her police detective partner's old-fashioned investigative legwork to assist the St. Louis PD in solving homicide cases. So far P.J. has helped end the spree of a cannibalistic killer (*Gray Matter*); played cat and mouse with a cunning computer hacker willing to kill anyone who tried to thwart his desire for revenge (*Fire Cracker*); and confronted the dangers of violent video games (*Chameleon*).

Shirley Kennett now lives in Eureka, Missouri, with her husband and son. Her thrillers are sure to make you look at the world of computer technology with a new perspective.

Combing Technology and the Path Not Chosen

Virtual Reality allows a user to define a world that exists only in the mind of a computer, and then to fully immerse himself in the sights, sounds and sensations of that world.

Because I follow new developments in the computer field in general, I had a casual interest in virtual reality (VR). But the use of VR in the P.J. Gray books was specifically intended to place the series in an area that might take off in the future.

Over and above the progressive improvement in crime scene techniques and forensic analysis, there have been two remarkable innovations in criminology in the last three decades: behavioral profiling and DNA fingerprinting. Each started off slowly and gained momentum. Now they are considered indispensable tools.

I feel that VR holds potential on a similar scale for a big leap forward in investigative technique, and I wanted to position my series on the leading edge. Besides, the more I dug into VR, the more I became fascinated with it.

P.J. is a psychologist as well as a computer expert. Although I don't have a psychology degree, I have taken graduate-level psychology courses. At one time I did plan to go into that field, applying for doctoral programs and gearing up for the clinical work that interested me. I've retained an interest in psychology and follow the developments in the field as an outsider with her nose pressed against the window.

With P.J., I saw an opportunity to take the path not chosen and see where it would lead me. I also felt she would bring valuable insight to her job in the police department with that background, and that it was a natural way to create tension with her computer-resistant partner, Detective Leo Schultz.

What really triggered my interest in VR was a trip to Disney World. I saw a demonstration of its use for entertainment purposes, a prototype system under development by Disney engineers. By the time I was on the plane flying home, I was already planning the use of VR in my series.

Adapting Reality to the Needs of Fiction

The VR technology P.J. has developed in the series is not currently in use by law enforcement. Simpler versions are available in large departments, such as the Los Angeles PD, but they differ from P.J.'s system in two respects: They aren't full-immersion VR, and they are not aided by artificial intelligence.

In full-immersion VR, the participant wears a head-mounted display (HMD), which blocks out sensory input from the real world. The HMD contains speakers so that outside noise is minimized, and two small display monitors, one in front of each eye. The monitors fill the participant's field of vision. Each monitor shows the same scene, but offset so that the images enter the eyes at the angle perceived in normal vision. (To experience how this works, hold a pencil at arm's length. Close one eye and look at it, then do the same with the other eye.)

During full-immersion VR the participant sees only what's on the monitors, and everything appears to be life-sized. Turning the head reveals a new scene. Various methods are used to enable the participant to move around within the virtual world.

When the HMD is not used, the VR world is confined to a regular computer monitor. The viewer sees things in miniature on the screen, with clever shading done to give a 3-D effect. This is called "looking through the window."

Lack of funds for research and equipment prevent more extensive use of VR, whether full immersion or simple window gazing, in law enforcement. Also, a new technique takes a while to catch on, as behavioral profiling did. I think time will cure both problems, as VR becomes cheaper to use and law enforcement professionals discover its potential.

Artificial intelligence means that the computer has been given the license to make guesses and extrapolations, providing a nonhuman viewpoint on the way things play out during a homicide re-creation. To my knowledge, no police department is using this add-on feature, at least not yet.

The Basis for the Premise

The most common current use of VR is courtroom presentation of a simple crime scene re-creation for the jury, in the looking-through-the-window mode. This is done only in high-profile cases where the client is willing to spend money for such an expensive tool, whether for the prosecution or the defense. Courtroom use is still controversial because it is possible to use many subtle ways to present a simulation of an incident in either a favorable or nonfavorable light. VR is not an objective, neutral tool—not a quantifiable thing like DNA fingerprinting.

Right now it is hard to say whether courtroom presentation will be squashed as too subjective or will blossom into the latest method of influencing a jury in all kinds of cases from homicides to automobile crashes.

Looking Further into the Future

I don't own VR equipment. An excellent setup would cost in the neighborhood of fifty to a hundred thousand dollars. Costs will come down in the future, making personal ownership more practical. I do have 3-D drawing tools and simple animation software that can run on high-end personal computers, and that gives me an opportunity to dabble in the field. I would love to be able to create the scenes I portray in the books and immerse myself in them, but all of that comes from my research and my imagination right now. As far as accuracy is concerned, there is a wealth of information about VR on the Internet, and those who are involved in research churn out formal papers regularly.

Because my work is fiction, I have a little leeway to invent things, as long as I keep the basics intact. For example, in the books there is a process called scanimation, taken from *scan* and *animate*. Scanimation involves scanning photos of people and having the computer fully animate them in the virtual world—turn them into walking, talking 3-D images.

In reality, this process does exist at the far leading edge of the field, but it is much more complex than I describe. It's been used in movie special effects at great cost and with elaborate equipment but has not filtered down into the type of environment P.J. Gray has. The P.J. books are not science fiction, though. Everything in them can be done now, just not in the casual way P.J. tosses them together in her basement office.

Villains—Real and Imagined

The spark for Pauley Mac, the villain in *Gray Matter*, came about one day in a long line in the grocery store. A woman waiting nearby was irritated with her children, who were pulling candy from the shelves and generally creating a small tornado around her shopping cart. One tripped over his own feet and fell to the floor. As tears began to flow, she hauled him up and mumbled "You don't have the brains God gave a dog."

It bothered me terribly. I still regret not approaching the woman and telling her about verbal abuse and self-esteem and anything I could think of that might have made enough of an impression to stop her from treating her children that way. That scene haunted me until that child became Pauley Mac in my mind—always trying to improve himself, belittled constantly and told he didn't have the brains of a dog.

I researched cannibalism and found that there is a history dating back thousands of years and spread throughout many societies of consuming body parts to absorb the strengths that were thought to reside there. In a few cases, these beliefs are still practiced today. So Pauley Mac acquired his alternate self named Dog by taking his parents' cruel sarcasm literally. The voices of his victims that foment inner turmoil add to the chaos.

Chameleon deals with the effects of violent video games on children. In it, P.J. begins to suspect that her twelve-year-old son, Thomas, and his new friend might be somehow connected to a series of murders at their school. My own Thomas is four years younger than P.J.'s son. At eight, the worlds of imagination and reality still overlap quite a bit. For a child who clings to belief in the tooth fairy and Santa Claus, it isn't much of a stretch to believe that the violence portrayed in games is real.

Second Thoughts

I gave P.J.'s son the same name as my own child because I thought it would help me identify with her more closely. Even their physical descriptions match. But this backfired when it came time to have the fictional Thomas associate with a killer.

Just seeing his name on the page in connection with bloody events gave me the shivers. Many scenes in my books are intense. To create them I have to live the scenes in my mind as vividly as possible. Putting Thomas into those scenes was emotionally harrowing. However, I won't water down any plots because of it.

The best plots and characterization, in my opinion, come when the author is willing to look into both the darkest and brightest places in the human heart. Putting the fictional Thomas in jeopardy has made me think deeply about and empathize more with parents whose lives have been invaded by violence.

My characters struggle with major issues, not superficial things. Both P.J. and Leo battle relationship and self-confidence insecurities. Leo's excess weight aggravates his arthritic knee, often hampering his ability to respond as quickly as he'd like. P.J. can't lose the extra pounds she put on during her divorce.

I wanted to give P.J. and Leo room to grow and change, to become more like each other in some ways, as people do who work closely together on matters of such intensity. Readers' lives are not unblemished, at least not by the time they've reached middle age as P.J. and Leo have. The comments and questions I've been getting indicate readers have responded strongly to and become caught up in the lives of P.J. and Leo, in addition to the cases they work on. And that's exactly what I had in mind.

Supporting Players

Merlin, P.J.'s mentor, whom she knows though their chat room connection and only by that name, is a shadowy but ever-present wisp that curls around the edges of P.J.'s life but is in some way central to it. While I don't have any firm plans to reveal Merlin's true identity, I have toyed around with a plot in which he vanishes after delivering an enigmatic plea for help to P.J., leaving her to figure out who he is and how she can help him.

Will Carpenter, the villain in *Fire Cracker*, whose computer name is Cracker, revealed that he was also one of Merlin's disciples. Needless to say, Merlin, who still doesn't know exactly which of his contacts is Cracker, isn't happy knowing that his intimate circle contains a cold-blooded killer.

Ambiguous Endings

I deliberately left the issue of Will Carpenter hanging at the end of the book. In my next book, *Cut Loose*, I return to it in a dramatic way when P.J. risks her relationship with Merlin in order to get in touch with Cracker—not to capture him, but to take advantage of his extraordinary ability to find people who want to stay hidden.

The Birth of a Suspense Author

I'm not sure how much of an influence growing up in a converted turn-of-the-century funeral home had on my choice of writing genre. I do know that I used to sneak into the basement with a flashlight to read when I was supposed to be doing chores or homework or getting ready for bed. I used to wonder what the grooves and drains in the floor were for until I figured it out in a flash of understanding. The knowledge didn't stop my nocturnal visits, though—it was the perfect place to read *Alfred Hitchcock* and *Ellery Queen* magazines.

Personal Goals

Now that I've passed the first hurdle of getting published, I have three goals as a writer.

The first is to improve my writing: to step out and take new challenges, to consciously study and enhance the expression of my creativity, to make each book better than the one before and to never take the easy path if the hard path results in a better book.

The second is to become enough of a commercial success to comfortably support myself and my family from my writing income.

The third goal is to reach out to those who are coming along after me and offer what assistance I can in terms of emotional support and practical advice to other writers.

++ JOHN LUTZ ++

Using Urban Settings in Psychological Suspense

Award-winning author John Lutz's *SWF Seeks Same* was filmed for the movies as *Single White Female*. *The Ex* became a major HBO movie. In addition to his suspense novels, he has two separate mystery series in print.

Setting plays a big part in every Lutz novel. New York City becomes a character all its own in *SWF Seeks Same*, aiding and abetting both villain and heroine in their need to become invisible.

Born in Dallas, Texas, John Lutz now lives in Webster Groves, Missouri. In addition to his two series and his stand-alone thrillers, this prolific author's short fiction has been included in several mystery and suspense anthologies. He has also contributed about two hundred stories to various magazines.

Mystery vs. Suspense

Every good novel contains an element of suspense. In mysteries it exists in varying degrees. A mystery classified as a suspense novel is one that emphasizes suspense rather than curiosity.

Curiosity holds the reader until the last page so he or she can discover how the jewels were stolen from the locked glass case in the middle of winter when the servants saw nothing and there was freshly fallen snow without footprints. . . . You get the idea.

In a suspense novel, the reader identifies with the characters and at a certain level vicariously experiences what they do, feels their trepidation, maybe even winces along with them when they feel physical pain. This might be so even if the ending is predictable.

The reader also feels *for* the characters in a suspense novel. If the time bomb is ticking away beneath the restaurant table while the hero or heroine is calmly sipping a second cup of coffee, we have suspense. When the waiter spills water that runs through the crack in the table and shorts the bomb's wiring, or the bomb is discovered by a crawling escapee from a nearby high chair and then disarmed, the reader feels relief.

There are other differences: A mystery requires the skillful planting of clues, more foreshadowing to make subsequent developments seem plausible, red herrings to divert the reader's suspicion, and the carefully controlled release of facts. But the key difference between the two types of books is that a suspense novel is primarily a shared emotional experience between the reader and the book's character. A mystery novel can simply be a puzzle that raises questions then answers them in ways that satisfy the reader. But a good one will also contain suspense.

Setting

My choice of a particular urban setting depends on what sort of novel, or scene, I'm writing. In *SWF Seeks Same*, teeming Manhattan provided the anonymity needed by one woman seeking to take over another's personality and life. And much of the novel took place in an old apartment building that contributed an air of menace.

In *Dancing With the Dead*, the dreary urban setting in which the main character was abused by her lover was a contrast to the contrived, gentle and softly lit romantic setting of a dance studio in which her male instructor treated her with the utmost respect. Different stories have different requirements.

Motivation

For normally streetwise city dwellers to ignore their internal warnings and plunge into dangerous situations as a book progresses, the writer must convince the reader of the characters' disorientation. Something such as fear, hate, love, manipulation by another character (as in *SWF*), weariness or displacement must compel them to let down their guard.

Motivation equals plausibility. In the case of Mary, in *Dancing With the Dead*, the fact that she had been conditioned as an enabler, tolerating and adjusting to her mother's alcoholism, made it more believable that she had a "victim" mind-set. She was yearning for another victimizer and would stay in an abusive relationship with a man she loved. The writer should consider motivation in its broad and interior sense, instead of simply manufacturing exterior reasons for characters taking certain actions.

Beginnings

An opening scene's primary function is to grab and hold the reader. But in fiction writing, almost everything must have more than one purpose. The trick is to write a scene that hooks the reader and also furnishes elements of character, mood, plot and theme.

In the opening scene of *SWF*, Allie's apartment building, the Cody Arms, is described as viewed by Allie from across the street. The building "looms like a medieval castle" whose gargoyles with chipped features are "leering at passersby," while on the street, cabs "growl and rattle past." So the main character and the setting have been introduced, along with an atmosphere of dread. The reader knows much about the book, if not the particulars, from the first few paragraphs. We're not in the New York the department of tourism would feature in its brochures.

The Ex begins with a tumultuous, beautiful woman escaping from a mental institution during a tornado, callously killing an employee in the process. So who's the tornado here? I think the opening chapter gives the reader a pretty good idea of how the book is going to progress.

How Setting Affects Plot

The key points of my books are developed during the plotting stage, added during revisions or sometimes simply inserted as they occur to me. I work from a synopsis written loosely enough so that I don't close any mental doors. During the actual composition, action (as opposed to plot) and character often provide opportunities that can be used to advantage.

For my books to have been set in rural or suburban areas as opposed to cities, their dynamics would have to have been completely different. Rather than being novels about "lost" people—a woman whose identity is being sapped by a psychotic roommate; one who feels her family slipping away at the hands of another lonely and desperate woman trying to claim it—both *SWF* and *The Ex* would have been about tormented and humiliated people with no place to hide. And, of course, they would have to have been plotted differently.

My suggestion for writers who might be contemplating urban settings for their suspense novels would be to utilize the built-in suspense of simply living in a large city.

If one person in ten thousand is a potential psychotic killer, you'll pass that statistic in human form on the street fairly often. The anonymity of a big city means the ever-present sense of sudden loss of identity—you are more likely to have an accident and lose your memory, or your wallet or purse, and not be able to prove who you are, or to be mistaken for someone else and suffer the consequences.

There is also a sense of the vertical in an urban setting, ironically added to a claustrophobic atmosphere; the threat is not only all around, but above and below. Remember that your character can be confronted by a larger array of unpleasant possibilities in an urban setting.

Pacing

The short chapters in my books are the result of both style and a conscious effort to generate suspense. Shorter chapters mean a faster pace, more opportunity for cliff-hanger endings to chapters and more points that can be used to emphasize and direct and hold the steady course of the novel. There is also a clearer pattern to be recalled later by the reader, when it's time to connect events to their foreshadowing.

The last chapter of *The Ex* wasn't in the original plot or synopsis. (In the book's final scene, the heroine and her family pass a jogger in the park who looks eerily like Deirdre, the dead antagonist.) Deirdre was supposed to take on a somewhat mythical form as the novel progressed, the embodiment of what every *young* wife fears—not the fresh young thing at the watercooler, but the wily older woman with her sexual hooks in the husband, more a force than an infatuation.

When the novel was virtually finished, it occurred to me that a whiff of immorality might add to that menace and mystique. Thus, the additional chapter. This is one of the reasons I don't work from a strict outline but prefer to leave doors open to possibilities.

The Writing Process

I revise as I go, then revise the day's work as a whole, then move on to the next day's work and the same process. Then I revise the finished manuscript, revise it again and keep revising until something (my exhausted muse?) tells me I've gotten all I can from the material. Not for everyone, but I like to revise. Love it, in fact.

Writing the Legal/ Political Thriller

Before he was a best-selling author, Richard North Patterson was a successful attorney. A former prosecutor on the Watergate case, Patterson chose as the protagonist for his first novel a man not unlike himself. *The Lasko Tangent*, which won an Edgar Award from the Mystery Writers of America for best first novel, introduced Christopher Paget and was published in 1979.

Fourteen years and three unrelated books later, Patterson revisited Paget in *Degree of Guilt*. His third book in the Paget trilogy, *Eyes of a Child*, followed in 1995.

Kirkus Reviews called *Eyes of a Child* "a miracle of agonizingly focused suspense," adding "The adversarial nature of American criminal justice has never been more brilliantly dramatized."

Patterson and his wife, Laurie, live with their family in San Francisco and on Martha's Vineyard.

Maturing as an Author

After I wrote *The Lasko Tangent*, I didn't want to write a serial character. Many people in my business have done well with that, but I felt that it was self-limiting. So as far as I was concerned, Paget was history. Three books intervened and then there were eight years where I didn't write at all. Then I essentially took a three-month leave from my law partnership to see whether I could still write a novel.

I no longer had to worry about being trapped by a serial character, but I had a limited time frame. My first thought was that it would be easier to return to a character I knew, and I thought about the idea of what would have happened to Paget over fourteen years. Back in the late seventies, I hadn't thought about his future. Now the possibilities intrigued me.

If you compare the first two Paget books, *The Lasko Tangent* and *Degree of Guilt*, you might think they were written by different authors. That first book was the work of a reasonably clever twenty-nine-year-old smart-ass. The second, actually my fifth published book, was the work of a man in his midforties who had seen and reflected on a lot of things.

Viewpoint

Another thing is that if you look at my second, third and fourth books, you will see an evolution from first to third person and to the use of multiple points of view. You see a growing maturity in the writing. You see the more Spartan writing style I use now. So if you look at what I wrote in the fourth book, *Private Screening*, even though eight years separate them, it's a lot easier to see *Degree of Guilt* upcoming.

In *Degree of Guilt* and *Eyes of a Child*, the third Paget book, I refer to the character as "Paget" rather than "he" when I'm in his viewpoint. This gave a bit of distance. You see things through his eyes, but there's also a narrative gloss. The point of view assumes a certain omniscience. So really the authorial mind, or the conscience of the novel, is looking at everybody.

Later on, in *Silent Witness* and *The Final Judgment* and my latest, *No Safe Place*, which is dramatically different from any of the others, I drop that. In their own points of view, characters are referred to by their first names. It struck me as more intimate and also evened out the cultural difference in referring to women by their first names and men by their last.

Motivation

I don't go through what I think is a silly exercise of trying to give characters entire biographies that I'm not going to use. I do think very hard about what their circumstances are, what they want, what they're like, how they got that way and how they're likely to react to particular circumstances.

Frequently what that means is that I'll go to psychiatrists or psychologists and say, "This is how I envision a particular character. And this is the experience he's had or response he's had. Now, what's his inner landscape look like, or what kind of experience might he have had to get that way?"

I try to build these characters inside out, and to me it's very important to make them psychologically real so that their behavior makes sense. I'm not only concerned with plot but with psychological consistency. So that when somebody does something surprising, if you think about it, you can say, yeah, that makes sense, I can see that.

No Safe Place is about a young Democratic presidential candidate who is running in the 2000 primaries against a sitting vice-president. One of the young candidate's problems is that the vice-president is holding the advantage of his incumbency. Another is that a *Newsweek*-type magazine, which I call *News World*, is attempting to prove that two years before, while my candidate was still married, he had an affair with a reporter who was covering him on the Hill and she had an abortion.

And his third problem is the contradiction that he's a pro-choice Catholic who has dared to say that he personally thinks that a fetus is a life. Nonetheless, he's being stalked by a guy who has just shot up an abortion clinic and now has decided to kill my candidate.

Other than that he doesn't have a problem in the world.

It was spooky to me that I finished this book in early October 1997 and then we had the Lewinsky thing and the abortion clinic bombing in Birmingham. Gun control also plays a big part in the book, and now we've had all these shootings.

I don't get any satisfaction in the coincidence, but none of those things are impossible to perceive. In fact, I think they are inevitable. I look at our society and its problems and try to figure out where they're going and very often they go there.

To achieve a balance in dealing with issues, I talk to a lot of people. In the case of *No Safe Place*, I interviewed a former president, a couple of senators, a cabinet member, people who had managed candidates in both parties in the last two elections, reporters, Secret Service people and advocates for various positions. I tried to bring a lot of different things to a novel that certainly doesn't lack a point of view but isn't oversimplified either.

Characterization

Until recently my favorite character from all my books has been Carolyn Masters from *The Final Judgment*. Now I have to say she's my favorite *female* character. The protagonist in *No Safe Place*, the young senator, is my favorite male character.

Carolyn was always interesting to me. I finally just had to figure out the whys. I mean, she's a mystery to me. I got to page four hundred or something in the manuscript for *Degree of Guilt* and I needed a judge. It could have been anyone, any gender, but Carolyn knocked at my psychic window and appeared. I liked her, so I thought I'd give her more to do in *Eyes of a Child*. Then she sort of came back in and said, "Look, now I want my own book." So I said, "Anything you want."

About ten or fifteen years ago a particular sort of fiction became popular—one in which somebody would get up in the morning, spend five pages just trying to figure whether she should leave her apartment, then finally she doesn't, and that sort of thing would go on for pages and pages. That just bores me to death.

The people that interest me are the ones who want something, for good or ill. I'm fascinated by what they do to get it and certainly by the unintended consequences of ambition and by why they have those ambitions in the first place.

I also think it's much more interesting to have a situation that is personally fateful for the principal character or characters. It should mean something to them in terms of their own lives. It's more suspenseful, but I also think it's more revealing of character. And I know the issues within a character that I want to address because I've gone through the psychological profile I talked about earlier.

In *No Safe Place* we see Kerry Kilcannon's childhood and his youth and his failed marriage and we know what's at stake for him when he seeks the presidency. We know what he's gone through to get there.

Outlining

I just started to write my next book, and I have folders here for every scene. They're in consecutive order, about eighty-eight folders. I'll change the order and something will surprise me as I go along, but I try to plot out my books as well as I can because I think the end should resonate back to the beginning. The plot should not only make logical sense, but the behavior of the characters should be consequential rather than arbitrary.

Lawyers are the most linear, afraid-to-screw-up people in the world and we're planners; we have to be. Particularly those of us who try big, complicated cases. You have to know where all the pieces fit, and you have to shape everything into a narrative that makes sense to a judge or a jury. Without being a lawyer I don't think I would have been able to develop such in-depth plots. Certainly, I would not have done so in the same way.

I try not to let one factor in my novels predominate, and I certainly don't want them to be seen as legal procedurals. I'm very careful to make sure the books are character driven as well as have what I hope to be an exciting plot. I really pay attention to maintaining that balance.

A Personal Observation

If someone asked me about my ultimate ambition with regard to my writing, I guess I would say, "To be the best suspense novelist of my generation." And by that I mean one who not only writes novels of real quality but provokes thought about why we are the way we are as people as well as about political and social issues. So that when people read one of my books, it has some real meaning to them and some real value and it lingers after they've put it down.

Writing a Series Character in Psychological Suspense

Mary Willis Walker's series protagonist, Molly Cates, is a journalist for the *Lone Star Monthly*. Molly is also a strong woman who tells it like it is yet isn't afraid to revise long-held opinions when necessary. Like most complex protagonists, she harbors personal demons that have influenced the decisions she's made in her life.

Research plays an important part in Walker's fiction. Her third novel, *Under the Beetle's Cellar*, centers on the ordeal of eleven children and one adult held captive in a buried school bus by an apocalyptic cult leader.

To insure that she portrayed her young hostages accurately, Walker enlisted the aid of a friend, a fourth-grade teacher who asked her students how they would pass the time in such a situation. The result is a chilling reality that lingers with the reader long after the book has ended.

Walker's first three books have all won or been nominated for top mystery awards. Her most recent, *All the Dead Lie Down*, forces series heroine Molly Cates to examine her life's motivation and question the foundation on which she's built her journalism career.

A former teacher, Walker resides in Austin, Texas.

Beginnings

I had my first book, *Zero at the Bone*, in mind for a possible series. Then my head was taken over by the Molly Cates voice so I switched to that. I had always thought about doing a series because it seemed like it would be fun to explore a character over time and because the conventional wisdom is that the way you develop a readership is with a series character.

Viewpoint

I wrote *The Red Scream*, my first Molly Cates book, from a limited third-person viewpoint. Then, for *Under the Beetle's Cellar*, I had this vision of an aboveground story and a belowground story and that required two viewpoints. I wanted those stories to touch one another in various ways the reader would recognize.

In *All the Dead Lie Down*, Molly's voice is written in past tense and Sarah Jane's [a homeless woman] in present tense. That decision was imposed on me by the characters. Sarah Jane came to me in present. I'd always done Molly Cates in past tense and continue to do so. But when Molly entered Sarah Jane's world, it felt right for her to come into present tense, too.

It sounds simple when I explain it, but it was very messy to work out. I think that's one of the things—experimenting with differing viewpoints and tenses—that is not adequately addressed in books about writing. Writing is rewriting. And so many things are really trial and error.

In *The Red Scream*, for instance, I didn't know I was going to do the poetry. [Each chapter of the book opens with a poem written by Walker's condemned anatagonist. The context and language of each open aids in revealing the character's background and mental state.] I started out introducing (serial killer) Louie Bronk through some of the things Molly had written about him, including his quotes. But I found it wasn't working well. I thought it was boring so I kept editing it out. Then, when I did the prison research, one of the prisoners gave me some poetry he had written, hoping I'd help him get it published, of course.

While it wasn't anything like Louie's poetry, it got me thinking about how much I'd like to try my hand at serial killer poetry. I hadn't known that desire was lurking in me, but once I sat down and started to write his poetry, I was just lost. I spent afternoons working on it, just doing it for my own use.

Then I started putting bits of poetry at the beginnings of chapters. I was sure my publisher would edit it out. It's pretty appalling stuff, but it ended up working. And she liked it! I wrote, of course, a lot more poetry than I ever used.

Research

Zero at the Bone used a zoo setting. Before I began to write the book I did a lot more than just talk to people at the zoo. I actually worked with the keepers at the Oklahoma City Zoo and also spent a lot of time in Dallas. Of all the research I've done, that was the hardest world to get access to. The first three zoos I approached about spending some time in their reptile house turned me down. Houston, my first choice, and San Antonio turned me down. Initially Dallas did, too. I ended up in Oklahoma City because my sister's on the board there. That helped, but I believe in using influence only when it's absolutely necessary.

I suppose that could be considered dangerous, but it has always interested me and it doesn't scare me at all, even at night. I like the illusion of being able to go anywhere, so I love doing research that feels a little bit risky. And I like riding with the police. I suppose that's as dangerous as it gets. You know you're right in the middle of a situation and you don't know what's going to happen next.

That's what I was saying before I was published. I'm a writer. I'm writing a novel and it has prison scenes in it. Will you tell me this; will you tell me that? And people are almost always willing to give you as much as they can. That's been one of the astonishing things I've learned. I'm still reticent about [interviewing] but once I get started I love it so much that it's hard to stop and actually get down to the hard work of writing because the research is so much fun.

To provide a balanced view of the death penalty, I had Molly interview family members of Louie Bronk's victims. A lot of my interest in victim crimes comes from a friend who is an organizer for victims groups around Texas. So, many of those scenes came from talking to people who had been, or had family members who had been, victims of violent crime.

Research excites me more than it frightens me. I got totally hooked on prisons when I started doing research for *The Red Scream* and ended up continuing along that line by writing the script for a documentary on women in prison. When I was researching *All the Dead Lie Down*, I hung out a lot along the Waller Creek area in Austin where a lot of the homeless people camp out.

Characterization

Characters have to come before plot or theme in a book. One of the things I like to do is put people who are opinionated up against really hard insoluble issues. I like to give Molly Cates a hard time on her issues and really challenge her thinking, such as with her ambivalence about the death penalty issue.

Publicly she takes the liberal opposed-to-capital-punishment view, but at heart she has some bloodlust. I like playing with that, with issues that really have two very powerful arguments on both sides or on several sides. So I pick my issues by things that I'm fascinated by and ambivalent about. Certainly gun control is one of those things. Yet the more I researched that for *All the Dead Lie Down*, the more ambivalent I became. I had a very major reaction against the easy access to guns and now I'm not so sure. So, I choose to write about that which I crave to know and research.

Plotting

Sometimes it's hard to keep track of the interaction between characters and subplots because I don't outline. What I do is take big chart-size paper and draw little diagrams of the various things going on simultaneously so I can see them. It ends up being a very messy-looking diagram of different running plots.

I need to visually see an overall picture because I sometimes feel overwhelmed by all the stuff going on as I get toward the end. It's important not to miss a loose end somewhere, but I seem to be incapable of doing a written outline. I keep trying and it never works out for me.

The Perils of Using a Series Protagonist

I think that there has to be common ground of some sort between a protagonist and a villain. Certainly the protagonist in a crime-based novel needs to have traits that allow her insight into the villain in some way, whether it be a streak of violence or a tendency to compulsiveness or whatever. I think a common ground makes for something with more reverberation.

In *The Red Scream*, I touched on Molly's obsession about the death of her father. The problem with doing something like that early on in a series is that you're really stuck with it.

I'm not much of an advance planner and hadn't really thought the situation out. But you have to go with whatever you've set in place, so I knew that eventually I'd have to have Molly deal with her history. I was just waiting until I felt ready to do it. *All the Dead Lie Down* seemed to be the right place.

Because the book wound up digging so deeply into Molly's psyche, I had trouble getting it to where I wanted it. I have horrible trouble with deadlines anyway; so I was definitely late with this particular book.

Advice for Others

I'm a beginner at fiction writing. I've been doing this for about twelve years and that isn't that long. My background is in English literature. What I've done most of my life is lie on my bed reading, which I think is the training ground for a writer.

I'm not much for giving advice, but when I do, it's that writers should first try to identify what it is that has always interested them and drawn them. Once they've identified that, they should run with it in some way.

I have found that the more I do that, the better my work is, even though it seems when I'm doing it to be so idiosyncratic that I don't know how it could interest anyone else. It turns out that it's more universal that way. It seems to be a paradox that the more you grow with your individual obsession, the more it will appeal to other people.

Writing Romantic Relationship Suspense

Booklist calls Marilyn Wallace's most recent novel, *Current Danger*, "a genuine page turner, an effective mix of mainstream mystery, suspense thriller, and police procedural." *Kirkus Reviews* agrees: "Wallace does her usual expert job of raising your blood pressure and keeping you from taking those deep, cleansing breaths." Such are the kudos for an author whose modern novels often read like classic gothic suspense.

A Single Stone explores the relationship between a couple whose daughter has been murdered. When a second child dies under similar circumstances, the wife, who was charged but released in their daughter's murder, becomes a suspect and is forced to confront the possibility that she's living with a killer.

In addition to authoring seven novels, Wallace is the editor of the award-winning *Sisters in Crime* anthology series and coeditor with Robert J. Randisi of the anthology *Deadly Allies*.

Marilyn Wallace lives in New York City.

Discovering the Thriller

I didn't actually choose to write suspense until my fourth book, *So Shall You Reap*. My first three were meant to be police procedurals. Two homicide detectives, Jay Goldstein and Carlos Cruz, shared the storytelling and a woman whose life was disrupted by a crime provided a third point of view. That her world was thrown into upheaval by events outside her control set up a challenge that became the heart of each book.

It wasn't until I'd written the third book that I realized that the form that had evolved seemed to enhance the what's-the-outcome-going-to-be aspect of the story. At that point I began to redefine what I was writing. As I embraced the concept, I discovered how much I enjoyed highlighting the suspense aspect of the storytelling. In a sense, suspense chose me.

Detective fiction certainly can be suspenseful, and suspense novels can include a level of conscious detection on the part of the protagonist. It's really a question of emphasis. The decision to retire my detectives came from the understanding that the heart of a series is the protagonist, and I discovered that I was increasingly drawn to exploring other characters in depth.

But characters have a way of surprising you. I was amused to discover that Jay Goldstein was the person to whom Teresa Gallagher, a cop who appeared briefly in *Lost Angel* and *Current Danger*, was engaged. Somehow, the alternate universe I've been creating in all the books hovers in my mind when I start writing something new, and it develops a rhythm and a logic of its own. In a way, all my books now are part of that created universe, as characters make references to people and events that first appeared in other books.

Revision

I do significant rewriting in every scene. Writing a first draft is an always difficult, sometimes painful process for me because it's such a juggling act. I'm still trying to find out who the characters are and what's happened to them. Discovery is exhilarating, but it's so consuming that I lack the mental energy to make the words say exactly what they should in first draft.

The hardest part of working this way is allowing those imperfect words and images to continue to exist until I get the first draft done. By now, I know enough about how I work to understand that it's in the rewriting that I'll earn the payoff of playing with language.

Keeping a Promise to the Reader

I believe that in the opening scene of a suspense novel, you establish a pact with the reader that says, "This is what you can expect from this book. These are the people and the issues and the mood." It's in the ending that you fulfill that promise, but it's the created expectations that make that ending satisfying or not. And in this world of so many books, so little time, writers have only a few paragraphs to capture the reader and convince him to make the commitment to spend several hours with these characters in this situation.

Setting and Atmosphere

When I wrote *So Shall You Reap*, I set out to write a New England gothic. Taconic Hills isn't really New England, and the book itself isn't exactly a gothic, but I was drawn to a place that evokes a mood, where the land and the buildings themselves may have been the only witnesses to significant events. The limited society of a small town, the disorientation that comes from realizing that people you think you know are harboring secrets that affect your life, the attachments people make to the physical world that surrounds them—these are such juicy elements of fiction.

Developing Ideas Into Plots

Each one is different, but generally a book begins with a situation that has some grip on my imagination and won't leave me alone. *The Seduction* began with an image of a bouquet of dead flowers tied with a black bow and evolved into a situation. Then I found myself wondering, *What if someone sent me a series of grotesque gifts tied in black ribbon?* I wrote the book to find out why someone would do that, and how the recipient of those weird gifts would react.

Most often, the kernel is a moment in my own life that has stayed with me, an emotional seed that keeps growing and becomes more urgent as time passes. Sometimes, it's an article that merges with questions I have about the way people behave toward one another. *Lost Angel* came from a moment in which I thought someone might be walking off with my young son and from a series of newspaper articles about a child custody battle that included accusations of satanic cult involvement. I found myself angry with those parents, wondering what they could have been thinking to allow their child to be the pawn in such a destructive game.

In some sense, when I write suspense fiction I'm trying to explain the mysteries of the world and human behavior to myself.

Character Motivation

The hallmark of the suspense novel is the need for the main character to confront a situation not of her own making in which she or someone she loves is in extreme danger. Such a situation demands that you dig deep to find your strengths, which in everyday life you may not have had reason to exercise. Can you imagine a woman accused of murdering her own child trying to heal and then being accused of another murder *not* changing?

The protagonist of *A Single Stone* was forced to find her strength because of the circumstances she was compelled to confront. Anyone who's been through such an extreme test cannot possibly emerge without being affected in a fundamental way, either by recognizing parts of herself or the world that she didn't understand before, or because her perspective is altered by what she's been through.

Pacing

Many of my books incorporate some version of a ticking time bomb as an aid to pacing. I love patterns—quilts, tiles, songs with refrains and chorus—and those time constructs are a way of creating a pattern in a book. Then I started to feel that "the ticking bomb" was becoming something I depended on, so I didn't count the passage of time on the page in *Current Danger*. But I did in my notes.

For suspense, the tension often can be kicked up a notch by dropping in on a potential villain. Watching the antagonist in *Current Danger* lie in wait for one of his victims gives readers a more disturbing sense of the depth of his distorted world.

The goal in a novel of suspense is to create in the reader a need to keep turning pages. Anything that slows the reader down, makes him ask, "Now, what's the writer doing here?" works against that end. Anything that makes the reader feel, "I have to know how this is going to turn out" works toward that end.

Choosing a Viewpoint Character

The choice of viewpoint character in each book is partly a result of asking the question, Whose book is this? I ask myself who is changed, who is tested, who has the most at stake in the book. Then I have to figure out whether that character has access to enough of the unfolding action and information to be the sole source for the reader. Keeping to a single viewpoint character allows maximum reader identification because they're discovering the unfolding story along with the protagonist.

The suspense tradition, however, suggests that the reading experience may be heightened when several threads are drawn inexorably together as the action progresses toward the ultimate confrontation, and for this, multiple points of view might work better. Even when that's the choice, I think it's most satisfying to focus on one of the characters and have the others be a supporting cast.

I choose that main character with the knowledge that I'm going to be spending a fair amount of time with her, so I have to like her from the start. And since one of the pleasures of being a writer is that you get to inhabit different lives, another part of the decision is that I have to be interested in what the character does in her everyday life, what she thinks, what personal, political or social issues she'll be dealing with.

Writing What You Know and Knowing What You Write

I've always interpreted the old write-what-you-know dictum loosely to mean write what you know *emotionally*. It's the writer's ability to capture an emotional experience that makes fiction feel authentic. I can extrapolate what it's like to have a mother disappear by recalling other feelings of loss, etc. But I discovered the value of research when I learned that if the other details are wrong, readers catch you out.

In *A Case of Loyalties*, I had a character ride a bicycle across the Oakland

Bay Bridge. I got several annoyed letters pointing out that, while you can ride across the Golden Gate Bridge, you can't do that on the other bridge across San Francisco Bay.

So Shall You Reap was a different situation. My husband and I had raised bees for a while when we lived in an upstate New York community not unlike Taconic Hills in size and topography. Calling on those memories was like doing research from an unwritten journal of my own life.

When I decided that Lee Montana, the photo editor in *The Seduction* who would never dream of shooting anything more than a photograph, would feel compelled to learn to use a gun to protect herself and her family, I decided I'd better find out what that was like. Her experience mirrors mine. The most astonishing thing about those three lessons was the nearly overwhelming feeling that I'd acquired the ability to [easily] kill another person, and the exhilaration I felt as my control grew. I tried to give those same feelings to Lee.

Research often uncovers such unexpected treasures for the writer. Here I thought I was going to get only the mechanics of guns and target practice, but I got something much richer to use in the book.

Dialogue

I believe a writer must have an ear for the way people speak, but this is a skill that can be cultivated. Dialogue serves so many functions, it's hard to make it work to your intention and have it sound natural at the same time. Dialogue reveals character, conveys information, fixes the time and place, sets up expectations, delivers back story, hides clues and conveys the emotional state of the speaker. Above all, it must entertain, and it must sound unforced.

Like other aspects of fiction, writers strive to improve the quality of their dialogue with practice. The more you do it, and the more objective you are when it's time to edit your own work, the more you learn about how to do it better next time. It's in the rewriting that most of my dialogue starts to sound the way I want it to. That's when I cut the speechiness, sharpen the indirectness, come up with the quirky characteristics that mark individual styles of communication.

Some writers probably do it right the first time because they have such a natural ear; I come closer each pass I make because I've trained myself to hear the clinkers and change them.

I listen differently when I'm writing, more intently, with the aim of figuring out why someone made me doubt what she said, why I believed his lies, what charms and what offends me about her conversation, who the person is behind all his words. I find myself assuming a character's physical posture. Somehow, the wisdom of the body allows the words to come closer to their emotional truth.

Books

American Automobile Association. *Tour Book—Arkansas, Kansas, Missouri, Oklahoma*. Heathrow, FL: AAA, 1996 edition.

Benchley, Peter. *Jaws*. Garden City, NY: Doubleday, 1974.

Berube, Margery S., director of editorial operations. *The American Heritage Dictionary*. Boston: Houghton Mifflin Company, 1982, 1985.

Bickham, Jack M. *Scene & Structure*. Cincinnati: Writer's Digest Books, 1993.

Block, Lawrence. *Writing the Novel: From Plot to Print*. Cincinnati: Writer's Digest Books, 1979.

Card, Orson Scott. *Characters & Viewpoint*. Cincinnati: Writer's Digest Books, 1988.

Castle, Mort, ed. *Writing Horror*. Cincinnati: Writer's Digest Books, 1997.

Cheney, Theodore A. Rees. *Getting the Words Right*. Cincinnati: Writer's Digest Books, 1983.

Chicago Manual of Style, The. 13th ed. Chicago: The University of Chicago Press, 1969, 1982.

Christie, Agatha. *The Murder of Roger Ackroyd*. New York: Dodd, Mead & Co., 1926, 1954.

Clancy, Tom. *The Hunt for Red October*. New York: Berkley, 1984.

———. *Clear and Present Danger*. New York: Putnam, 1989.

Clark, Mary Higgins. *The Cradle Will Fall*. New York: Simon & Schuster, 1980.

———. *Stillwatch*. New York: Simon & Schuster, 1984.

Clark, Thomas. *Queries & Submissions*. Cincinnati: Writer's Digest Books, 1995.

Connelly, Michael. *The Poet*. New York: Little, Brown & Co., 1996.

———. *Blood Work*. New York: Little, Brown & Co., 1998.

Cussler, Clive. *Raise The Titanic*. New York: Pocket Books, 1976.

———. *Flood Tide*. New York: Simon & Schuster, 1997.

du Maurier, Daphne. *Rebecca*. New York: Doubleday & Co., 1938

Fielding, Joy. *See Jane Run.* New York: William Morrow & Co. Inc., 1991.

Gerritsen, Tess. *Harvest.* New York: Pocket Books, 1996.

Gilstrap, John. *At All Costs.* New York: Watner Books, 1998.

———. *Nathan's Run.* New York: HarperCollins, 1996.

Goldstein, Norm, ed. *Associated Press Style Book and Libel Manual.* Reading, MA: Perseus Books, 1998.

Grisham, John. *A Time to Kill.* New York: Dell, reprinted by permission from Wynwood Press, 1989.

———. *The Chamber.* New York: Doubleday, 1994.

———. *The Firm.* New York: Doubleday, 1991.

Guide to Literary Agents. Cincinnati: Writer's Digest Books, updated annually.

Hailey, Arthur. *Airport.* New York: Doubleday, 1968.

Hallard, Karen, managing ed. *1998 Literary Market Place.* New Providence, NJ: R.R. Bowker, 1997.

Harris, Thomas. *The Silence of the Lambs.* New York: St. Martin's Press, 1988.

Hunter, Jessie. *One, Two, Buckle My Shoe.* New York: Simon & Schuster, 1997.

Kelman, Judith. *More Than You Know.* New York: Bantam Books, 1996.

Lutz, John. *The Ex.* New York: Kensington Publishing Co., 1996.

———. *S.W.F. Seeks Same.* New York: St. Martin's Press, 1990.

Marshall, Evan. *The Marshall Plan for Novel Writing.* Cincinnati: Writer's Digest Books, 1998.

Nance, John J. *Pandora's Clock.* New York: Doubleday, 1995.

Neff, Jack, Glenda Neff, Don Prues and the editors of *Writer's Market. Formatting and Submitting Your Manuscript.* Cincinnati: Writer's Digest Books, 2000.

Novel & Short Story Writer's Market. Cincinnati: Writer's Digest Books, updated annually.

Patterson, Richard North. *Silent Witness.* New York: Ballantine Books, 1996.

Skillman, Trish Macdonald. *Someone to Watch Over.* New York: Dell, 1994.

———. *Buried Secrets.* New York: Dell, 1995.

Strunk, William Jr., E.B. White. *The Elements of Style.* New York: MacMillan Publishing Co., Inc., 1979.

Tobias, Ronald B. *Theme & Strategy.* Cincinnati: Writer's Digest Books, 1989.

Walker, Mary Willis. *All the Dead Lie Down.* New York: Doubleday 1998.

———. *The Red Scream.* New York: Doubleday, 1994.

———. *Under the Beetle's Cellar.* New York: Doubleday, 1995.

Wallace, Marilyn. *Lost Angel.* New York: Bantam, 1996.

———. *The Seduction.* New York: Doubleday, 1993,

———. *A Single Stone.* New York: Doubleday, 1991.

Writer's Market. Cincinnati: Writer's Digest Books, updated annually.

Periodicals

Blythe, Hal, Charlie Sweet. "Telling Stories Within Your Stories." *Writer's Digest*, January 1994, p. 44.

Chamberlain, Erna. Review of *Nathan's Run* by John Gilstrap. *Library Journal*, February 1, 1996, vol. 121, no. 2, p. 97.

Kress, Nancy. "Where Are We?" *Writer's Digest*, July 1993, p. 10.

———. "So Bad They're Good." *Writer's Digest*, May 1995, p. 8.

———. "Putting It All Together." *Writer's Digest*, November 1995, p. 10.

Miksanek, Tony MD. *JAMA*, January 15, 1997. vol. 277, no. 3, p. 265.

Miller, Ronald C. Review of *Inca Gold* by Clive Cussler. *Armchair Detective*, Fall 1994, p. 496.

Orlofsky, Michael. "The Power of Place." *Writer's Digest*, October 1994, p. 40.

Review of *Eyes of a Child* by Richard North Patterson. *Kirkus Reviews*, October 15, 1994.

Review of *Current Danger* by Marilyn Wallace. *Kirkus Reviews*, January 1, 1998.

Rowen, John. Review of *Current Danger* by Marilyn Wallace. *Booklist*, February 1, 1998, vol. 94, no. 11, p. 905.

Seidman, Michael. "Creating Characters Who Create Your Story." *Writer's Digest*, December, 1996, p. 24.

Sweeten-Shults, Lana. "Video Patrol with Lana Sweeten-Shults." *Wichita Falls Times Record News*, 1997.

Truscott, Lucian IV. *Los Angeles Times Book Review*, February 18, 1996, p.4.

Index

A

Above Suspicion (MacInnes), 21-22
Acronyms, 179
Action theme, 152
Action-adventure
    characterization in, 25-28
    Cussler on, 205-210
    dialogue in, 134
    endings, 208
    experimentation in, 208
    goals and motivation in, 108-110
    notable titles in, 20-21
    plot in, 50-51
    political thriller and, 12
    special considerations for, 209
    style for, 171-172
    as suspense category, 7, 11-12
    technology in, 206-207
Adjectives, 178
Adverbs, 178-179
Against the Wind (Freedman), 21
Agent
    contract negotiation and, 187
    meeting, 189-190
    relationship with, 188-189
    requirements of, 186
    specialization of, 187
    submitting manuscript without, 186
Airport (Hailey), 77-78, 263
All the Dead Lie Down (Walker), 75, 145, 173, 250-251, 253-254, 264
Ambler, Eric, 21
American Heritage Dictionary, The, 17, 262
Andromeda Strain, The (Crichton), 21
Antagonist
    action adventure, 109-110
    dialogue between protagonist and, 28
    as POV character, 92-93
    legal thriller, 111
    medical thriller, 112
    political thriller, 114-115
    psychological suspense, 115-116
    romantic relationship suspense, 117-118
    techno-thriller, 120
    theme and, 155-156
    women-in-jeopardy suspense, 119
    See also Villain
Antecedents, pronoun, 182
Armageddon, 11
Armchair Detective magazine, 205, 264
Associated Press Stylebook and Libel Manual, 167, 263
Association of Author's Representatives (AAR), 192
At All Costs (Gilstrap), 66-67, 114-115, 168, 174, 224-229, 263
Atmosphere, 73-74, 77-79, 257. *See also* Setting
Author bias
    style and, 170
    theme and, 153-154

B

Back story, 95-105
    case study, 95-98
    dumping, 95
    flashbacks, 100-102
    in isolated sections, 102-103
    plot background, 98-100
    revealing, 95-98, 104-105
    what to include in, 103-104
Bad Seed, The, 213
Beginnings
    endings that set, 159-160
    opening lines, 211-212
    opening scene, 257
    plot and, 41-42
    psychological suspense, 242-243
    series character and, 250-251
Behavior, characterization and, 215
Ben Kincaid series (Bernhardt), 21
Benchley, Peter, 20, 43, 262
Berent, Mark, 20
Bernhardt, William, 21
Berube, Margery S., 262

Bias, author, 153-154, 170
Bickham, Jack M., 138, 262
Black Echo, The (Connelly), 198
Black Ice, The, 201
Block, Lawrence, 9, 166, 262
Blood Relative (Hougan), 23
Blood Work (Connelly), 127, 174, 198-199, 202, 262
Bloodstream (Gerritsen), 21, 218-219
Blythe, Hal, 130, 264
Bond, James, 12, 21, 25-26, 31, 74, 108, 171, 205-206
Booklist magazine, 255, 264
Bosch, Harry, 198-199, 201-202
Brain Dead (Dreyer), 21
Brigance, Jake, 110-111
Brighton, Carolyn, 114-115, 229
Brighton, Jake, 66-67, 114-115, 229
Brown, Dale, 23, 32
Buried Secrets (Skillman), 24, 36, 49, 104, 131, 191, 263

C

Card, Orson Scott, 24, 262
Carpenter, Will, 238
Case of Loyalties, A (Wallace), 71, 259
Castle, Mort, 4, 262
Catch phrases, 127-128
Cates, Molly, 22, 34, 145, 154-155, 250-254
Chamber, The (Grisham), 154, 263
Chamberlain, Erna, 264
Chameleon (Kennett), 120, 233, 236
Chandler, Raymond, 204
Chapters
    final, 165
    first page of, 184
    length of, 168
    short, 243-244
Characterization, 24-40
    action adventure, 25-28
    behavior and, 215
    Connelly on, 200-201
    dialogue as tool for, 124
    goals and motivation. *See* Goals and motivation
    Kennett on, 237
    legal thriller, 29-30, 248-249
    medical thriller, 30

    narrative passages and, 172
    political thriller, 30, 248-249
    psychological suspense, 28-30, 227
    romantic relationship suspense, 28-30
    series character, 253
    setting and, 68-69
    supporting players, 36-38
    techno-thriller, 25-28
    as theme, 152
    viewpoint characters, 38-40
    women-in-jeopardy suspense, 28-30, 231-232
    See also Characters
Characters
    dialogue as window to, 123. *See also* Dialogue
    histories of individual. *See* Back story
    observations of other, 28
    point of view, 91-94
    profiles of main, 49
    theme and interaction of, 155
    viewpoint, 38-40. *See also* Point of view
    voice of, 125-128
    See also Characterization
Characters & Viewpoint (Card), 24, 262
Cheney, Theodore A. Rees, 175, 262
Chicago Hope, 134, 222
Chicago Manual of Style, The, 167, 182, 262
Child-jep suspense
    plot in, 18, 63-64
    villains in, 34
    See also Women-in-jeopardy suspense
Children, harming, 18
Chocolate Man, The, 35-36, 42, 46-48, 74, 104, 144
Christie, Agatha, 6, 92, 262
Circular Staircase, The (Rinehart), 22
Clancy, Tom, 7, 14, 19-21, 23, 25-27, 32, 42, 44, 87, 94, 145, 162-163, 174, 262
Clark, Mary Higgins, 22, 78-79, 130, 174, 230, 262
Clark, Thomas, 262
Clear and Present Danger (Clancy), 14, 21, 113-114, 262
Cliché, 177
Cliff-hanger
    conflict and tension through, 44-46
    endings, 222-223, 244

Climax, 48, 138, 140, 160
Coffin for Dimitrios, A (Ambler), 21
Coma (Cook), 21
Conflict
    creating, 43-44
    defined, 43
    dialogue and, 123
    pacing and, 138-139
    plot and, 42-46
    See also Conflict and tension
Conflict and tension
    cliff-hangers and, 44-46
    deadlines and, 44-46
    dialogue and, 43
    plot twists and, 43-44
Connelly, Michael, 22, 82, 89-90, 127, 142,
    171, 174, 198-204, 262
Content, revising, 175-176
Contract negotiation
    agents and, 187
    editors and, 186
Cook, Robin, 21
Coonts, Stephen, 23, 32
Cornwell, Patricia, 23, 32
Cradle Will Fall, The (Clark), 78-79, 262
Crichton, Michael, 21
Crime
    in mystery novel, 5
    in psychological suspense, 198-204
Crime scene techniques, 234
Crisis, 138-140, 168
Cruz, Carlos, 256
Current Danger (Wallace), 255-256, 258, 264
Cussler, Clive, 12, 20, 31, 78, 87, 93, 205-210,
    262, 264
Cut Loose (Kennett), 238

D

Dancing With the Dead (Lutz), 241-242
Danger, suspense and, 6
Dante's Peak, 11
Davenport, Lucas, 22
Day of the Jackal, The (Forsyth), 21
Deadlines
    conflict and tension through, 44-46
    organizing through, 49
Deadly Allies anthology, 255
Deaver, Jeff, 22

Deep Impact, 11
Degree of Guilt (Patterson), 245-246, 248
Description, language of, 181
Details
    manuscript, 182-183
    of setting, 68-71
Dialogue, 122-136
    anecdotes in, 130
    arguments in, 129
    balance in narrative and, 136
    conflict, tension and, 43, 123
    as dominating, 168
    emotion and, 132-134
    internal, 28, 39, 107, 156
    natural, 131-132, 169
    position of, 169-170
    in psychological suspense, 224-225
    revising, 179-180
    in romantic relationship suspense,
        260-261
    secrets suggested through, 128-129
    slang, 125, 132
    stilted, 169
    "story within a story" in, 130
    suspense categories and, 134-136
    voice and, 125-128
    writer's ear for, 260
Dickens, Charles, 151-152
Diction, 126
Dirk Pitt series (Cussler), 20, 93. *See also* Pitt,
    Dirk
Don't Cry Now (Fielding), 213-214
Doyle, Arthur Conan (Sir), 6
Dragon (Cussler), 207-208
Drew, Nancy, 46-47
Dreyer, Eileen, 21
du Maurier, Daphne, 4, 22, 262
Dumps, 95

E

Eagle Station (Berent), 20
Edgar Award, 198, 245
Editor
    activities of, 186
    changing, 187
    as reader, 107
    unagented material and, 193

Elements of Fiction Writing series, The, 24, 139-140

Elements of Style, The (Strunk and White), 166-167, 263

Emotional effect, as theme, 152

Emotion
capturing, 259
dialogue and, 132-134
endings and, 164
revealing hero's, 26-27
short sentences and, 180
suspense and, 6
See also Emotional effect

Endings, 157-165
action adventure, 208
ambiguous, 162, 238
cliff-hanger, 222-223, 244. *See also* Cliff-hanger
inappropriate, 150
postscripts, 162-164
proper, 164-165
psychological suspense, 228-229
readers' emotions and, 164
satisfying, 212-213
that set beginnings, 159-160
too soon, 160-162
ultimate, 160-162
in women-in-jeopardy suspense, 212-213

English grammar, 180

Epic saga, pacing in, 137

ER, 134, 222

Ex, The (Lutz), 34, 37, 240, 242-244, 263

Eyes of a Child (Patterson), 245-246, 248, 264

F

Fatal Attraction, 17, 107

Fem-jep suspense
movies, 106
plot in, 63-64
villains in, 34
See also Women-in-jeopardy suspense

Fielding, Joy, 22, 81, 84, 118-119, 211-217, 263

Final Judgment, The (Patterson), 21, 246, 248

Fire Cracker (Kennett), 233

Firm, The (Grisham), 12-13, 21, 263

First-person point of view, 82-84, 172

advantage of, 232
POV characters for, 91-92

Flashbacks
back story and, 100-102
motivation through, 107
verb tense for, 182-183

Fleming, Ian, 12, 21, 25, 206

Flight of the Intruder (Coonts), 23

Flood Tide (Cussler), 78, 205-207, 209, 262

Follett, Ken, 21

Foreshadowing
building suspense with, 225-226
placement in paragraph, 181
plot and, 46-47

Formatting and Submitting Your Manuscript (Neff, Neff and Prues), 184, 190, 263

Forsyth, Frederick, 21

Freedman, J.F., 21

G

Gallagher, Teresa, 256

Gerritsen, Tess, 14, 21, 35, 75, 89, 218-223, 263

Getting the Words Right (Cheney), 175, 262

Gilstrap, John, 22, 47, 66-67, 98-100, 114, 163, 168, 174, 188, 224-229, 263, 264

Goals and motivation, 18, 106-121
action adventure, 108-110
legal thriller, 110-111
medical thriller, 111-112
obstacles and, 108
political thriller, 112-115
psychological suspense, 115-117
techno-thriller, 119-120
testing, 121
tips for, 120-121
women-in-jeopardy suspense, 118-119

Goldstein, Jay, 256

Gone With the Wind (Mitchell), 137

Gothic suspense, 17

Grafton, Jake, 32

Grafton, Sue, 6

Gray, P.J., 23, 233-234, 236-238. *See also* P.J. Gray series

Gray Matter (Kennett), 233, 236

Grisham, John, 12-13, 21, 110-111, 154, 156, 174, 263

Guide to Literary Agents, 185, 189, 192, 263

H

Hailey, Arthur, 77-78, 263
Harris, Thomas, 7, 16, 28, 263
Harvest (Gerritsen), 14, 35, 218, 220, 263
Header, 184
Heartbreaker (Robards), 22
Hemingway, Ernest, 210
Hero
 action adventure, 12, 25-28
 death of, 163
 legal thriller, 29-30
 techno-thriller, 25-28
 See also Heroine; Protagonist
Heroine
 women-in-jeopardy suspense, 18
 See also Hero, Protagonist
Hitchcock, Alfred, 239
Holmes, Sherlock, 6
Hougan, Carolyn, 23
House on the Hill, The (Kelman), 230-231
Hunter, Jessie, 23, 33, 35-36, 42, 46, 74, 89,
 104, 144, 263
Hunt for Red October, The (Clancy), 7, 19, 23,
 25-28, 32, 42, 44, 94, 145, 162, 174, 262
Hush Little Darlings (Kelman), 232

I

Ideas
 developing plots from, 257
 identifying story, 221
 universal theme, 151
If I Should Die (Kelman), 230-231
In Search Of series, 76
Incident of suspense, 7
Internal dialogue, 28
 characterization through, 39
 motivation through, 107
 theme revealed through, 156
 women-in-jeopardy suspense and, 212
Internet
 research on, 72
 See also Web site
Interviewing experts, 75-76

J

Jake Grafton series (Coonts), 32
James Bond series (Fleming), 21. *See also* Bond,
 James

Jaws (Benchley), 20, 43, 262
Jefferies, Cal, 123
Jones, Indiana, 11, 31, 205
Journal of the American Medical Association, 218
Joyce, James, 210
Justice series (Bernhardt), 21

K

Kay Scarpetta series (Cornwell), 23, 32
Kelman, Judith, 19, 23, 78, 134, 230-232, 263
Kennedy, John F., 168
Kennett, Shirley, 23, 120, 233-239
Key to Rebecca, The (Follett), 21
Kilcannon, Kerry, 249
Kincaid, Ben, 21
Kirkus Reviews, 245, 255, 264
Koontz, Dean, 230
Kress, Nancy, 31, 45, 264

L

Lasko Tangent, The (Patterson), 245-246
le Carré, John, 21, 35
Lecter, Hannibal, 16, 28, 116, 144
Legal thriller
 characterization in, 29-30, 248-249
 dialogue in, 134-135
 goals and motivation in, 110-111
 motivation in, 247-248
 notable titles, 21
 Patterson on, 245-249
 plot in, 53-54
 POV character in, 92
 as suspense category, 7, 12-13
 viewpoint in, 246
 villains in, 34
Lethal Weapon, 106
Library Journal, 224, 264
Life Support (Gerritsen), 14, 218-220
Limited (singular) third-person point of view,
 84-87, 92-93, 251
Lincoln, Abraham, 168
Literary agent. *See* Agent
Literary Market Place (LMP), 185, 192, 263
Lost Angel (Wallace), 23, 174, 256-257
Lucas Davenport series (Sanford), 22
Lutz, John, 22, 34, 37, 49, 240-244, 263

M

Mac, Pauley, 236-237

McCaleb, Terry, 127
McEvoy, Jack, 82, 90, 142-143
MacInnes, Helen, 21-22
McLanahan, Patrick, 32
Maiden's Grave, A (Deaver), 22
Manuscript
  preparing, 182-183
  submitting. *See* Submission strategies
Margins, 184
Marshall, Evan, 190-191, 263
Marshall Plan for Novel Writing, The (Marshall), 190, 263
Masters, Carolyn, 248
Medical thriller
  characterization in, 30
  cliff-hanger endings in, 222-223
  dialogue in, 134-135
  Gerritsen on, 218-223
  goals and motivation in, 111-112
  insider's knowledge for, 220
  notable titles, 21
  plot in, 55-56
  popularity of, 218-219
  reality and fiction in, 222
  research for, 220-221
  setting for, 66
  specialized terms in, 220
  stories, 219, 221
  as suspense category, 7, 13-14
  villains in, 34-35
Metaphors, mixed, 177
Midnovel slump, 147-149
Miksanek, Tony, 218, 264
Miller, Ronald C., 205, 264
Millhone, Kinsey, 6
Misplaced modifiers, 182
Missing Pieces (Fielding), 211, 215-216
Mixed points of view, 89-90
Molly Cates series (Walker), 22. *See also* Cates, Molly
Mood. *See* Atmosphere
Mordecai, Samuel, 44
More Than You Know (Kelman), 78, 134, 263
Motivation
  flashbacks and, 107
  legal/political thriller, 247-248
  psychological suspense, 15-16, 242
  romantic relationship suspense, 258

women-in-jeopardy suspense, 18
  See also Goals and motivation
Movies
  action-adventure, 11
  goals and motivation in, 106, 108
Multiple third-person point of view, 87-90, 93-94
Murder of Roger Ackroyd, The (Christie), 92, 262
Mystery
  pacing in, 137
  suspense vs., 5, 10, 240-241
Mystery Writers of America, Edgar Award, 198, 245

N

Nance, John J., 21, 30, 34, 111-112, 263
Nancy Drew series, 46-47
Narrative
  balance in dialogue and, 136
  characterization through, 40, 172
  revising, 179-180
Nathan's Run (Gilstrap), 22, 98-100, 163, 168, 188, 224, 226-227, 263, 264
Neff, Glenda, 184, 263
Neff, Jack, 184, 263
Nina Reilly series (O'Shaughnessy), 21
No Safe Place (Patterson), 15, 246-249
Nouns, 178
Novel & Short Story Writer's Market, 185, 263

O

Omniscient point of view, 38, 80-82
One, Two, Buckle My Shoe (Hunter), 23, 33, 35-36, 46-48, 89, 263
Opening lines, 211
Orett, Linda, 100-101
Orlofsky, Michael, 264
O'Shaughnessy, Perri, 21
Outlining
  character-profile technique, 49
  charting vs., 253
  Connelly on, 202
  Patterson on, 249

P

Pacing, 137-150
  components of, 138-140

crises and, 140-141
inappropriate endings and, 150
inconsistency and, 149
midnovel slump and, 147-149
problems, 141-143
providing information and, 144
psychological suspense and, 243-244
romantic relationship suspense and,
258-259
showing vs. telling, 145
simplicity and, 144-145
slow beginning, 141
timidity and, 149-150
too little too late, 143-144
too much too soon, 141-143
transitions, 145-157
unnecessary scenes, 147
Page numbers, 184
Paget, Christopher, 245-246
Pandora's Clock (Nance), 21, 30, 34, 111-112,
263
Paragraph
foreshadowing in, 181
length of, 168
single-sentence, 181
Parker, Robert B., 5
Patrick McClanahan series (Brown), 32
Patterson, Richard North, 15, 21, 48, 102-103,
245-249, 263, 264
Pedophiles, 18
Phrases, catch, 127-128
Phrasing, 126
Physical reactions, 28
"Pit and the Pendulum, The" (Poe), 4
Pitt, Dirk, 12, 20, 31-32, 87, 108, 134,
205-209
P.J. Gray series, 23. *See also* Gray, P.J.
Plot
action adventure, 50-51, 207-208
assembling scenes for, 48
background and, 98-100
basics of, 41-49
beginning and, 41-42
case studies in, 50-64
child-jep suspense, 18, 63-64
conflict, tension and, 42-46
evolution of, 215-217
Kennett on, 237

legal thriller, 53-54
medical thriller, 55-56
political thriller, 56-58
psychological suspense, 58-61
rhythm of suspense and, 47-48
romantic relationship suspense, 62-63,
257
setting and, 66-67, 243
subplots, 148-149, 176
techno-thriller, 51-53
twists, 43-44, 140
women-in-jeopardy suspense, 18,
63-64, 215-217
Poe, Edgar Allan, 4, 152
Poet, The (Connelly), 22, 82, 89-90, 142, 171,
198, 202, 262
Point of view (POV)
characters, 91-94
first-person, 82-84, 91-92, 172, 232
in legal/political thriller, 246
limited third-person, 84-87, 92-93, 251
mixed, 89-90
multiple, 87-90, 93-94, 246
omniscient, 38, 80-94
in psychological suspense, 225
second-person, 82
series character and, 251-252
shifting, 232
tense and, 90-91
Poirot, Hercule, 6
Political/techno-thriller, 15. *See also* Political
thriller; Techno-thriller
Political thriller
action adventure in, 12
characterization in, 30, 248-249
dialogue in, 135
goals in, 112-115
motivation in, 112-115, 247-248
notable titles, 21-22
Patterson on, 245-249
plot in, 56-58
as suspense category, 7, 14-15
technology in. *See* Political/
techno-thriller
viewpoint in, 246
villains in, 35
writing style for, 172
Postscripts, 162-164

Presumed Innocent (Turow), 21
Prey series (Sandford), 22
Private Screening (Patterson), 246
Pronoun antecedents, 182
Protagonist
    action adventure, 108-109
    dialogue between antagonist and, 28
    legal thriller, 110-111
    medical thriller, 111-112
    political thriller, 112-115
    as POV character, 91-93
    psychological suspense, 15-16, 28-30,
      115
    romantic relationship suspense, 17,
      28-30, 117
    series. *See* Series character
    supporting players and, 36
    techno-thriller, 119-120
    theme and, 156
    women-in-jeopardy suspense, 28-30,
      118-119
    See also Hero; Heroine
Prues, Don, 184, 263
Psychological suspense
    beginnings, 242-243
    characterization and, 28-30, 227
    crime-based, Connelly on, 198-204
    dialogue in, 135, 224-225
    endings for, 228-229
    Fielding on, 211-217
    foreshadowing and, 225-226
    goals and motivation in, 115-117
    issue-driven, Gilstrap on, 224-229
    legal thriller as, 13
    motivation and, 242
    mystery vs. suspense, 240-241
    notable titles, 22
    pacing in, 243-244
    personal experience and, 228
    plot in, 58-61, 243, 253
    point of view in, 225
    POV characters in, 92, 94
    realism and, 228
    research for, 252-253
    series character in, 250-254
    setting and, 241-243
    stand-alone vs. series, 198-199
    as suspense category, 7, 15-16

theme, 227
urban settings in, Lutz on, 240-244
violence in, 226-227
writing style for, 172
Publisher
    book titles and, 173
    finding. *See* Submission strategies
Punctuation, 182

Q

Queen, Ellery, 239
Queries & Submissions (Clark), 262
Query
    to agent, 188
    to editor, 193-194

R

Raise the Titanic (Cussler), 87, 205, 262
Ramius, Marko, 32, 42
Randisi, Robert J., 255
Reading, writing and, 8-9
Rebecca (du Maurier), 4, 16, 22, 262
Red herrings
    backgrounds for, 36
    introducing, 144
    supporting players as, 37
    in women-in-jeopardy suspense, 231
Red Scream, The (Walker), 75, 154-155,
    173-174, 251, 254, 264
Reilly, Nina, 21
Research
    Connelly on, 199-200
    experts and, 75-77
    library, 76
    medical thriller, 220-221
    psychological suspense, 252-253
    setting, 71-72, 213-214
    women-in-jeopardy suspense, 231
Resolution, 48, 138-139, 168
Revision
    content and structure, 175-176
    sentence structure, 179-182
    as ultimate tool, 175
    Wallace on, 256
    word choice and, 177-179
    word and sentence placement, 179-182
Rhythm
    of good writing, 180

of suspense, 47
Rinehart, Mary Roberts, 22
Robards, Karen, 22
Romantic relationship suspense
    characterization in, 28-30
    dialogue in, 135-136, 260-261
    goals in, 117-118
    motivation in, 117-118, 258
    multiple POVs in, 93-94
    notable titles, 22
    opening scene of, 257
    pacing in, 137, 258-259
    plot in, 62-63, 257
    POV characters in, 92
    revising, 256
    setting and atmosphere of, 257
    as suspense category, 8, 16-17
    viewpoint character for, 259
    villains in, 34
    Wallace on, 255-261
    writing style for, 172
Rowen, John, 264
Russia House, The (le Carré), 21
Ryan, Jack, 25-28, 32, 113-114, 163

S

Sandford, John, 22
Scandal, political, 15
Scarpetta, Kay, 23, 32
Scene
    before climax, 165
    opening, 257
    as pacing component, 138
    unnecessary, 147
Scene & Structure (Bickham), 138, 262
Sea Hunters, The, 205
Second-person point of view, 82
Seduction, The (Wallace), 90-91, 257, 264
See Jane Run (Fielding), 22, 81, 84, 118-119,
    211-212, 215, 263
Seidman, Michael, 24-25, 264
Sensory cues, 65-66
Sentences
    compound, 180
    length of, 168
    short, 180
Sequel, 138
Serial killer, 7, 35, 90, 149, 155-156

Series books
    mysteries as, 5
    stand-alone book vs., 198-199
    suspense in, 17
Series character
    beginnings and, 250-251
    characterization for, 253
    development of, 206
    perils of using, 253-254
    in psychological suspense, 250-254
    as registered trademark, 209
    restrictions on, 208
    viewpoint and, 251-252
    See also names of specific characters
Setting, 65-79
    characterization and, 68-69
    details of, 68-71
    experts on, 75-77
    plot and, 66-67, 243
    research for, 71-72, 213-214
    sensory cues and, 65-66
    urban, 240-244
ShawGuides, 189
Shock Wave (Cussler), 208
Silence of the Lambs, The (Harris), 7, 16, 28,
    116, 263
Silent Witness (Patterson), 102-103, 246, 263
Single Stone, A (Wallace), 17, 100, 255, 258,
    264
Single White Female, 240. *See also* SWF Seeks
    Same
Singular third-person point of view. *See* Lim-
    ited third-person point of view
Sisters in Crime series, 255
Someone to Watch Over (Skillman), 39, 49, 94,
    102-104, 121-123, 128-129, 141, 191, 263
Someone's Watching (Kelman), 23, 230-231
So Shall You Reap (Wallace), 255, 257, 260
Speed, 11
Spelling, 182
Spenser, 5
Spy Who Came In From the Cold, The (le Carré),
    35
Starling, Clarice, 16, 28-29, 116
Stillwatch (Clark), 130, 174, 262
Strunk, William, Jr., 166, 263
Style, 166-172
    chapter length and, 168

defined, 167
dialogue position and, 169-170
identifying your, 170-171
as invisible, 170
paragraph length and, 168
sentence length and, 168
as sound and cadence, 167
suspense categories and, 171-172
Subplots, 148-149, 176
Submission strategies
agents, 186-189
editors, 193-194
post-query, 194-195
reference books, 185-186
writers conferences, 189-193
Supporting players, 36-38, 238
Suspense
atmosphere of, 74
categories of, 7-8, 11-23. *See also indi-*
vidual categories
defining, 4-10
as emotional, 6
gothic, 17
incident of, 7
mystery vs., 5, 10, 240-241
plot and, 46-47. *See also* Plot
rhythm of, 47-48
series, 17
Sweet, Charlie, 130, 264
Sweeten-Shults, Lana, 31, 264
SWF Seeks Same (Lutz), 22, 240-243, 263
Synopsis, 49, 190

T

Techno-thriller
ambiguous endings in, 238
characterization in, 25-28
cutting-edge technology and, 233-239
dialogue in, 134
future in, 236
goals and motivation in, 119-120
notable titles, 23
plot in, 51-53
POV characters in, 94
premise in, 235-236
reality and fiction in, 234-235
"scanimation" in, 236
supporting players in, 238

as suspense category, 19-20
villains in, 236-237
virtual reality and, 233-236
writing style for, 172
Tell Me No Secrets (Fielding), 213-215
Tense. *See* Verbs, tense
Tension
creating, 43-44
defined, 43
as dialogue plus conflict, 123
in limited third-person POV, 86
plot and, 42-46
speech patterns and, 132
See also Conflict and tension
Terrorist activities, 15
Theme, 151-156
character interaction and, 155
characterization and, 215
defined, 151
identifying, 152-153
integrating, 154-155
psychological suspense and, 227
subtlety of, 153-154
universal ideas, 151
Theme & Strategy (Tobias), 151, 263
Third-person point of view
limited, 84-87, 92-93
multiple, 87-90
Time to Kill, A (Grisham), 13, 110-111, 174, 263
Tin Man, The (Brown), 23
Titanic, 138
Titles, 173-174
Tobias, Ronald B., 151, 263
Tone, 127, 176
Toxin (Cook), 21
Transitions, 145-157
Traymore, Pat, 130
Truscott, Lucian, IV, 198, 264
Turow, Scott, 21
Twister, 11

U

Ulysses (Joyce), 210
Under the Beetle's Cellar (Walker), 22, 29, 34, 42, 250-251, 264

V

Verbs
  tense, 90-91, 102, 182-183
  tricky, 183
  word choice and, 177-178
Viewpoint. *See* Point of view (POV)
Viewpoint character, 38-40, 259
Villain
  beginning with, 42
  defined (Kress), 31
  by genre, 34
  mind of, 33
  motivation of, 109, 120-121
  nasty, 31-33
  as observed by others, 34
  in psychological suspense, 15-16
  in techno-thriller, 236-237
  undisclosed, 35-36, 129, 176
  in women-in-jeopardy suspense, 18
Violence
  pacing and, 149
  validity of, 226-227
Voice, 125-128
  age and, 125-126
  catch phrases, 127-128
  diction and, 126
  phrasing and, 126
  tone and, 127
  word choice and, 126
Vonnegut, Kurt, 200

W

Walker, Mary Willis, 22, 29, 34, 42, 44, 48, 75, 145, 154, 156, 173-174, 250-254, 264
Wallace, Marilyn, 17, 23, 71, 90-91, 100, 131, 140, 174, 255-261, 264
Wheat, Carolyn, 10
Where Are the Children? (Clark), 22
Where Shadows Fall (Kelman), 232
White, E.B., 166, 263
Wolfe, Thomas, 210
Women-in-jeopardy suspense
  characterization in, 28-30, 231-232
  dialogue in, 136
  Fielding on, 211-217
  goals and motivation in, 118-119
  issue-driven, Kelman on, 230-232
  multiple POVs in, 93-94
  notable titles, 22-23
  plot in, 63-64, 215-217
  POV characters in, 92
  research for, 231
  as suspense category, 8, 17-19
  villains in, 34
  writing style for, 172
  See also Fem-jep suspense
Word choice, 126, 173-184
  acronyms, 179
  adjectives, 178
  adverbs, 178-179
  nouns, 178
  power of, 168
  revision and, 175, 177-179
  title, 173-174
  verbs, 177-178
Writers conferences, 189-193
Writer's Digest magazine, 25, 31, 45, 166, 264
Writer's Digest Books
  conference lists, 189
  The Elements of Fiction Writing Series, 24, 138-139
Writer's Market (Writer's Digest Books), 184-185, 264
"Write what you know," 214-215, 259-260
Writing, first rule of, 8
Writing environment, Connelly on, 199-200
Writing Horror (Castle), 4, 262
Writing the Novel: From Plot to Print (Block), 9, 166, 262
Writing process
  Connelly on, 201-202
  Fielding on, 217
  Lutz on, 244
Writing style. *See* Style

Z

Zero at the Bone (Walker), 250, 252

More Exciting Books
for Thriller Writers!

2000 Novel & Short Story Writer's Market—Get the information you need to get your short stories and novels published. You'll discover listings on fiction publishers, plus original articles on fiction writing techniques; detailed subject categories to help you target appropriate publishers; and interviews with writers, publishers and editors! *#10625/$24.99/675 pages/paperback*

Malicious Intent: A Writer's Guide to How Criminals Think—Create unforgettable villains with the help of this guide to criminal psychology. You'll explore the fact and fiction of who these people are, why they commit their crimes, how they choose their victims and more! *#10413/$16.99/240 pages/paperback*

Modus Operandi: A Writer's Guide to How Criminals Work—From murder to arson to prostitution, two seasoned detectives show you how to create masterful crimes while still dropping enough clues to let the good guys catch the bad guys. *#10414/$16.99/224 pages/paperback*

Cause of Death: A Writer's Guide to Death, Murder & Forensic Medicine—Discover how to accurately "kill-off" your characters as you are led step-by-step through the process of trauma, death and burial. *#10318/$16.99/240 pages/paperback*

Rip-Off: A Writer's Guide to Crimes of Deception—From street-level shell games to high-stakes real estate swindles, professional PI Fay Faron profiles the con artists, the cons and the victims. She provides you with the facts on classic scams like three-card monte, identity theft, insurance fraud, "white-collar" crime and Internet rip-offs. *#10570/$16.99/240 pages/paperback*

Body Trauma: A Writer's Guide to Wounds and Injuries—Here you'll find graphic explanations of serious bodily damage. You'll be able to work backward, deciding how severe a character's wounds should be and then writing the action that causes the pain. You'll put your characters in harm's way and mistreat them—believably—to within an inch of their fictional lives. *#10488/$16.99/240 pages/paperback*

Deadly Doses: A Writer's Guide to Poisons—This invaluable book for thriller writers provides you with information on hundreds of poisons, including their forms, symptoms, methods of administration and reactions. All entries are cross-referenced for accuracy and ease of use to cut your research time in half! *#10177/$16.99/298 pages/paperback*

The Writer's Complete Crime Reference Book—An incredible encyclopedia of hard-to-find facts about the ways of criminals and cops, prosecutors and defenders, victims and juries. Everything you might need for writing great mysteries and thrillers is at your fingertips. *#10371/$19.99/304 pages*

Lights and Sirens—All writers need to capture real-life drama and detail in their work. This fascinating book takes you through every dramatic step of search and rescue and emergency scenarios, from the accident scene and the injuries to the rescuers and the paramedics. *#10550/$16.99/272 pages/paperback*

Writing the Novel From Plot to Print—Lawrence Block, recently named Grand Master of Mystery Writing, covers every step of the novel writing and selling process to help you to deliver a salable manuscript to the right editor's desk. *#2747/$14.99/218 pages*